ISBN 0-8373-5338-6

MW00676557

New **RUDMAN'S QUESTIONS
AND ANSWERS ON THE...**

**College-Level Examination Program
Subject Test In...**

ANATOMY, PHYSIOLOGY AND MICROBIOLOGY

Test Preparation Study Guide

Questions and Answers

NATIONAL LEARNING CORPORATION

PASSBOOK®

NOTICE

PASSBOOK® SERIES

THE *PASSBOOK® SERIES* has been created to prepare applicants and candidates for the ultimate academic battlefield — the examination room.

At some time in our lives, each and every one of us may be required to take an examination — for validation, matriculation, admission, qualification, registration, certification, or licensure.

Based on the assumption that every applicant or candidate has met the basic formal educational standards, has taken the required number of courses, and read the necessary texts, the *PASSBOOK® SERIES* furnishes the one special preparation which may assure passing with confidence, instead of failing with insecurity. Examination questions — together with answers — are furnished as the basic vehicle for study so that the mysteries of the examination and its compounding difficulties may be eliminated or diminished by a sure method.

This book is meant to help you pass your examination provided that you qualify and are serious in your objective.

The entire field is reviewed through the huge store of content information which is succinctly presented through a provocative and challenging approach — the question-and-answer method.

A climate of success is established by furnishing the correct answers at the end of each test.

You soon learn to recognize types of questions, forms of questions, and patterns of questioning. You may even begin to anticipate expected outcomes.

You perceive that many questions are repeated or adapted so that you can gain acute insights, which may enable you to score many sure points.

You learn how to confront new questions, or types of questions, and to attack them confidently and work out the correct answers.

You note objectives and emphases, and recognize pitfalls and dangers, so that you may make positive educational adjustments.

Moreover, you are kept fully informed in relation to new concepts, methods, practices, and directions in the field.

You discover that you are actually taking the examination all the time: you are preparing for the examination by "taking" an examination, not by reading extraneous and/or supererogatory textbooks.

In short, this PASSBOOK®, used directedly, should be an important factor in helping you to pass your test.

NONTRADITIONAL EDUCATION

Students returning to school as adults bring more varied experience to their studies than do the teenagers who begin college shortly after graduating from high school. As a result, there are numerous programs for students with nontraditional learning curves. Hundreds of colleges and universities grant degrees to people who cannot attend classes at a regular campus or have already learned what the college is supposed to teach.

You can earn nontraditional education credits in many ways:

- Passing standardized exams
- Demonstrating knowledge gained through experience
- Completing campus-based coursework, and
- Taking courses off campus

Some methods of assessing learning for credit are objective, such as standardized tests. Others are more subjective, such as a review of life experiences.

With some help from four hypothetical characters – Alice, Vin, Lynette, and Jorge – this article describes nontraditional ways of earning educational credit. It begins by describing programs in which you can earn a high school diploma without spending 4 years in a classroom. The college picture is more complicated, so it is presented in two parts: one on gaining credit for what you know through course work or experience, and a second on college degree programs. The final section lists resources for locating more information.

Earning High School Credit

People who were prevented from finishing high school as teenagers have several options if they want to do so as adults. Some major cities have back-to-school programs that allow adults to attend high school classes with current students. But the more practical alternatives for most adults are to take the General Educational Development (GED) tests or to earn a high school diploma by demonstrating their skills or taking correspondence classes.

Of course, these options do not match the experience of staying in high school and graduating with one's friends. But they are viable alternatives for adult learners committed to meeting and, often, continuing their educational goals.

GED Program

Alice quit high school her sophomore year and took a job to help support herself, her younger brother, and their newly widowed mother. Now an adult, she wants to earn her high school diploma – and then go on to college. Because her job as head cook and her family responsibilities keep her busy during the day, she plans to get a high school equivalency diploma. She will study for, and take, the GED tests. Every year, about half a million adults earn their high school credentials this way. A GED diploma is accepted in lieu of a high school one by more than 90 percent of employers, colleges, and universities, so it is a good choice for someone like Alice.

The GED testing program is sponsored by the American Council on Education and State and local education departments. It consists of examinations in five subject areas: Writing, science, mathematics, social studies, and literature and the arts. The tests also measure skills such as analytical ability, problem solving, reading comprehension, and ability to understand and apply information. Most of the questions are multiple choice; the writing test includes an essay section on a topic of general interest.

Eligibility rules for taking the exams vary, but some states require that you must be at least 18. Tests are given in English, Spanish, and French. In addition to standard print, versions in large print, Braille, and audiocassette are also available. Total time allotted for the tests is 7 1/2 hours.

The GED tests are not easy. About one-fourth of those who complete the exams every year do not pass. Passing scores are established by administering the tests to a sample of graduating high school seniors. The minimum standard score is set so that about one-third of graduating seniors would not pass the tests if they took them.

Because of the difficulty of the tests, people need to prepare themselves to take them. Often, they start by taking the Official GED Practice Tests, usually available through a local adult education center. Centers are listed in your phone book's blue pages under "Adult Education," "Continuing Education," or "GED." Adult education centers also have information about GED preparation classes and self-study materials. Classes are generally arranged to accommodate adults' work schedules. National Learning Corporation publishes several study guides that aim to thoroughly prepare test-takers for the GED.

School districts, colleges, adult education centers, and community organizations have information about GED testing schedules and practice tests. For more information, contact them, your nearest GED testing center, or:

GED Testing Service
One Dupont Circle, NW, Suite 250
Washington, DC 20036-1163
1(800) 62-MY GED (626-9433)
(202) 939-9490

Skills Demonstration

Adults who have acquired high school level skills through experience might be eligible for the National External Diploma Program. This alternative to the GED does not involve any direct instruction. Instead, adults seeking a high school diploma must demonstrate mastery of 65 competencies in 8 general areas: Communication; computation; occupational preparedness; and self, social, consumer, scientific, and technological awareness.

Mastery is shown through the completion of the tasks. For example, a participant could prove competency in computation by measuring a room for carpeting, figuring out the amount of carpet needed, and computing the cost.

Before being accepted for the program, adults undergo an evaluation. Tests taken at one of the program's offices measure reading, writing, and mathematics abilities. A take-home segment includes a self-assessment of current skills, an individual skill evaluation, and an occupational interest and aptitude test.

Adults accepted for the program have weekly meetings with an assessor. At the meeting, the assessor reviews the participant's work from the previous week. If the task has not been completed properly, the assessor explains the mistake. Participants continue to correct their errors until they master each competency. A high school diploma is awarded upon proven mastery of all 65 competencies.

Fourteen States and the District of Columbia now offer the External Diploma Program. For more information, contact:

External Diploma Program
One Dupont Circle, NW, Suite 250
Washington, DC 20036-1193
(202) 939-9475

Correspondence and Distance Study

Vin dropped out of high school during his junior year because his family's frequent moves made it difficult for him to continue his studies. He promised himself at the time he dropped out that he would someday finish the courses needed for his diploma. For people like Vin, who prefer to earn a traditional diploma in a nontraditional way, there are about a dozen accredited courses of study for earning a high school diploma by correspondence, or distance study. The programs are either privately run, affiliated with a university, or administered by a State education department.

Distance study diploma programs have no residency requirements, allowing students to continue their studies from almost any location. Depending on the course of study, students need not be enrolled full time and usually have more flexible schedules for finishing their work. Selection of courses ranges from vo-tech to college prep, and some programs place different emphasis on the types of diplomas offered. University affiliated schools, for example, allow qualified students to take college courses along with their high school ones. Students can then apply the college credits toward a degree at that university or transfer them to another institution.

Taking courses by distance study is often more challenging and time consuming than attending classes, especially for adults who have other obligations. Success depends on each student's motivation. Students usually do reading assignments on their own. Written exercises, which they complete and send to an instructor for grading, supplement their reading material.

A list of some accredited high schools that offer diplomas by distance study is available free from the Distance Education and Training Council, formerly known as the National Home Study Council. Request the "DETC Directory of Accredited Institutions" from:

The Distance Education and Training Council
1601 18th Street, NW.
Washington, DC 20009-2529
(202) 234-5100

Some publications profiling nontraditional college programs include addresses and descriptions of several high school correspondence ones. See the Resources section at the end of this article for more information.

Getting College Credit For What You Know

Adults can receive college credit for prior coursework, by passing examinations, and documenting experiential learning. With help from a college advisor, nontraditional students should assess their skills, establish their educational goals, and determine the number of college credits they might be eligible for.

Even before you meet with a college advisor, you should collect all your school and training records. Then, make a list of all knowledge and abilities acquired through

3

experience, no matter how irrelevant they seem to your chosen field. Next, determine your educational goals: What specific field do you wish to study? What kind of a degree do you want? Finally, determine how your past work fits into the field of study. Later on, you will evaluate educational programs to find one that's right for you.

People who have complex educational or experiential learning histories might want to have their learning evaluated by the Regents Credit Bank. The Credit Bank, operated by Regents College of the University of the State of New York, allows people to consolidate credits earned through college, experience, or other methods. Special assessments are available for Regents College enrollees whose knowledge in a specific field cannot be adequately evaluated by standardized exams. For more information, contact the Regents Credit Bank at:

Regents College
7 Columbia Circle
Albany, NY 12203-5159
(518) 464-8500

Credit For Prior College Coursework

When Lynette was in college during the 1970s, she attended several different schools and took a variety of courses. She did well in some classes and poorly in others. Now that she is a successful business owner and has more focus, Lynette thinks she should forget about her previous coursework and start from scratch. Instead, she should start from where she is.

Lynette should have all her transcripts sent to the colleges or universities of her choice and let an admissions officer determine which classes are applicable toward a degree. A few credits here and there may not seem like much, but they add up. Even if the subjects do not seem relevant to any major, they might be counted as elective credits toward a degree. And comparing the cost of transcripts with the cost of college courses, it makes sense to spend a few dollars per transcript for a chance to save hundreds, and perhaps thousands, of dollars in books and tuition.

Rules for transferring credits apply to all prior coursework at accredited colleges and universities, whether done on campus or off. Courses completed off campus, often called extended learning, include those available to students through independent study and correspondence. Many schools have extended learning programs; Brigham Young University, for example, offers more than 300 courses through its Department of Independent Study. One type of extended learning is distance learning, a form of correspondence study by technological means such as television, video and audio, CD-ROM, electronic mail, and computer tutorials. See the Resources section at the end of this article for more information about publications available from the National University Continuing Education Association.

Any previously earned college credits should be considered for transfer, no matter what the subject or the grade received. Many schools do not accept the transfer of courses graded below a C or ones taken more than a designated number of years ago. Some colleges and universities also have limits on the number of credits that can be transferred and applied toward a degree. But not all do. For example, Thomas Edison State College, New Jersey's State college for adults, accepts the transfer of all 120 hours of credit required for a baccalaureate degree – provided all the credits are transferred from regionally accredited schools, no more than 80 are at the junior college level, and the student's grades overall and in the field of study average out to C.

To assign credit for prior coursework, most schools require original transcripts. This means you must complete a form or send a written, signed request to have your transcripts released directly to a college or university. Once you have chosen the schools you want to apply to, contact the schools you attended before. Find out how much each transcript costs, and ask them to send your transcripts to the ones you are applying to. Write a letter that includes your name (and names used during attendance, if different) and dates of attendance, along with the names and addresses of the schools to which your transcripts should be sent. Include payment and mail to the registrar at the schools you have attended. The registrar's office will process your request and send an official transcript of your coursework to the colleges or universities you have designated.

Credit For Noncollege Courses

Colleges and universities are not the only ones that offer classes. Volunteer organizations and employers often provide formal training worth college credit. The American Council on Education has two programs that assess thousands of specific courses and make recommendations on the amount of college credit they are worth. Colleges and universities accept the recommendations or use them as guidelines.

One program evaluates educational courses sponsored by government agencies, business and industry, labor unions, and professional and voluntary organizations. It is the Program on Noncollegiate Sponsored Instruction (PONSI). Some of the training seminars Alice has participated in covered topics such as food preparation, kitchen safety, and nutrition. Although she has not yet earned her GED, Alice can earn college credit because of her completion of these formal job-training seminars. The number of credits each seminar is worth does not hinge on Alice's current eligibility for college enrollment.

The other program evaluates courses offered by the Army, Navy, Air Force, Marines, Coast Guard, and Department of Defense. It is the Military Evaluations Program. Jorge has never attended college, but the engineering technology classes he completed as part of his military training are worth college credit. And as an Army veteran, Jorge is eligible for a service that takes the evaluations one step further. The Army/American Council on Education Registry Transcript System (AARTS) will provide Jorge with an individualized transcript of American Council on Education credit recommendations for all courses he completed, the military occupational specialties (MOS's) he held, and examinations he passed while in the Army. All Army and National Guard enlisted personnel and veterans who enlisted after October 1981 are eligible for the transcript. Similar services are being considered by the Navy and Marine Corps.

To obtain a free transcript, see your Army Education Center for a 5454R transcript request form. Include your name, Social Security number, basic active service date, and complete address where you want the transcript sent. Mail your request to:

AARTS Operations Center
415 McPherson Ave.
Fort Leavenworth, KS 66027-1373

Recommendations for PONSI are published in *The National Guide to Educational Credit for Training Programs;* military program recommendations are in *The Guide to the Evaluation of Educational Experiences in the Armed Forces.* See the Resources section at the end of this article for more information about these publications.

Former military personnel who took a foreign language course through the Defense Language Institute may request course transcripts by sending their name, Social Security number, course title, duration of the course, and graduation date to:

Commandant, Defense Language Institute
Attn: ATFL-DAA-AR
Transcripts
Presidio of Monterey
Monterey, CA 93944-5006

Not all of Jorge's and Alice's courses have been assessed by the American Council on Education. Training courses that have no Council credit recommendation should still be assessed by an advisor at the schools they want to attend. Course descriptions, class notes, test scores, and other documentation may be helpful for comparing training courses to their college equivalents. An oral examination or other demonstration of competency might also be required.

There is no guarantee you will receive all the credits you are seeking – but you certainly won't if you make no attempt.

Credit By Examination

Standardized tests are the best-known method of receiving college credit without taking courses. These exams are often taken by high school students seeking advanced placement for college, but they are also available to adult learners. Testing programs and colleges and universities offer exams in a number of subjects. Two U.S. Government institutes have foreign language exams for employees that also may be worth college credit.

It is important to understand that receiving a passing score on these exams does not mean you get college credit automatically. Each school determines which test results it will accept, minimum scores required, how scores are converted for credit, and the amount of credit, if any, to be assigned. Most colleges and universities accept the American Council on Education credit recommendations, published every other year in the 250-page *Guide to Educational Credit by Examination*. For more information, contact:

The American Council on Education
Credit by Examination Program
One Dupont Circle, Suite 250
Washington, DC 20036-1193
(202) 939-9434

Testing programs:

You might know some of the five national testing programs by their acronyms or initials: CLEP, ACT PEP: RCE, DANTES, AP, and NOCTI. (The meanings of these initialisms are explained below.) There is some overlap among programs; for example, four of them have introductory accounting exams. Since you will not be awarded credit more than once for a specific subject, you should carefully evaluate each program for the subject exams you wish to take. And before taking an exam, make sure you will be awarded credit by the college or university you plan to attend.

CLEP (College-Level Examination Program), administered by the College Board, is the most widely accepted of the national testing programs; more than 2,800 accredited schools award credit for passing exam scores. Each test covers material taught in basic undergraduate courses. There are five general exams – English composition, humanities, college mathematics, natural sciences, and social sciences and history – and many subject exams. Most exams are entirely multiple-choice, but English composition exams may include an essay section. For more information, contact:

CLEP
P.O. Box 6600
Princeton, NJ 08541-6600
(609) 771-7865

ACT PEP: RCE (American College Testing Proficiency Exam Program: Regents College Examinations) tests are given in 38 subjects within arts and sciences, business, education, and nursing. Each exam is recommended for either lower- or upper-level credit. Exams contain either objective or extended response questions, and are graded according to a standard score, letter grade, or pass/fail. Fees vary, depending on the subject and type of exam. For more information or to request free study guides, contact:

ACT PEP: Regents College Examinations
P.O. Box 4014
Iowa City, IA 52243
(319) 337-1387
(New York State residents must contact Regents College directly.)

DANTES (Defense Activity for Nontraditional Education Support) standardized tests are developed by the Educational Testing Service for the Department of Defense. Originally administered only to military personnel, the exams have been available to the public since 1983. About 50 subject tests cover business, mathematics, social science, physical science, humanities, foreign languages, and applied technology. Most of the tests consist entirely of multiple-choice questions. Schools determine their own administering fees and testing schedules. For more information or to request free study sheets, contact:

DANTES Program Office
Mail Stop 31-X
Educational Testing Service
Princeton, NJ 08541
1(800) 257-9484

The AP (Advanced Placement) Program is a cooperative effort between secondary schools and colleges and universities. AP exams are developed each year by committees of college and high school faculty appointed by the College Board and assisted by consultants from the Educational Testing Service. Subjects include arts and languages, natural sciences, computer science, social sciences, history, and mathematics. Most tests are 2 or 3 hours long and include both multiple-choice and essay questions. AP courses are available to help students prepare for exams, which are offered in the spring. For more information about the Advanced Placement Program, contact:

Advanced Placement Services
P.O. Box 6671
Princeton, NJ 08541-6671
(609) 771-7300

NOCTI (National Occupational Competency Testing Institute) assessments are designed for people like Alice, who have vocational-technical skills that cannot be evaluated by other tests. NOCTI assesses competency at two levels: Student/job ready and teacher/experienced worker. Standardized evaluations are available for occupations such as auto-body repair, electronics, mechanical drafting, quantity food preparation, and upholstering. The tests consist of multiple-choice questions and a performance component. Other services include workshops, customized assessments, and pre-testing. For more information, contact:

NOCTI
500 N. Bronson Ave.
Ferris State University
Big Rapids, MI 49307
(616) 796-4699

Colleges and universities:

Many colleges and universities have credit-by-exam programs, through which students earn credit by passing a comprehensive exam for a course offered by the institution. Among the most widely recognized are the programs at Ohio University, the University of North Carolina, Thomas Edison State College, and New York University.

Ohio University offers about 150 examinations for credit. In addition, you may sometimes arrange to take special examinations in non-laboratory courses offered at Ohio University. To take a test for credit, you must enroll in the course. If you plan to transfer the credit earned, you also need written permission from an official at your school. Books and study materials are available, for a cost, through the university. Exams must be taken within 6 months of the enrollment date; most last 3 hours. You may arrange to take the exam off campus if you do not live near the university.

Ohio University is on the quarter-hour system; most courses are worth 4 quarter hours, the equivalent of 3 semester hours. For more information, contact:

Independent Study
Tupper Hall 302
Ohio University
Athens, OH 45701-2979
1(800) 444-2910
(614) 593-2910

The University of North Carolina offers a credit-by-examination option for 140 independent study (correspondence) courses in foreign languages, humanities, social sciences, mathematics, business administration, education, electrical and computer engineering, health administration, and natural sciences. To take an exam, you must request and receive approval from both the course instructor and the independent studies department. Exams must be taken within six months of enrollment, and you may register for no more than two at a time. If you are not near the University's Chapel Hill campus, you may take your exam under supervision at an accredited college, university, community college, or technical institute. For more information, contact:

Independent Studies
CB #1020, The Friday Center
UNC-Chapel Hill
Chapel Hill, NC 27599-1020
1(800) 862-5669 / (919) 962-1134

The Thomas Edison College Examination Program offers more than 50 exams in liberal arts, business, and professional areas. Thomas Edison State College administers tests twice a month in Trenton, New Jersey; however, students may arrange to take their tests with a proctor at any accredited American college or university or U.S. military base. Most of the tests are multiple choice; some also include short answer or essay questions. Time limits range from 90 minutes to 4 hours, depending on the exam. For more information, contact:

Thomas Edison State College
TECEP, Office of Testing and Assessment
101 W. State Street
Trenton, NJ 08608-1176
(609) 633-2844

New York University's Foreign Language Program offers proficiency exams in more than 40 languages, from Albanian to Yiddish. Two exams are available in each language: The 12-point test is equivalent to 4 undergraduate semesters, and the 16-point exam may lead to upper level credit. The tests are given at the university's Foreign Language Department throughout the year.

Proof of foreign language proficiency does not guarantee college credit. Some colleges and universities accept transcripts only for languages commonly taught, such as French and Spanish. Nontraditional programs are more likely than traditional ones to grant credit for proficiency in other languages.

For an informational brochure and registration form for NYU's foreign language proficiency exams, contact:

New York University
Foreign Language Department
48 Cooper Square, Room 107
New York, NY 10003
(212) 998-7030

Government institutes:

The Defense Language Institute and Foreign Service Institute administer foreign language proficiency exams for personnel stationed abroad. Usually, the tests are given at the end of intensive language courses or upon completion of service overseas. But some people – like Jorge, who knows Spanish – speak another language fluently and may be allowed to take a proficiency exam in that language before completing their tour of duty. Contact one of the offices listed below to obtain transcripts of those scores. Proof of proficiency does not guarantee college credit, however, as discussed above.

To request score reports from the Defense Language Institute for Defense Language Proficiency Tests, send your name, Social Security number, language for which you were tested, and, most importantly, when and where you took the exam to:

Commandant, Defense Language Institute
Attn: ATFL-ES-T
DLPT Score Report Request
Presidio of Monterey
Monterey, CA 93944-5006

To request transcripts of scores for Foreign Service Institute exams, send your name, Social Security number, language for which you were tested, and dates or year of exams to:

Foreign Service Institute
Arlington Hall
4020 Arlington Boulevard
Rosslyn, VA 22204-1500
Attn: Testing Office (Send your request to the attention of the testing office of the foreign language in which you were tested)

Credit For Experience

Experiential learning credit may be given for knowledge gained through job responsibilities, personal hobbies, volunteer opportunities, homemaking, and other experiences. Colleges and universities base credit awards on the knowledge you have attained, not for the experience alone. In addition, the knowledge must be college level; not just any learning will do. Throwing horseshoes as a hobby is not likely to be worth college credit. But if you've done research on how and where the sport originated, visited blacksmiths, organized tournaments, and written a column for a trade journal – well, that's a horseshoe of a different color.

Adults attempting to get credit for their experience should be forewarned: Having your experience evaluated for college credit is time-consuming, tedious work – not an easy shortcut for people who want quick-fix college credits. And not all experience, no matter how valuable, is the equivalent of college courses.

Requesting college credit for your experiential learning can be tricky. You should get assistance from a credit evaluations officer at the school you plan to attend, but you should also have a general idea of what your knowledge is worth. A common method for converting knowledge into credit is to use a college catalog. Find course titles and descriptions that match what you have learned through experience, and request the number of credits offered for those courses.

Once you know what credit to ask for, you must usually present your case in writing to officials at the college you plan to attend. The most common form of presenting experiential learning for credit is the portfolio. A portfolio is a written record of your knowledge along with a request for equivalent college credit. It includes an identification and description of the knowledge for which you are requesting credit, an explanatory essay of how the knowledge was gained and how it fits into your educational plans, documentation that you have acquired such knowledge, and a request for college credit. Required elements of a portfolio vary by schools but generally follow those guidelines.

In identifying knowledge you have gained, be specific about exactly what you have learned. For example, it is not enough for Lynette to say she runs a business. She must identify the knowledge she has gained from running it, such as personnel management, tax law, marketing strategy, and inventory review. She must also include brief descriptions about her knowledge of each to support her claims of having those skills.

The essay gives you a chance to relay something about who you are. It should address your educational goals, include relevant autobiographical details, and be well organized, neat, and convey confidence. In his essay, Jorge might first state his goal of becoming an engineer. Then he would explain why he joined the Army, where he got hands-on training and experience in developing and servicing electronic equipment.

This, he would say, led to his hobby of creating remote-controlled model cars, of which he has built 20. His conclusion would highlight his accomplishments and tie them to his desire to become an electronic engineer.

Documentation is evidence that you've learned what you claim to have learned. You can show proof of knowledge in a variety of ways, including audio or video recordings, letters from current or former employers describing your specific duties and job performance, blueprints, photographs or artwork, and transcripts of certifying exams for professional licenses and certification – such as Alice's certification from the American Culinary Federation. Although documentation can take many forms, written proof alone is not always enough. If it is impossible to document your knowledge in writing, find out if your experiential learning can be assessed through supplemental oral exams by a faculty expert.

Earning a College Degree

Nontraditional students often have work, family, and financial obligations that prevent them from quitting their jobs to attend school full time. Can they still meet their educational goals? Yes.

More than 150 accredited colleges and universities have nontraditional bachelor's degree programs that require students to spend little or no time on campus; over 300 others have nontraditional campus-based degree programs. Some of those schools, as well as most junior and community colleges, offer associate's degrees nontraditionally. Each school with a nontraditional course of study determines its own rules for awarding credit for prior coursework, exams, or experience, as discussed previously. Most have charges on top of tuition for providing these special services.

Several publications profile nontraditional degree programs; see the Resources section at the end of this article for more information. To determine which school best fits your academic profile and educational goals, first list your criteria. Then, evaluate nontraditional programs based on their accreditation, features, residency requirements, and expenses. Once you have chosen several schools to explore further, write to them for more information. Detailed explanations of school policies should help you decide which ones you want to apply to.

Get beyond the printed word – especially the glowing words each school writes about itself. Check out the schools you are considering with higher education authorities, alumni, employers, family members, and friends. If possible, visit the campus to talk to students and instructors and sit in on a few classes, even if you will be completing most or all of your work off campus. Ask school officials questions about such things as enrollment numbers, graduation rate, faculty qualifications, and confusing details about the application process or academic policies. After you have thoroughly investigated each prospective college or university, you can make an informed decision about which is right for you.

Accreditation

Accreditation is a process colleges and universities submit to voluntarily for getting their credentials. An accredited school has been investigated and visited by teams of observers and has periodic inspections by a private accrediting agency. The initial review can take two years or more.

Regional agencies accredit entire schools, and professional agencies accredit either specialized schools or departments within schools. Although there are no national accrediting standards, not just any accreditation will do. Countless "accreditation associations" have been invented by schools, many of which have no academic programs and sell phony degrees, to accredit themselves. But 6 regional and about 80 professional accrediting associations in the United States are recognized by the U.S. Department of Education or the Commission on Recognition of Postsecondary Accreditation. When checking accreditation, these are the names to look for. For more information about accreditation and accrediting agencies, contact:

Institutional Participation Oversight Service Accreditation and State Liaison Division
U.S. Department of Education
ROB 3, Room 3915
600 Independence Ave., SW
Washington, DC 20202-5244
(202) 708-7417

Because accreditation is not mandatory, lack of accreditation does not necessarily mean a school or program is bad. Some schools choose not to apply for accreditation, are in the process of applying, or have educational methods too unconventional for an accrediting association's standards. For the nontraditional student, however, earning a degree from a college or university with recognized accreditation is an especially important consideration. Although nontraditional education is becoming more widely accepted, it is not yet mainstream. Employers skeptical of a degree earned in a nontraditional manner are likely to be even less accepting of one from an unaccredited school.

Program Features

Because nontraditional students have diverse educational objectives, nontraditional schools are diverse in what they offer. Some programs are geared toward helping students organize their scattered educational credits to get a degree as quickly as possible. Others cater to those who may have specific credits or experience but need assistance in completing requirements. Whatever your educational profile, you should look for a program that works with you in obtaining your educational goals.

A few nontraditional programs have special admissions policies for adult learners like Alice, who plan to earn their GEDs but want to enroll in college in the meantime. Other features of nontraditional programs include individualized learning agreements, intensive academic counseling, cooperative learning and internship placement, and waiver of some prerequisites or other requirements – as well as college credit for prior coursework, examinations, and experiential learning, all discussed previously.

Lynette, whose primary goal is to finish her degree, wants to earn maximum credits for her business experience. She will look for programs that do not limit the number of credits awarded for equivalency exams and experiential learning. And since well-documented proof of knowledge is essential for earning experiential learning credits, Lynette should make sure the program she chooses provides assistance to students submitting a portfolio.

Jorge, on the other hand, has more credits than he needs in certain areas and is willing to forego some. To become an engineer, he must have a bachelor's degree; but because he is accustomed to hands-on learning, Jorge is interested in getting experience as he gains more technical skills. He will concentrate on finding schools with strong cooperative education, supervised fieldwork, or internship programs.

Residency Requirements

Programs are sometimes deemed nontraditional because of their residency requirements. Many people think of residency for colleges and universities in terms of tuition, with in-state students paying less than out-of-state ones. Residency also may refer to where a student lives, either on or off campus, while attending school.

But in nontraditional education, residency usually refers to how much time students must spend on campus, regardless of whether they attend classes there. In some nontraditional programs, students need not ever step foot on campus. Others require only a very short residency, such as one day or a few weeks. Many schools have standard residency requirements of several semesters but schedule classes for evenings or weekends to accommodate working adults.

Lynette, who previously took courses by independent study, prefers to earn credits by distance study. She will focus on schools that have no residency requirement. Several colleges and universities have nonresident degree completion programs for adults with some college credit. Under the direction of a faculty advisor, students devise a plan for earning their remaining credits. Methods for earning credits include independent study, distance learning, seminars, supervised fieldwork, and group study at arranged sites. Students may have to earn a certain number of credits through the degree-granting institution. But many programs allow students to take courses at accredited schools of their choice for transfer toward their degree.

Alice wants to attend lectures but has an unpredictable schedule. Her best course of action will be to seek out short residency programs that require students to attend seminars once or twice a semester. She can take courses that are televised and videotape them to watch when her schedule permits, with the seminars helping to ensure that she properly completes her coursework. Many colleges and universities with short residency requirements also permit students to earn some credits elsewhere, by whatever means the student chooses.

Some fields of study require classroom instruction. As Jorge will discover, few colleges and universities allow students to earn a bachelor's degree in engineering entirely through independent study. Nontraditional residency programs are designed to accommodate adults' daytime work schedules. Jorge should look for programs offering evening, weekend, summer, and accelerated courses.

Tuition and Other Expenses

The final decisions about which schools Alice, Jorge, and Lynette attend may hinge in large part on a single issue: Cost. And rising tuition is only part of the equation. Beginning with application fees and continuing through graduation fees, college expenses add up.

Traditional and nontraditional students have some expenses in common, such as the cost of books and other materials. Tuition might even be the same for some courses, especially for colleges and universities offering standard ones at unusual times. But for nontraditional programs, students may also pay fees for services such as credit or transcript review, evaluation, advisement, and portfolio assessment.

Students are also responsible for postage and handling or setup expenses for independent study courses, as well as for all examination and transcript fees for transferring credits. Usually, the more nontraditional the program, the more detailed the fees. Some schools charge a yearly enrollment fee rather than tuition for degree completion candidates who want their files to remain active.

Although tuition and fees might seem expensive, most educators tell you not to let money come between you and your educational goals. Talk to someone in the financial aid department of the school you plan to attend or check your library for publications about financial aid sources. The U.S. Department of Education publishes a guide to Federal aid programs such as Pell Grants, student loans, and work-study. To order the free 74-page booklet, *The Student Guide: Financial Aid from the U.S. Department of Education,* contact:

Federal Student Aid Information Center
P.O. Box 84
Washington, DC 20044
1 (800) 4FED-AID (433-3243)

Resources

Information on how to earn a high school diploma or college degree without following the usual routes is available from several organizations and in numerous publications. Information on nontraditional graduate degree programs, available for master's through doctoral level, though not discussed in this article, can usually be obtained from the same resources that detail bachelor's degree programs.

National Learning Corporation publishes study guides for all of these exams, for both general examinations and tests in specific subject areas. To order study guides, or to browse their catalog featuring more than 5,000 titles, visit NLC online at www.passbooks.com, or contact them by phone at (800) 632-8888.

Organizations

Adult learners should always contact their local school system, community college, or university to learn about programs that are readily available. The following national organizations can also supply information:

American Council on Education
One Dupont Circle
Washington, DC 20036-1193
(202) 939-9300

Within the American Council on Education, the Center for Adult Learning and Educational Credentials administers the National External Diploma Program, the GED Program, the Program on Noncollegiate Sponsored Instruction, the Credit by Examination Program, and the Military Evaluations Program.

College-Level Examination Program (CLEP)

1. WHAT IS CLEP?

CLEP stands for the College-Level Examination Program, sponsored by the College Board. It is a national program of credit-by-examination that offers you the opportunity to obtain recognition for college-level achievement. No matter when, where, or how you have learned – by means of formal or informal study – you can take CLEP tests. If the results are acceptable to your college, you can receive credit.

You may not realize it, but you probably know more than your academic record reveals. Each day you, like most people, have an opportunity to learn. In private industry and business, as well as at all levels of government, learning opportunities continually occur. If you read widely or intensively in a particular field, think about what you read, discuss it with your family and friends, you are learning. Or you may be learning on a more formal basis by taking a correspondence course, a television or radio course, a course recorded on tape or cassettes, a course assembled into programmed tests, or a course taught in your community adult school or high school.

No matter how, where, or when you gained your knowledge, you may have the opportunity to receive academic credit for your achievement that can be counted toward an undergraduate degree. The College-Level Examination Program (CLEP) enables colleges to evaluate your achievement and give you credit. A wide range of college-level examinations are offered by CLEP to anyone who wishes to take them. Scores on the tests are reported to you and, if you wish, to a college, employer, or individual.

2. WHAT ARE THE PURPOSES OF THE COLLEGE-LEVEL EXAMINATION PROGRAM?

The basic purpose of the College-Level Examination Program is to enable individuals who have acquired their education in nontraditional ways to demonstrate their academic achievement. It is also intended for use by those in higher education, business, industry, government, and other fields who need a reliable method of assessing a person's educational level.

Recognizing that the real issue is not how a person has acquired his education but what education he has, the College Level Examination Program has been designed to serve a variety of purposes. The basic purpose, as listed above, is to enable those who have reached the college level of education in nontraditional ways to assess the level of their achievement and to use the test results in seeking college credit or placement.

In addition, scores on the tests can be used to validate educational experience obtained at a nonaccredited institution or through noncredit college courses.

Some colleges and universities may use the tests to measure the level of educational achievement of their students, and for various institutional research purposes.

Other colleges and universities may wish to use the tests in the admission, placement, and guidance of students who wish to transfer from one institution to another.

Businesses, industries, governmental agencies, and professional groups now accept the results of these tests as a basis for advancement, eligibility for further training, or professional or semi-professional certification.

Many people are interested in the examination simply to assess their own educational progress and attainment.

The college, university, business, industry, or government agency that adopts the tests in the College-Level Examination Program makes its own decision about how it will use and interpret the test scores. The College Board will provide the tests, score them, and report the results either to the individuals who took the tests or the college or agency that administered them. It does NOT, and cannot, award college credit, certify college equivalency, or make recommendations regarding the standards these institutions should establish for the use of the test results.

Therefore, if you are taking the tests to secure credit from an institution, you should FIRST ascertain whether the college or agency involved will accept the scores. Each institution determines which CLEP tests it will accept for credit and the amount of credit it will award. If you want to take tests for college credit, first call, write, or visit the college you wish to attend to inquire about its policy on CLEP scores, as well as its other admission requirements.

The services of the program are also available to people who have been requested to take the tests by an employer, a professional licensing agency, a certifying agency, or by other groups that recognize college equivalency on the basis of satisfactory CLEP scores. You may, of course, take the tests SOLELY for your own information. If you do, your scores will be reported only to you.

While neither CLEP nor the College Board can evaluate previous credentials or award college credit, you will receive, with your scores, basic information to help you interpret your performance on the tests you have taken.

3. WHAT ARE THE COLLEGE-LEVEL EXAMINATIONS?

In order to meet different kinds of curricular organization and testing needs at colleges and universities, the College-Level Examination Program offers 35 different subject tests falling under five separate general categories: Composition and Literature, Foreign Languages, History and Social Sciences, Science and Mathematics, and Business.

4. WHAT ARE THE SUBJECT EXAMINATIONS?

The 35 CLEP tests offered by the College Board are listed below:

COMPOSITION AND LITERATURE:
- American Literature
- Analyzing and Interpreting Literature
- English Composition
- English Composition with Essay
- English Literature
- Freshman College Composition
- Humanities

FOREIGN LANGUAGES
- French
- German
- Spanish

HISTORY AND SOCIAL SCIENCES
- American Government
- Introduction to Educational Psychology
- History of the United States I: Early Colonization to 1877
- History of the United States II: 1865 to the Present
- Human Growth and Development
- Principles of Macroeconomics
- Principles of Microeconomics
- Introductory Psychology
- Social Sciences and History
- Introductory Sociology
- Western Civilization I: Ancient Near East to 1648
- Western Civilization II: 1648 to the Present

SCIENCE AND MATHEMATICS
- College Algebra
- College Algebra-Trigonometry
- Biology
- Calculus
- Chemistry
- College Mathematics
- Natural Sciences
- Trigonometry
- Precalculus

BUSINESS
- Financial Accounting
- Introductory Business Law
- Information Systems and Computer Applications
- Principles of Management
- Principles of Marketing

CLEP Examinations cover material taught in courses that most students take as requirements in the first two years of college. A college usually grants the same amount of credit to students earning satisfactory scores on the CLEP examination as it grants to students successfully completing the equivalent course.

Many examinations are designed to correspond to one-semester courses; some, however, correspond to full-year or two-year courses.

Each exam is 90 minutes long and, except for English Composition with Essay, is made up primarily of multiple-choice questions. Some tests have several other types of questions besides multiple choice. To see a more detailed description of a particular CLEP exam, visit www.collegeboard.com/clep.

The English Composition with Essay exam is the only exam that includes a required essay. This essay is scored by college English faculty designated by CLEP and does not require an additional fee. However, other Composition and Literature tests offer optional essays, which some college and universities require and some do not. These essays are graded by faculty at the individual institutions that require them and require an additional $10 fee. Contact the particular institution to ask about essay requirements, and check with your test center for further details.

All 35 CLEP examinations are administered on computer. If you are unfamiliar with taking a test on a computer, consult the CLEP Sampler online at www.collegeboard.com/clep. The Sampler contains the same tutorials as the actual exams and helps familiarize you with navigation and how to answer different types of questions.

Points are not deducted for wrong or skipped answers – you receive one point for every correct answer. Therefore it is best that an answer is supplied for each exam question, whether it is a guess or not. The number of correct answers is then converted to a formula score. This formula, or "scaled," score is determined by a statistical process called *equating*, which adjusts for slight differences in difficulty between test forms and ensures that your score does not depend on the specific test form you took or how well others did on the same form. The scaled scores range from 20 to 80 – this is the number that will appear on your score report.

To ensure that you complete all questions in the time allotted, you would probably be wise to skip the more difficult or perplexing questions and return to them later. Although the multiple-choice items in these tests are carefully designed so as not to be tricky, misleading, or ambiguous, on the other hand, they are not all direct questions of factual information. They attempt, in their way, to elicit a response that indicates your knowledge or lack of knowledge of the material in question or your ability or inability to use or interpret a fact or idea. Thus, you should concentrate on answering the questions as they appear to be without attempting to out-guess the testmakers.

5. WHAT ARE THE FEES?

The fee for all CLEP examinations is $55. Optional essays required by some institutions are an additional $10.

6. WHEN ARE THE TESTS GIVEN?

CLEP tests are administered year-round. Consult the CLEP website (www.collegeboard.com/clep) and individual test centers for specific information.

7. WHERE ARE THE TESTS GIVEN?

More than 1,300 test centers are located on college and university campuses throughout the country, and additional centers are being established to meet increased needs. Any accredited collegiate institution with an explicit and publicly available policy of credit by examination can become a CLEP test center. To obtain a list of these centers, visit the CLEP website at www.collegeboard.com/clep.

8. HOW DO I REGISTER FOR THE COLLEGE-LEVEL EXAMINATION PROGRAM?

Contact an individual test center for information regarding registration, scheduling and fees. Registration/admission forms can also be obtained on the CLEP website.

9. MAY I REPEAT THE COLLEGE-LEVEL EXAMINATIONS?

You may repeat any examination providing at least six months have passed since you were last administered this test. If you repeat a test within a period of time less than six months, your scores will be cancelled and your fees forfeited. To repeat a test, check the appropriate space on the registration form.

10. WHEN MAY I EXPECT MY SCORE REPORTS?

With the exception of the English Composition with Essay exam, you should receive your score report instantly once the test is complete.

11. HOW SHOULD I PREPARE FOR THE COLLEGE-LEVEL EXAMINATIONS?

This book has been specifically designed to prepare candidates for these examinations. It will help you to consider, study, and review important content, principles, practices, procedures, problems, and techniques in the form of varied and concrete applications.

12. QUESTIONS AND ANSWERS APPEARING IN THIS PUBLICATION

The College-Level Examinations are offered by the College Board. Since copies of past examinations have not been made available, we have used equivalent materials, including questions and answers, which are highly recommended by us as an appropriate means of preparing for these examinations.

If you need additional information about CLEP Examinations, visit www.collegeboard.com/clep.

THE COLLEGE-LEVEL EXAMINATION PROGRAM

How The Program Works

CLEP examinations are administered at many colleges and universities across the country, and most institutions award college credit to those who do well on them. The examinations provide people who have acquired knowledge outside the usual educational settings the opportunity to show that they have learned college-level material without taking certain college courses.

The CLEP examinations cover material that is taught in introductory-level courses at many colleges and universities. Faculties at individual colleges review the tests to ensure that they cover the important material taught in their courses. Colleges differ in the examinations they accept; some colleges accept only two or three of the examinations while others accept nearly all of them.

Although CLEP is sponsored by the College Board and the examinations are scored by Educational Testing Service (ETS), neither of these organizations can award college credit. Only accredited colleges may grant credit toward a degree. When you take a CLEP examination, you may request that a copy of your score report be sent to the college you are attending or plan to attend. After evaluating your scores, the college will decide whether or not to award you credit for a certain course or courses, or to exempt you from them. If the college gives you credit, it will record the number of credits on your permanent record, thereby indicating that you have completed work equivalent to a course in that subject. If the college decides to grant exemption without giving you credit for a course, you will be permitted to omit a course that would normally be required of you and to take a course of your choice instead.

What the Examinations Are Like

The examinations consist mostly of multiple-choice questions to be answered within a 90-minute time limit. Additional information about each CLEP examination is given in the examination guide and on the CLEP website.

<u>Where To Take the Examinations</u>

CLEP examinations are administered throughout the year at the test centers of approximately 1,300 colleges and universities. On the CLEP website, you will find a list of institutions that award credit for satisfactory scores on CLEP examinations. Some colleges administer CLEP examinations to their own students only. Other institutions administer the tests to anyone who registers to take them. If your college does not administer the tests, contact the test centers in your area for information about its testing schedule.

Once you have been tested, your score report will be available instantly. CLEP scores are kept on file at ETS for 20 years; and during this period, for a small fee, you may have your transcript sent to another college or to anyone else you specify. (Your scores will never be sent to anyone without your approval.)

APPROACHING A COLLEGE ABOUT CLEP

The following sections provide a step-by-step approach to learning about the CLEP policy at a particular college or university. The person or office that can best assist students desiring CLEP credit may have a different title at each institution, but the following guidelines will lead you to information about CLEP at any institution.

Adults returning to college often benefit from special assistance when they approach a college. Opportunities for adults to return to formal learning in the classroom are now widespread, and colleges and universities have worked hard to make this a smooth process for older students. Many colleges have established special service offices that are staffed with trained professionals who understand the kinds of problems facing adults returning to college. If you think you might benefit from such assistance, be sure to find out whether these services are available at your college.

<u>How to Apply for College Credit</u>

STEP 1. Obtain the General Information Catalog and a copy of the CLEP policy from the colleges you are considering. If you have not yet applied for admission, ask for an admissions application form too.

Information about admissions and CLEP policies can be obtained by contacting college admissions offices or finding admissions information on the school websites. Tell the admissions officer that you are a prospective student and that you are interested in applying for admission and CLEP credit. Ask for a copy of the publication in which the college's complete CLEP policy is explained. Also get the name and the telephone number of the person to contact in case you have further questions about CLEP.

At this step, you may wish to obtain information from external degree colleges. Many adults find that such colleges suit their needs exceptionally well.

STEP 2. If you have not already been admitted to the college you are considering, look at its admission requirements for undergraduate students to see if you can qualify.

This is an important step because if you can't get into college, you can't get college credit for CLEP. Nearly all colleges require students to be admitted and to enroll in one or more courses before granting the students CLEP credit.

Virtually all public community colleges and a number of four-year state colleges have open admission policies for in-state students. This usually means that they admit anyone who has graduated from high school or has earned a high school equivalency diploma.

If you think you do not meet the admission requirements, contact the admissions office for an interview with a counselor. Colleges do sometimes make exceptions, particularly for adult applicants. State why you want the interview and ask what documents you should bring with you or send in advance. (These materials may include a high school transcript, transcript of previous college work, completed application for admission, etc.) Make an extra effort to have all the information requested in time for the interview.

During the interview, relax and be yourself. Be prepared to state honestly why you think you are ready and able to do college work. If you have already taken CLEP examinations and scored high enough to earn credit, you have shown that you are able to do college work. Mention this achievement to the admissions counselor because it may increase your chances of being accepted. If you have not taken a CLEP examination, you can still improve your chances of being accepted by describing how your job training or independent study has helped prepare you for college-level work. Tell the counselor what you have learned from your work and personal experiences.

STEP 3. Evaluate the college's CLEP policy.

Typically, a college lists all its academic policies, including CLEP policies, in its general catalog. You will probably find the CLEP policy statement under a heading such as Credit-by-Examination, Advanced Standing, Advanced Placement, or External Degree Program. These sections can usually be found in the front of the catalog.

Many colleges publish their credit-by-examination policies in a separate brochure, which is distributed through the campus testing office, counseling center, admissions office, or registrar's office. If you find a very general policy statement in the college catalog, seek clarification from one of these offices.

Review the material in the section of this guide entitled Questions to Ask About a College's CLEP Policy. Use these guidelines to evaluate the college's CLEP policy. If you have not yet taken a CLEP examination, this evaluation will help you decide which examinations to take and whether or not to take the free-response or essay portion. Because individual colleges have different CLEP policies, a review of several policies may help you decide which college to attend.

STEP 4. If you have not yet applied for admission, do so early.

Most colleges expect you to apply for admission several months before you enroll, and it is essential that you meet the published application deadlines. It takes time to process your application for admission; and if you have yet to take a CLEP examination, it will be some time before the college receives and reviews your score report. You will probably want to take some, if not all, of the CLEP examinations you are interested in before you enroll so you know which courses you need not register for. In fact, some colleges require that all CLEP scores be submitted before a student registers.

Complete all forms and include all documents requested with your application(s) for admission. Normally, an admissions decision cannot be reached until all documents have been submitted and evaluated. Unless told to do so, do not send your CLEP scores until you have been officially admitted.

STEP 5. Arrange to take CLEP examination(s) or to submit your CLEP score(s).

You may want to wait to take your CLEP examinations until you know definitely which college you will be attending. Then you can make sure you are taking tests your college will accept for credit. You will also be able to request that your scores be sent to the college, free of charge, when you take the tests.

If you have already taken CLEP examinations, but did not have a copy of your score report sent to your college, you may request the College Board to send an official transcript at any time for a small fee. Use the Transcript Request Form that was sent to you with your score report. If you do not have the form, you may find it online at www.collegeboard.com/clep.

Your CLEP scores will be evaluated, probably by someone in the admissions office, and sent to the registrar's office to be posted on your permanent record once you are enrolled. Procedures vary from college to college, but the process usually begins in the admissions office.

STEP 6. Ask to receive a written notice of the credit you receive for your CLEP score(s).

A written notice may save you problems later, when you submit your degree plan or file for graduation. In the event that there is a question about whether or not you earned CLEP credit, you will have an official record of what credit was awarded. You may also need this verification of course credit if you go for academic counseling before the credit is posted on your permanent record.

STEP 7. Before you register for courses, seek academic counseling.

A discussion with your academic advisor can prevent you from taking unnecessary courses and can tell you specifically what your CLEP credit will mean to you. This step may be accomplished at the time you enroll. Most colleges have orientation sessions for new students prior to each enrollment period. During orientation, students are usually assigned an academic advisor who then gives them individual help in developing long-range plans and a course schedule for the next semester. In conjunction with this counseling, you may be asked to take some additional tests so that you can be placed at the proper course level.

External Degree Programs

If you have acquired a considerable amount of college-level knowledge through job experience, reading, or noncredit courses, if you have accumulated college credits at a variety of colleges over a period of years, or if you prefer studying on your own rather than in a classroom setting, you may want to investigate the possibility of enrolling in an external degree program. Many colleges offer external degree programs that allow you to earn a degree by passing examinations (including CLEP), transferring credit from other colleges, and demonstrating in other ways that you have satisfied the educational requirements. No classroom attendance is required, and the programs are open to out-of-state candidates as well as residents. Thomas A. Edison State College in New Jersey and Charter Oaks College in Connecticut are fully accredited independent state colleges; the New York program is part of the state university system and is also fully accredited. If you are interested in exploring an external degree, you can write for more information to:

Charter Oak College
The Exchange, Suite 171
270 Farmington Avenue
Farmington, CT 06032-1909

Regents External Degree Program
Cultural Education Center
Empire State Plaza
Albany, New York 12230

Thomas A. Edison State College
101 West State Street
Trenton, New Jersey 08608

Many other colleges also have external degree or weekend programs. While they often require that a number of courses be taken on campus, the external degree programs tend to be more flexible in transferring credit, granting credit-by-examination, and allowing independent study than other traditional programs. When applying to a college, you may wish to ask whether it has an external degree or weekend program.

Questions to Ask About a College's CLEP Policy

Before taking CLEP examinations for the purpose of earning college credit, try to find the answers to these questions:

1. Which CLEP examinations are accepted by this college?

A college may accept some CLEP examinations for credit and not others - possibly not the one you are considering. The English faculty may decide to grant college English credit based on the CLEP English Composition examination, but not on the Freshman College Composition examination. Or, the mathematics faculty may decide to grant credit based on the College Mathematics to non-mathematics majors only, requiring majors to take an examination in algebra, trigonometry, or calculus to earn credit. For these reasons, it is important that you know the specific CLEP tests for which you can receive credit.

2. Does the college require the optional free-response (essay) section as well as the objective portion of the CLEP examination you are considering?

Knowing the answer to this question ahead of time will permit you to schedule the optional essay examination when you register to take your CLEP examination.

3. Is credit granted for specific courses? If so, which ones?

You are likely to find that credit will be granted for specific courses and the course titles will be designated in the college's CLEP policy. It is not necessary, however, that credit be granted for a specific course in order for you to benefit from your CLEP credit. For instance, at many liberal arts colleges, all students must take certain types of courses; these courses may be labeled the core curriculum, general education requirements, distribution requirements, or liberal arts requirements. The requirements are often expressed in terms of credit hours. For example, all students may be required to take at least six hours of humanities, six hours of English, three hours of mathematics, six hours of natural science, and six hours of social science, with no particular courses in these disciplines specified. In these instances, CLEP credit may be given as 6 hrs. English credit or 3 hrs. Math credit without specifying for which English or mathematics courses credit has been awarded. In order to avoid possible disappointment, you should know before taking a CLEP examination what type of credit you can receive and whether you will only be exempted from a required course but receive no credit.

4. How much credit is granted for each examination you are considering, and does the college place a limit on the total amount of CLEP credit you can earn toward your degree?

Not all colleges that grant CLEP credit award the same amount for individual tests. Furthermore, some colleges place a limit on the total amount of credit you can earn through CLEP or other examinations. Other colleges may grant you exemption but no credit toward your degree. Knowing several colleges' policies concerning these issues may help you decide which college you will attend. If you think you are capable of passing a number of CLEP examinations, you may want to attend a college that will allow you to earn credit for all or most of them. For example, the state external degree programs grant credit for most CLEP examinations (and other tests as well).

5. What is the required score for earning CLEP credit for each test you are considering?

Most colleges publish the required scores or percentile ranks for earning CLEP credit in their general catalog or in a brochure. The required score may vary from test to test, so find out the required score for each test you are considering.

6. What is the college's policy regarding prior course work in the subject in which you are considering taking a CLEP test?

Some colleges will not grant credit for a CLEP test if the student has already attempted a college-level course closely aligned with that test. For example, if you successfully completed English 101 or a comparable course on another campus, you will probably not be permitted to receive CLEP credit in that subject, too. Some colleges will not permit you to earn CLEP credit for a course that you failed.

7. Does the college make additional stipulations before credit will be granted?

It is common practice for colleges to award CLEP credit only to their enrolled students. There are other stipulations, however, that vary from college to college. For example, does the college require you to formally apply for or accept CLEP credit by completing and signing a form? Or does the college require you to validate your CLEP score by successfully completing a more advanced course in the subject? Answers to these and other questions will help to smooth the process of earning college credit through CLEP.

The above questions and the discussions that follow them indicate some of the ways in which colleges' CLEP policies can vary. Find out as much as possible about the CLEP policies at the colleges you are interested in so you can choose a college with a policy that is compatible with your educational goals. Once you have selected the college you will attend, you can find out which CLEP examinations your college recognizes and the requirements for earning CLEP credit.

DECIDING WHICH EXAMINATIONS TO TAKE

If You're Taking the Examinations for College Credit or Career Advancement:

Most people who take CLEP examinations do so in order to earn credit for college courses. Others take the examinations in order to qualify for job promotions or for professional certification or licensing. It is vital to most candidates who are taking the tests for any of these reasons that they be well prepared for the tests they are taking so that they can advance as rapidly as possible toward their educational or career goals.

It is usually advisable that those who have limited knowledge in the subjects covered by the tests they are considering enroll in the college courses in which that material is taught. Those who are uncertain about whether or not they know enough about a subject to do well on a particular CLEP test will find the following guidelines helpful.

There is no way to predict if you will pass a particular CLEP examination, but answers to the questions under the seven headings below should give you an indication of whether or not you are likely to succeed.

1. Test Descriptions

Read the description of the test provided. Are you familiar with most of the topics and terminology in the outline?

2. Textbooks

Examine the suggested textbooks and other resource materials following the test descriptions in this guide. Have you recently read one or more of these books, or have you read similar college-level books on this subject? If you have not, read through one or more of the textbooks listed, or through the textbook used for this course at your college. Are you familiar with most of the topics and terminology in the book?

3. Sample Questions

The sample questions provided are intended to be typical of the content and difficulty of the questions on the test. Although they are not an exact miniature of the test, the proportion of the sample questions you can answer correctly should be a rough estimate of the proportion of questions you will be able to answer correctly on the test.

Answer as many of the sample questions for this test as you can. Check your answers against the correct answers. Did you answer more than half the questions correctly?

Because of variations in course content at different institutions, and because questions on CLEP tests vary from easy to difficult - with most being of moderate difficulty - the average student who passes a course in a subject can usually answer correctly about half the questions on the corresponding CLEP examination. Most colleges set their passing scores near this level, but some set them higher. If your college has set its required score above the level required by most colleges, you may need to answer a larger proportion of questions on the test correctly.

4. Previous Study

Have you taken noncredit courses in this subject offered by an adult school or a private school, through correspondence, or in connection with your job? Did you do exceptionally well in this subject in high school, or did you take an honors course in this subject?

5. Experience

Have you learned or used the knowledge or skills included in this test in your job or life experience? For example, if you lived in a Spanish-speaking country and spoke the language for a year or more, you might consider taking the Spanish examination. Or, if you have worked at a job in which you used accounting and finance skills, Principles of Accounting would be a likely test for you to take. Or, if you have read a considerable amount of literature and attended many art exhibits, concerts, and plays, you might expect to do well on the Humanities exam.

6. Other Examinations

Have you done well on other standardized tests in subjects related to the one you want to take? For example, did you score well above average on a portion of a college entrance examination covering similar skills, or did you obtain an exceptionally high score on a high school equivalency test or a licensing examination in this subject? Although such tests do not cover exactly the same material as the CLEP examinations and may be easier, persons who do well on these tests often do well on CLEP examinations, too.

7. Advice

Has a college counselor, professor, or some other professional person familiar with your ability advised you to take a CLEP examination?

If your answer was yes to questions under several of the above headings, you probably have a good chance of passing the CLEP examination you are considering. It is unlikely that you would have acquired sufficient background from experience alone. Learning gained through reading and study is essential, and you will probably find some additional study helpful before taking a CLEP examination.

If You're Taking the Examinations to Prepare for College

Many people entering college, particularly adults returning to college after several years away from formal education, are uncertain about their ability to compete with other college students. They wonder whether they have sufficient background for college study, and those who have been away from formal study for some time wonder whether they have forgotten how to study, how to take tests, and how to write papers. Such people may wish to improve their test-taking and study skills prior to enrolling in courses.

One way to assess your ability to perform at the college level and to improve your test-taking and study skills at the same time is to prepare for and take one or more CLEP examinations. You need not be enrolled in a college to take a CLEP examination, and you may have your scores sent only to yourself and later request that a transcript be sent to a college if you then decide to apply for credit. By reviewing the test descriptions and sample questions, you may find one or several subject areas in which you think you have substantial knowledge. Select one examination, or more if you like, and carefully read at least one of the textbooks listed in the bibliography for the test. By doing this, you will get a better idea of how much you know of what is usually taught in a college-level course in that subject. Study as much material as you can, until you think you have a good grasp of the subject matter. Then take the test at a college in your area. It will be several weeks before you receive your results, and you may wish to begin reviewing for another test in the meantime.

To find out if you are eligible for credit for your CLEP score, you must compare your score with the score required by the college you plan to attend. If you are not yet sure which college you will attend, or whether you will enroll in college at all, you should begin to follow the steps outlined. It is best that you do this before taking a CLEP test, but if you are taking the test only for the experience and to familiarize yourself with college-level material and requirements, you might take the test before you approach a college. Even if the college you decide to attend does not accept the test you took, the experience of taking such a test will enable you to meet with greater confidence the requirements of courses you will take.

You will find information about how to interpret your scores in WHAT YOUR SCORES MEAN, which you will receive with your score report, and which can also be found online at the CLEP website. Many colleges follow the recommendations of the American Council on Education (ACE) for setting their required scores, so you can use this information as a guide in determining how well you did. The ACE recommendations are included in the booklet.

If you do not do well enough on the test to earn college credit, don't be discouraged. Usually, it is the best college students who are exempted from courses or receive credit-by-examination. The fact that you cannot get credit for your score means that you should probably enroll in a college course to learn the material. However, if your score was close to the required score, or if you feel you could do better on a second try or after some additional study, you may retake the test after six months. Do not take it sooner or your score will not be reported and your fee will be forfeited.

If you do earn the score required to earn credit, you will have demonstrated that you already have some college-level knowledge. You will also have a better idea whether you should take additional CLEP examinations. And, what is most important, you can enroll in college with confidence, knowing that you do have the ability to succeed.

PREPARING TO TAKE CLEP EXAMINATIONS

Having made the decision to take one or more CLEP examinations, most people then want to know if it is worthwhile to prepare for them - how much, how long, when, and how should they go about it? The precise answers to these questions vary greatly from individual to individual. However, most candidates find that some type of test preparation is helpful.

Most people who take CLEP examinations do so to show that they have already learned the important material that is taught in a college course. Many of them need only a quick review to assure themselves that they have not forgotten some of what they once studied, and to fill in some of the gaps in their knowledge of the subject. Others feel that they need a thorough review and spend several weeks studying for a test. A few wish to take a CLEP examination as a kind of final examination for independent study of a subject instead of the college course. This last group requires significantly more study than those who only need to review, and they may need some guidance from professors of the subjects they are studying.

The key to how you prepare for CLEP examinations often lies in locating those skills and areas of prior learning in which you are strong and deciding where to focus your energies. Some people may know a great deal about a certain subject area, but may not test well. These individuals would probably be just as concerned about strengthening their test-taking skills as they are about studying for a specific test. Many mental and physical skills are used in preparing for a test. It is important not only to review or study for the examinations, but to make certain that you are alert, relatively free of anxiety, and aware of how to approach standardized tests. Suggestions on developing test-taking skills and preparing psychologically and physically for a test are given. The following section suggests ways of assessing your knowledge of the content of a test and then reviewing and studying the material.

Using This Study Guide

Begin by carefully reading the test description and outline of knowledge and skills required for the examination, if given. As you read through the topics listed there, ask yourself how much you know about each one. Also note the terms, names, and symbols that are mentioned, and ask yourself whether you are familiar with them. This will give you a quick overview of how much you know about the subject. If you are familiar with nearly all the material, you will probably need a minimum of review; however, if less than half of it is familiar, you will probably require substantial study to do well on the test.

If, after reviewing the test description, you find that you need extensive review, delay answering the sample question until you have done some reading in the subject. If you complete them before reviewing the material, you will probably look for the answers as you study, and then they will not be a good assessment of your ability at a later date.

If you think you are familiar with most of the test material, try to answer the sample questions.

Apply the test-taking strategies given. Keeping within the time limit suggested will give you a rough idea of how quickly you should work in order to complete the actual test.

Check your answers against the answer key. If you answered nearly all the questions correctly, you probably do not need to study the subject extensively. If you got about half the questions correct, you ought o review at least one textbook or other suggested materials on the subject. If you answered less than half the questions correctly, you will probably benefit from more extensive reading in the subject and thorough study of one or more textbooks. The textbooks listed are used at many colleges but they are not the only good texts. You will find helpful almost any standard text available to you., such as the textbook used at your college, or earlier editions of texts listed. For some examinations, topic outlines and textbooks may not be available. Take the sample tests in this book and check your answers at the end of each test. Check wrong answers.

Suggestions for Studying

The following suggestions have been gathered from people who have prepared for CLEP examinations or other college-level tests.

1. Define your goals and locate study materials

First, determine your study goals. Set aside a block of time to review the material provided in this book, and then decide which test(s) you will take. Using the suggestions, locate suitable resource materials. If a preparation course is offered by an adult school or college in your area, you might find it helpful to enroll.

2. Find a good place to study

To determine what kind of place you need for studying, ask yourself questions such as: Do I need a quiet place? Does the telephone distract me? Do objects I see in this place remind me of things I should do? Is it too warm? Is it well lit? Am I too comfortable here? Do I have space to spread out my materials? You may find the library more conducive to studying than your home. If you decide to study at home, you might prevent interruptions by other household members by putting a sign on the door of your study room to indicate when you will be available.

3. Schedule time to study

To help you determine where studying best fits into your schedule, try this exercise: Make a list of your daily activities (for example, sleeping, working, and eating) and estimate how many hours per day you spend on each activity. Now, rate all the activities on your list in order of their importance and evaluate your use of time. Often people are astonished at how an average day appears from this perspective. They may discover that they were unaware how large portions of time are spent, or they learn their time can be scheduled in alternative ways. For example, they can remove the least important activities from their day and devote that time to studying or another important activity.

4. Establish a study routine and a set of goals

In order to study effectively, you should establish specific goals and a schedule for accomplishing them. Some people find it helpful to write out a weekly schedule and cross out each study period when it is completed. Others maintain their concentration better by writing down the time when they expect to complete a study task. Most people find short periods of intense study more productive than long stretches of time. For example, they may follow a regular schedule of several 20- or 30-minute study periods with short breaks between them. Some people like to allow themselves rewards as they complete each study goal. It is not essential that you accomplish every goal exactly within your schedule; the point is to be committed to your task.

5. Learn how to take an active role in studying.

If you have not done much studying for some time, you may find it difficult to concentrate at first. Try a method of studying, such as the one outlined below, that will help you concentrate on and remember what you read.

a. First, read the chapter summary and the introduction. Then you will know what to look for in your reading.

b. Next, convert the section or paragraph headlines into questions. For example, if you are reading a section entitled, The Causes of the American Revolution, ask yourself: *What were the causes of the American Revolution?* Compose the answer as you read the paragraph. Reading and answering questions aloud will help you understand and remember the material.

c. Take notes on key ideas or concepts as you read. Writing will also help you fix concepts more firmly in your mind. Underlining key ideas or writing notes in your book can be helpful and will be useful for review. Underline only important points. If you underline more than a third of each paragraph, you are probably underlining too much.

d. If there are questions or problems at the end of a chapter, answer or solve them on paper as if you were asked to do them for homework. Mathematics textbooks (and some other books) sometimes include answers to some or all of the exercises. If you have such a book, write your answers before looking at the ones given. When problem-solving is involved, work enough problems to master the required methods and concepts. If you have difficulty with problems, review any sample problems or explanations in the chapter.

e. To retain knowledge, most people have to review the material periodically. If you are preparing for a test over an extended period of time, review key concepts and notes each week or so. Do not wait for weeks to review the material or you will need to relearn much of it.

Psychological and Physical Preparation

Most people feel at least some nervousness before taking a test. Adults who are returning to college may not have taken a test in many years or they may have had little experience with standardized tests. Some younger students, as well, are uncomfortable with testing situations. People who received their education in countries outside the United States may find that many tests given in this country are quite different from the ones they are accustomed to taking.

Not only might candidates find the types of tests and the kinds of questions on them unfamiliar, but other aspects of the testing environment may be strange as well. The physical and mental stress that results from meeting this new experience can hinder a candidate's ability to demonstrate his or her true degree of knowledge in the subject area being tested. For this reason, it is important to go to the test center well prepared, both mentally and physically, for taking the test. You may find the following suggestions helpful.

1. Familiarize yourself, as much as possible, with the test and the test situation before the day of the examination. It will be helpful for you to know ahead of time:

a. How much time will be allowed for the test and whether there are timed subsections.

b. What types of questions and directions appear on the examination.

c. How your test score will be computed.

d. How to properly answer the questions on the computer (See the CLEP Sample on the CLEP website)

e. In which building and room the examination will be administered. If you don't know where the building is, locate it or get directions ahead of time.

f. The time of the test administration. You might wish to confirm this information a day or two before the examination and find out what time the building and room will be open so that you can plan to arrive early.

g. Where to park your car or, if you wish to take public transportation, which bus or train to take and the location of the nearest stop.

h. Whether smoking will be permitted during the test.

i. Whether there will be a break between examinations (if you will be taking more than one on the same day), and whether there is a place nearby where you can get something to eat or drink.

2. Go to the test situation relaxed and alert. In order to prepare for the test:

a. Get a good night's sleep. Last minute cramming, particularly late the night before, is usually counterproductive.

b. Eat normally. It is usually not wise to skip breakfast or lunch on the day of the test or to eat a big meal just before the test.

c. Avoid tranquilizers and stimulants. If you follow the other directions in this book, you won't need artificial aids. It's better to be a little tense than to be drowsy, but stimulants such as coffee and cola can make you nervous and interfere with your concentration.

d. Don't drink a lot of liquids before the test. Having to leave the room during the test will disturb your concentration and take valuable time away from the test.

e. If you are inclined to be nervous or tense, learn some relaxation exercises and use them before and perhaps during the test.

3. Arrive for the test early and prepared. Be sure to:

a. Arrive early enough so that you can find a parking place, locate the test center, and get settled comfortably before testing begins. Allow some extra time in case you are delayed unexpectedly.

b. Take the following with you:

- Your completed Registration/Admission Form
- Two forms of identification – one being a government-issued photo ID with signature, such as a driver's license or passport
- Non-mechanical pencil
- A watch so that you can time your progress (digital watches are prohibited)
- Your glasses if you need them for reading or seeing the chalkboard or wall clock

c. Leave all books, papers, and notes outside the test center. You will not be permitted to use your own scratch paper; it will be provided. Also prohibited are calculators, cell phones, beepers, pagers, photo/copy devices, radios, headphones, food, beverages, and several other items.

d. Be prepared for any temperature in the testing room. Wear layers of clothing that can be removed if the room is too hot but will keep you warm if it is too cold.

4. When you enter the test room:

a. Sit in a seat that provides a maximum of comfort and freedom from distraction.

b. Read directions carefully, and listen to all instructions given by the test administrator. If you don't understand the directions, ask for help before test timing begins. If you must ask a question after the test has begun, raise your hand and a proctor will assist you. The proctor can answer certain kinds of questions but cannot help you with the test.

c. Know your rights as a test taker. You can expect to be given the full working time allowed for the test(s) and a reasonably quiet and comfortable place in which to work. If a poor test situation is preventing you from doing your best, ask if the situation can be remedied. If bad test conditions cannot be remedied, ask the person in charge to report the problem in the Irregularity Report that will be sent to ETS with the answer sheets. You may also wish to contact CLEP. Describe the exact circumstances as completely as you can. Be sure to include the test date and name(s) of the test(s) you took. ETS will investigate the problem to make sure it does not happen again, and, if the problem is serious enough, may arrange for you to retake the test without charge.

TAKING THE EXAMINATIONS

A person may know a great deal about the subject being tested, but not do as well as he or she is capable of on the test. Knowing how to approach a test is an important part of the testing process. While a command of test-taking skills cannot substitute for knowledge of the subject matter, it can be a significant factor in successful testing.

Test-taking skills enable a person to use all available information to earn a score that truly reflects his or her ability. There are different strategies for approaching different kinds of test questions. For example, free-response questions require a very different tack than do multiple-choice questions. Other factors, such as how the test will be graded, may also influence your approach to the test and your use of test time. Thus, your preparation for a test should include finding out all you can about the test so that you can use the most effective test-taking strategies.

Before taking a test, you should know approximately how many questions are on the test, how much time you will be allowed, how the test will be scored or graded, what types of questions and directions are on the test, and how you will be required to record your answers.

Taking Multiple-Choice Tests

1. Listen carefully to the instructions given by the test administrator and read carefully all directions before you begin to answer the questions.

2. Note the time that the test administrator starts timing the test. As you proceed, make sure that you are not working too slowly. You should have answered at least half the questions in a section when half the time for that section has passed. If you have not reached that point in the section, speed up your pace on the remaining questions.

3. Before answering a question, read the entire question, including all the answer choices. Don't think that because the first or second answer choice looks good to you, it isn't necessary to read the remaining options. Instructions usually tell you to select the best answer. Sometimes one answer choice is partially correct, but another option is better; therefore, it is usually a good idea to read all the answers before you choose one.

4. Read and consider every question. Questions that look complicated at first glance may not actually be so difficult once you have read them carefully.

5. Do not puzzle too long over any one question. If you don't know the answer after you've considered it briefly, go on to the next question. Make sure you return to the question later.

6. Make sure you record your response properly.

7. In trying to determine the correct answer, you may find it helpful to cross out those options that you know are incorrect, and to make marks next to those you think might be correct. If you decide to skip the question and come back to it later, you will save yourself the time of reconsidering all the options.

8. Watch for the following key words in test questions:

all	generally	never	perhaps
always	however	none	rarely
but	may	not	seldom
except	must	often	sometimes
every	necessary	only	usually

When a question or answer option contains words such as always, every, only, never, and none, there can be no exceptions to the answer you choose. Use of words such as often, rarely, sometimes, and generally indicates that there may be some exceptions to the answer.

9. Do not waste your time looking for clues to right answers based on flaws in question wording or patterns in correct answers. Professionals at the College Board and ETS put

a great deal of effort into developing valid, reliable, fair tests. CLEP test development committees are composed of college faculty who are experts in the subject covered by the test and are appointed by the College Board to write test questions and to scrutinize each question that is included on a CLEP test. Committee members make every effort to ensure that the questions are not ambiguous, that they have only one correct answer, and that they cover college-level topics. These committees do not intentionally include trick questions. If you think a question is flawed, ask the test administrator to report it, or contact CLEP immediately.

Taking Free-Response or Essay Tests

If your college requires the optional free-response or essay portion of a CLEP Composition and Literature exams, you should do some additional preparation for your CLEP test. Taking an essay test is very different from taking a multiple-choice test, so you will need to use some other strategies.

The essay written as part of the English Composition and Essay exam is graded by English professors from a variety of colleges and universities. A process called holistic scoring is used to rate your writing ability.

The optional free-response essays, on the other hand, are graded by the faculty of the college you designate as a score recipient. Guidelines and criteria for grading essays are not specified by the College Board or ETS. You may find it helpful, therefore, to talk with someone at your college to find out what criteria will be used to determine whether you will get credit. If the test requires essay responses, ask how much emphasis will be placed on your writing ability and your ability to organize your thoughts as opposed to your knowledge of subject matter. Find out how much weight will be given to your multiple-choice test score in comparison with your free-response grade in determining whether you will get credit. This will give you an idea where you should expend the greatest effort in preparing for and taking the test.

Here are some strategies you will find useful in taking any essay test:

1. Before you begin to write, read all questions carefully and take a few minutes to jot down some ideas you might include in each answer.

2. If you are given a choice of questions to answer, choose the questions you think you can answer most clearly and knowledgeably.

3. Determine in what order you will answer the questions. Answer those you find the easiest first so that any extra time can be spent on the more difficult questions.

4. When you know which questions you will answer and in what order, determine how much testing time remains and estimate how many minutes you will devote to each question. Unless suggested times are given for the questions or one question appears to require more or less time than the others, allot an equal amount of time to each question.

5. Before answering each question, indicate the number of the question as it is given in the test book. You need not copy the entire question from the question sheet, but it will be helpful to you and to the person grading your test if you indicate briefly the topic you are addressing – particularly if you are not answering the questions in the order in which they appear on the test.

6. Before answering each question, read it again carefully to make sure you are interpreting it correctly. Underline key words, such as those listed below, that often appear in free-response questions. Be sure you know the exact meaning of these words before taking the test.

analyze	demonstrate	enumerate	list
apply	derive	explain	outline
assess	describe	generalize	prove
compare	determine	illustrate	rank
contrast	discuss	interpret	show
define	distinguish	justify	summarize

If a question asks you to outline, define, or summarize, do not write a detailed explanation; if a question asks you to analyze, explain, illustrate, interpret, or show, you must do more than briefly describe the topic.

For a current listing of CLEP Colleges

where you can get credit and be tested, write:

CLEP, P.O. Box 6600, Princeton, NJ 08541-6600

Or e-mail: clep@ets.org, or call: (609) 771-7865

HOW TO TAKE A TEST

You have studied long, hard and conscientiously.

With your official admission card in hand, and your heart pounding, you have been admitted to the examination room.

You note that there are several hundred other applicants in the examination room waiting to take the same test.

They all appear to be equally well prepared.

You know that nothing but your best effort will suffice. The "moment of truth" is at hand: you now have to demonstrate objectively, in writing, your knowledge of content and your understanding of subject matter.

You are fighting the most important battle of your life—to pass and/or score high on an examination which will determine your career and provide the economic basis for your livelihood.

What extra, special things should you know and should you do in taking the examination?

BEFORE THE TEST

YOUR PHYSICAL CONDITION IS IMPORTANT

If you are not well, you can't do your best work on tests. If you are half asleep, you can't do your best either. Here are some tips:

1) Get about the same amount of sleep you usually get. Don't stay up all night before the test, either partying or worrying—DON'T DO IT!
2) If you wear glasses, be sure to wear them when you go to take the test. This goes for hearing aids, too.
3) If you have any physical problems that may keep you from doing your best, be sure to tell the person giving the test. If you are sick or in poor health, you really cannot do your best on any test. You can always come back and take the test some other time.

AT THE TEST

EXAMINATION TECHNIQUES

1) Read the general instructions carefully. These are usually printed on the first page of the exam booklet. As a rule, these instructions refer to the timing of the examination; the fact that you should not start work until the signal and must stop work at a signal, etc. If there are any *special* instructions, such as a choice of questions to be answered, make sure that you note this instruction carefully.

2) When you are ready to start work on the examination, that is as soon as the signal has been given, read the instructions to each question booklet, underline any key words or phrases, such as *least, best, outline, describe* and the like. In this way you will tend to answer as requested rather than discover on reviewing your paper that you *listed without describing*, that you selected the *worst* choice rather than the *best* choice, etc.

3) If the examination is of the objective or multiple-choice type – that is, each question will also give a series of possible answers: A, B, C or D, and you are called upon to select the best answer and write the letter next to that answer on your answer paper – it is advisable to start answering each question in turn. There may be anywhere from 50 to 100 such questions in the three or four hours allotted and you can see how much time would be taken if you read through all the questions before beginning to answer any. Furthermore, if you come across a question or group of questions which you know would be difficult to answer, it would undoubtedly affect your handling of all the other questions.

4) If the examination is of the essay type and contains but a few questions, it is a moot point as to whether you should read all the questions before starting to answer any one. Of course, if you are given a choice – say five out of seven and the like – then it is essential to read all the questions so you can eliminate the two which are most difficult. If, however, you are asked to answer all the questions, there may be danger in trying to answer the easiest one first because you may find that you will spend too much time on it. The best technique is to answer the first question, then proceed to the second, etc.

5) Time your answers. Before the exam begins, write down the time it started, then add the time allowed for the examination and write down the time it must be completed, then divide the time available somewhat as follows:
   • If 3-1/2 hours are allowed, that would be 210 minutes. If you have 80 objective-type questions, that would be an average of 2-1/2 minutes per question. Allow yourself no more than 2 minutes per question, or a total of 160 minutes, which will permit about 50 minutes to review.
   • If for the time allotment of 210 minutes there are 7 essay questions to answer, that would average about 30 minutes a question. Give yourself only 25 minutes per question so that you have about 35 minutes to review.

6) The most important instruction is to *read each question* and make sure you know what is wanted. The second most important instruction is to *time yourself properly* so that you answer every question. The third most important instruction is to *answer every question*. Guess if you have to but include something for each question. Remember that you will receive no credit for a blank and will probably receive some credit if you write something in answer to an essay question. If you guess a letter – say "B" for a multiple-choice question – you may have guessed right. If you leave a blank as an answer to a multiple-choice question, the examiners may respect your

feelings but it will not add a point to your score. Some exams may penalize you for wrong answers, so in such cases *only*, you may not want to guess unless you have some basis for your answer.

7) Suggestions
   a. Objective-type questions
      1. Examine the question booklet for proper sequence of pages and questions
      2. Read all instructions carefully
      3. Skip any question which seems too difficult; return to it after all other questions have been answered
      4. Apportion your time properly; do not spend too much time on any single question or group of questions
      5. Note and underline key words – *all, most, fewest, least, best, worst, same, opposite,* etc.
      6. Pay particular attention to negatives
      7. Note unusual option, e.g., unduly long, short, complex, different or similar in content to the body of the question
      8. Observe the use of "hedging" words – *probably, may, most likely,* etc.
      9. Make sure that your answer is put next to the same number as the question
      10. Do not second-guess unless you have good reason to believe the second answer is definitely more correct
      11. Cross out original answer if you decide another answer is more accurate; do not erase until you are ready to hand your paper in
      12. Answer all questions; guess unless instructed otherwise
      13. Leave time for review

   b. Essay questions
      1. Read each question carefully
      2. Determine exactly what is wanted. Underline key words or phrases.
      3. Decide on outline or paragraph answer
      4. Include many different points and elements unless asked to develop any one or two points or elements
      5. Show impartiality by giving pros and cons unless directed to select one side only
      6. Make and write down any assumptions you find necessary to answer the questions
      7. Watch your English, grammar, punctuation and choice of words
      8. Time your answers; don't crowd material

8) Answering the essay question

Most essay questions can be answered by framing the specific response around several key words or ideas. Here are a few such key words or ideas:

M's: manpower, materials, methods, money, management
P's: purpose, program, policy, plan, procedure, practice, problems, pitfalls, personnel, public relations

a. Six basic steps in handling problems:
   1. Preliminary plan and background development
   2. Collect information, data and facts
   3. Analyze and interpret information, data and facts
   4. Analyze and develop solutions as well as make recommendations
   5. Prepare report and sell recommendations
   6. Install recommendations and follow up effectiveness

b. Pitfalls to avoid
   1. *Taking things for granted* – A statement of the situation does not necessarily imply that each of the elements is necessarily true; for example, a complaint may be invalid and biased so that all that can be taken for granted is that a complaint has been registered
   2. *Considering only one side of a situation* – Wherever possible, indicate several alternatives and then point out the reasons you selected the best one
   3. *Failing to indicate follow up* – Whenever your answer indicates action on your part, make certain that you will take proper follow-up action to see how successful your recommendations, procedures or actions turn out to be
   4. *Taking too long in answering any single question* – Remember to time your answers properly

EXAMINATION SECTION

ANATOMIC SCIENCES
EXAMINATION SECTION

TEST 1

DIRECTIONS: Each question or incomplete statement is followed by several suggested answers or completions. Select the one that BEST answers the question or completes the statement. *PRINT THE LETTER OF THE CORRECT ANSWER IN THE SPACE AT THE RIGHT.*

1. Cerebrospinal fluid can be aspirated MOST safely by inserting the needle between the third and the fourth lumbar vertebrae because
   A. there is more space between the laminae of these two vertebrae
   B. the subarachnoid space does not extend below lumbar 4
   C. there is less danger of entering the internal vertebral plexus at this level
   D. the spinal cord usually does not extend below lumbar 2
   E. there are no important nerves in this part of the vertebral canal

1.___

2. An efferent lymphatic channel and an afferent lymphatic channel in lymph nodes *differ* in that the efferent vessel
   A. is located in the hilus region of the gland, whereas the afferent vessel enters the gland elsewhere
   B. contains numerous myeloid white blood cells, whereas the afferent vessel will contain few, if any, white blood cells
   C. has no valve structure, whereas the afferent vessel has a valve component
   D. is lined partially with reticuloendothelial cells, whereas the afferent vessel is lined totally with endothelial cells
   E. none of the above

2.___

3. The lesser omentum is a
   A. peritoneal fold connecting the lesser curvature of the stomach and the first part of the duodenum to the liver
   B. part of the peritoneal cavity separated from the greater sac
   C. layer of retroperitoneal fat around the kidneys
   D. mesentery connecting the liver to the anterior abdominal wall
   E. none of the above

3.___

4. A synapse between an axon of one neuron and a dendrite of another neuron is characterized by
   A. being nonpolarized and by being mere contacts between two neurons
   B. causing a slight delay in impulse transmission and by preventing impulse flow in two directions
   C. having anatomic continuity between the neurons and by being more difficult to fatigue than nerve processes

4.___

    D. being easily fatigued and by allowing fiber degenera-
       tion to pass from one neuron to the next neuron in
       the chain
    E. none of the above

5. The anterior boundary of the posterior mediastinum is the   5.___
    A. manubrium
    B. sternal angle
    C. body of the sternum
    D. pericardium on anterior aspect of the heart
    E. pericardium on posterior aspect of the heart

6. Compared with the left primary bronchus, the right primary   6.___
   bronchus is
    A. straighter, shorter, and larger
    B. more curved, longer, and smaller
    C. straighter, longer, and larger
    D. the same in size and structure
    E. none of the above

7. The appearance of striated muscle is a reflection of the   7.___
    A. location of sarcosomes
    B. striations in the sarcolemma
    C. fragmentation of mitochondria
    D. contraction waves along the muscle
    E. arrangement of macromolecular units in the myofibril

8. The sympathetic innervation to structures of the head and   8.___
   neck is distributed via the
    A. blood vessels
    B. fascial planes
    C. hyoid musculature
    D. cranial nerves III, VII, IX, and X
    E. none of the above

9. Hassall's bodies, as found in the thymus gland, represent   9.___
    A. occluded blood vessels
    B. vestiges of epithelium
    C. remnants of Rathke's pouch
    D. aggregations of degenerated lymphocytes
    E. all of the above

10. The heart is contained in the   10.___
    A. middle mediastinum   B. superior mediastinum
    C. anterior mediastinum   D. posterior mediastinum
    E. none of the above

11. The nasobuccal membrane ruptures at about   11.___
    A. 3 weeks in utero   B. 5 weeks in utero
    C. 9-10 weeks in utero   D. 3 months in utero
    E. birth

12. The intrinsic muscle that extends from the dorsum of the   12.___
   tongue toward the ventral surface is known as the
    A. verticalis   B. transversus
    C. superior longitudinalus   D. inferior longitudinalus
    E. none of the above

13. The respiratory portion of the respiratory system is
    characterized by
       A. possessing cartilage and by being actively under
          autonomic nervous system control
       B. serving for the O_2-CO_2 exchange and by being lined by
          a visceral layer of pleura
       C. containing alveolar lymphocytes as a component of the
          wall and by being supplied with blood from the bronchial
          vessels
       D. having simple squamous epithelium as a lining and by
          having scattered smooth muscle cells in some of its walls
       E. none of the above   13.___

14. The constricted passage between the mouth and the pharynx   14.___
    is called the
       A. fauces   B. vestibule
       C. valleculae   D. tonsillar fossa
       E. none of the above

15. The common carotid artery usually bifurcates at the level   15.___
    of the
       A. thyroid isthmus
       B. cricoid cartilage
       C. angle of the mandible
       D. superior border of the thyroid cartilage
       E. none of the above

16. The ascending aorta differs from the superior vena cava   16.___
    in that the aorta has
       A. a thicker tunica adventitia
       B. smooth muscle in the tunica media
       C. more elastic tissue in the tunica media
       D. longitudinal muscle in the tunica adventitia
       E. none of the above

17. Oxyphil cells are characteristic of which organ?   17.___
       A. Pineal body
       B. Thyroid gland
       C. Adrenal medulla
       D. Parathyroid gland
       E. Exocrine portion of pancreas

18. From the standpoint of lesser to greater size, which of   18.___
    the following sequences of leukocytes is CORRECT?
       A. Basophil, neutrophil, eosinophil, monocyte
       B. Neutrophil, eosinophil, monocyte, basophil
       C. Eosinophil, monocyte, basophil, neutrophil
       D. Monocyte, basophil, neutrophil, eosinophil
       E. None of the above

19. In surgical excision of the parotid gland, which of the   19.___
    following structures may be damaged?
       A. Submandibular duct
       B. Motor nerves to the temporal muscle
       C. Facial nerve, external carotid artery, auriculo-
          temporal nerve
       D. Lesser occipital nerve, spinal accessory nerve,
          hypoglossal nerve
       E. All of the above

20. Which of the following concerning the thyroid gland is   20.___
    CORRECT?
    A. Histologically, the thyroid gland has its parenchymal
       cells arranged as rounded follicles containing colloid
       material. If the follicles undergo atrophy in an
       adult, the condition of acromegaly ensues.
    B. TSH from pars anterior of the pituitary regulates
       thyroid gland activity. If the amount of TSH is
       deficient, epithelial cells of the follicles change
       from squamous to cuboidal shape.
    C. Parafollicular (C) cells in the thyroid gland elaborate
       calcitonin. This hormone tends to increase the blood
       calcium level in contrast to parathormone which tends
       to lower the blood calcium level.
    D. Follicular epithelium in instances of simple goiter is
       tall columnar. These tall cells are present because
       they are elaborating excess colloid material which
       causes the follicles to become enlarged.
    E. None of the above

21. The pigment granules of the basal cells of the epithelium   21.___
    of the gingiva originate in
    A. connective tissue fibers B. surface epithelial cells
    C. macrophages   D. melanoblasts
    E. neuroblasts

22. Which of the following is surrounded partly by connective   22.___
    tissue and partly by epithelium, contains lymphoid follicles,
    contains a cortex and a medulla, has no lymph sinuses, and
    is penetrated by a number of crypts?
    A. Spleen   B. Thymus
    C. Lymph node   D. Palatine tonsil
    E. Cortex

23. Which of the following lymph nodes are found along the   23.___
    course of the external jugular vein?
    A. Deep cervical nodes   B. Submandibular nodes
    C. Jugolodigastric nodes   D. Superficial cervical nodes
    E. Tracheal nodes

24. ALL of the following structures open into the right   24.___
    atrium EXCEPT the
    A. coronary sinus   B. pulmonary veins
    C. inferior vena cava   D. superior vena cava
    E. smallest cardiac veins

25. ALL of the following cell types secrete the substance   25.___
    with which they are paired EXCEPT
    A. Sertoli's cells - testosterone
    B. corpus luteum - progesterone
    C. alpha cells of pancreas - glucagon
    D. chromaffin cells of adrenal - catecholamines
    E. all of the above are correct

KEY (CORRECT ANSWERS)

1. D	11. B
2. A	12. A
3. A	13. D
4. B	14. A
5. E	15. D
6. A	16. C
7. E	17. D
8. A	18. A
9. B	19. C
10. A	20. A

21. D
22. D
23. D
24. B
25. A

TEST 2

DIRECTIONS: Each question or incomplete statement is followed by several suggested answers or completions. Select the one that BEST answers the question or completes the statement. *PRINT THE LETTER OF THE CORRECT ANSWER IN THE SPACE AT THE RIGHT.*

1. Which of the following tissues would be LEAST affected
   after destruction of the anterior lobe of the hypophysis?
   A. Thyroid epithelium
   B. Medulla of the adrenal gland
   C. Interstitial cells of the testis
   D. Zona fasciculata of the adrenal gland
   E. Spermatogenic epithelium of the testis

   1.___

2. Which of the following structures is in contact with the
   thyroid gland?
   A. Vagus nerve
   B. Phrenic nerve
   C. Thoracic duct
   D. Thyroarytenoid muscle
   E. Recurrent (inferior) laryngeal nerve

   2.___

3. Which of the following groups of muscles is supplied by
   the facial nerve?
   A. Buccinator, frontal, nasalis, masseter
   B. Masseter, temporal, medial pterygoid, lateral pterygoid
   C. Orbicularis oris, orbicularis oculi, stapedius,
      platysma
   D. Cremaster, risorius, levator anguli oris, zygomaticus
      major
   E. All of the above

   3.___

4. Which of the following muscles receive innervation from
   the fifth nerve?
   A. Mylohyoid, anterior belly of digastric, and tensor
      tympani
   B. Mylohyoid, anterior and posterior bellies of digastric,
      stapedius, and tensor tympani
   C. Mylohyoid, anterior belly of digastric geniohyoid, and
      tensor tympani
   D. Mylohyoid, anterior belly of digastric, platysma,
      tensor tympani, and stapedius
   E. None of the above

   4.___

5. Which of the following is a pure serous gland?
   A. Sublingual gland   B. Glands of Brunner
   C. Submandibular gland   D. Glands of von Ebner
   E. Glands of Blandin-Nuhn

   5.___

6. Fibrocartilage is characterized by   6.___
    A. being found in intervertebral disks, and by having parallel collagenous fibers
    B. having the ability to grow by apposition, and by developing from endoderm
    C. containing considerable nonsulfated mucopolysaccharides, and by appearing "glasslike" in life
    D. becoming calcified to form bone, and by lacking blood vessels
    E. none of the above

7. The external carotid artery contributes to the blood   7.___
supply of the nasal cavity via
    A. facial artery - superior labial artery - angular arteries
    B. lingual artery - deep lingual - internal nasal arteries
    C. occipital artery - ascending palatine - posterior nasal arteries
    D. maxillary artery - sphenopalatine - posterior lateral nasal arteries
    E. superficial temporal artery - transverse facial - external nasal arteries

8. Characteristics of the duodenum include   8.___
    I. tall columnar epithelium
   II. stratified squamous epithelium
 III. parietal and chief cells
  IV. Paneth's cells
   V. mucous glands in the submucosa
  VI. Peyer's patches

The CORRECT answer is:
    A. I, III, IV   B. I, IV, V
    C. I, V, VI   D. II, III, IV
    E. II, IV, V

9. A sinusoidal arrangement of blood vessels is found in the   9.___
    I. hypophysis   II. spleen
 III. kidney   IV. liver

The CORRECT answer is:
    A. I, II   B. I, II, IV
    C. I, III   D. II, III, IV
    E. I, II, III

10. The thyroid is derived from   10.___
    A. ectoderm of the stomodeum
    B. mesoderm of the third branchial arch
    C. endoderm between the first and the second branchial arches
    D. somites C_3 through C_5
    E. ectoderm of the first branchial arch

11. Skin is composed of   11.___
   A. epidermis, dermis, and hypodermis
   B. epidermis and hypodermis
   C. dermis and hypodermis
   D. epidermis and dermis
   E. all of the above

12. Two features which characterize the hypophysis are its   12.___
   A. development from endoderm and its location in the posterior cranial fossa
   B. blood supply by the external carotid artery and its development from Rathke's pouch
   C. anterior lobe having parenchymal cells arranged in cords and its development from ectoderm
   D. location in a depression in the anterior cranial fossa and its secretion of a hormone which controls calcium metabolism
   E. none of the above

13. Which statement indicates a TRUE similarity between skin of the forearm and skin of the palm?   13.___
   A. Both types contain sebaceous glands.
   B. The stratum germinativum is present in each.
   C. A stratum lucidum is present in each.
   D. The thickness of the epidermis is about the same.
   E. None of the above

14. Which of the following groups of organs are all retro-peritoneal?   14.___
   A. Kidney, adrenal, and rectum
   B. Pancreas, stomach, and ovary
   C. Kidney, transverse colon, and ovary
   D. Ureter, gallbladder, and transverse colon
   E. Pancreas, transverse colon, and descending colon

15. Lymph from the superior lateral quadrant of the mammary gland drains first into lymph nodes located adjacent to what vein?   15.___
   A. Axillary   B. Brachial
   C. Cephalic   D. Subclavian
   E. Internal thoracic

16. Of the lymphoid tissues in the body, which are considered as being subepithelial and nonencapsulated?   16.___
   A. Tonsils and thymus gland
   B. Peyer's patches and tonsils
   C. Thymus gland and lymph nodes
   D. Lymph nodes and aggregated nodules
   E. Thymus gland and aggregated nodules

17. Which artery is MOST concerned with the blood supply to the upper lip?   17.___
   A. Facial
   B. Maxillary
   C. External nasal
   D. Greater palatine
   E. Anterior superior alveolar

18. Which of the following statements concerning skin is   18.___
    CORRECT?
    A. The dermis contains a wider variety of nerve endings
       than does the epidermis.
    B. The epidermis is derived from mesenchyme.
    C. Areas without sebaceous glands have no stratum.
    D. In thick skin, as on the sole of the foot, the base-
       ment membrane is lacking.
    E. None of the above

19. What is the major change in bone matrix during its   19.___
    mineralization?
    A. Cells develop processes
    B. Water content decreases
    C. Haversian systems enlarge
    D. Ground substance aggregates
    E. Collagenous fibrils are formed

20. Epithelial cells in oral mucosa appear more adherent to   20.__
    each other in selective sites known as
       A. autosomes   B. lysosomes
       C. ribosomes   D. desmosomes
       E. karyosomes

21. The dura mater is the   22.___
       A. outer layer of the meninges
       B. inner layer of the meninges
       C. membrane covering peripheral nerve fibers
       D. membrane which lines the ventricles
       E. membrane covering the brain

22. Circulating blood elements involved in antibody production 22.___
    are
       A. neutrophils   B. lymphocytes
       C. erythrocytes   D. thrombocytes
       E. plasma cells

23. The greater peritoneal sac is placed in communication   23.___
    with the lesser peritoneal sac by means of the
       A. aortic hiatus   B. inguinal canal
       C. epiploic foramen   D. lesser pelvic aperture
       E. superior pelvic aperture

24. Total destruction of the third cranial nerve would result   24.___
    in paralysis of
       A. all extrinsic muscles of the eye and sphincter pupillae
       B. all rectus muscles of the eye, levator palpebrae and
          dilator pupillae
       C. superior, medial and inferior rectus, levator palpebrae
          and dilator pupillae
       D. superior, medial and inferior rectus, inferior oblique,
          levator palpebrae and sphincter pupillae
       E. the entire body

25. Neuroepithelial cells are *most likely* to be found in
    A. simple columnar epithelium of the stomach
    B. pseudostratified epithelium of the trachea
    C. stratified squamous epithelium of the tongue
    D. simple cuboidal epithelium of the kidney tubule
    E. any of the above

25.____

KEY (CORRECT ANSWERS)

1. B	11. D		
2. E	12. C		
3. C	13. B		
4. A	14. A		
5. D	15. A		
6. A	16. B		
7. D	17. A		
8. B	18. A		
9. B	19. B		
10. C	20. D		

21. A
22. B
23. C
24. D
25. C

EXAMINATION SECTION
TEST 1

DIRECTIONS: Each question or incomplete statement is followed by several suggested answers or completions. Select the one that BEST answers the question or completes the statement. *PRINT THE LETTER OF THE CORRECT ANSWER IN THE SPACE AT THE RIGHT.*

1. Which of the following structures pass through the parotid gland?   1.___
   I. Facial nerve
   II. Retromandibular vein
   III. External carotid artery
   IV. Superficial temporal artery
   V. Branches of the great auricular nerve

   The CORRECT answer is:
   A. I, II, III   B. I, II, IV
   C. I, III, V   D. II, III, V
   E. all of the above

2. Which of the following is NOT correct concerning the adrenal medulla?   2.___
   A. Has the same embryologic origin as sympathetic ganglia
   B. Is separated from the surrounding cortex of gland by a capsule of collagen fibers
   C. Is composed of many cells containing membrane-bound osmiophilic granules
   D. Has an intrinsic stroma consisting primarily of a network of reticular fibers
   E. Is connected with the surrounding cortex of gland by a capsule of collagen fibers

3. Increased resistance to pulmonary blood flow in the lungs would cause a strain on which chamber of the heart?   3.___
   A. Left atrium   B. Right atrium
   C. Left ventricle   D. Right ventricle
   E. All of the above

4. Which of the following is a cytoplasmic inclusion?   4.___
   A. Endoplasmic reticulum   B. Golgi apparatus
   C. Free ribosome   D. Mitochondria
   E. Glycogen

5. From which pharyngeal pouches do the parathyroid glands develop?   5.___
   A. First and second   B. Second and third
   C. Third and fourth   D. Fourth and fifth
   E. Third and fifth

6. Which of the following endocrine glands possesses, within it, a vascular portal system?   6.___
   A. Hypophysis   B. Thyroid gland
   C. Suprarenal gland   D. Parathyroid gland
   E. Islet of Langerhans

7. Which lymphatic organ has efferent and afferent lymphatic   7.___
   vessels?
   A. Spleen   B. Thymus
   C. Lymph node   D. Palatine tonsil
   E. Pharyngeal tonsil

8. Epithelial surface variations whose *primary* purpose is   8.___
   to increase functional surface area are
   A. cilia   B. flagella
   C. microvilli   D. macrovilli
   E. all of the above

9. The infrahyoid muscles receive their motor innervation   9.___
   from
   A. the vagus nerve
   B. the pharyngeal plexus
   C. supraclavicular nerves
   D. branches of the cervical plexus
   E. branches of the myenteric plexus

10. The hypophysis is characterized by a(n)   10.___
    A. pars nervosa with beta cells
    B. pars tuberalis with alpha cells
    C. pars nervosa without Herring bodies
    D. pars intermedius with alpha and beta cells
    E. anterior lobe with alpha and beta cells

11. The buccopharyngeal membrane is composed of   11.___
    A. ectoderm and endoderm
    B. ectoderm and mesoderm
    C. mesoderm and endoderm
    D. ectoderm, mesoderm, and endoderm
    E. ectoderm *only*

12. Bile is conducted   12.___
    A. away from the liver by the cystic duct
    B. away from the small intestine by the common bile duct
    C. into and out of the gallbladder by the common bile duct
    D. away from the liver and into the cystic duct by the
       common hepatic duct
    E. toward the liver by the cystic duct

13. Thin myofilaments and thick myofilaments are observed in   13.___
    the masseter muscle in E/M preparations. The thick filaments
    A. consist of actin
    B. are present in the I bands
    C. are crossed by the Z line
    D. are present only in the A band
    E. consist of both actin and myosin

14. The major structures forming the root of the lung are   14.___
    A. bronchus, phrenic nerve, bronchial arteries, and veins
    B. bronchus, azygos vein, and pulmonary artery
    C. bronchus, bronchial arteries, and veins
    D. bronchus, pulmonary artery, and veins
    E. bronchus, azygos vein, and phrenic nerve

15. The middle pharyngeal constrictor attaches to the   15.___
    A. mandible   B. hyoid bone
    C. cricoid cartilage   D. pterygomandibular raphe
    E. lateral pterygoid plate

16. The left kidney is in visceral contact anteriorly with the 16.___
    A. ileum   B. liver
    C. stomach   D. duodenum
    E. inferior vena cava

17. Mineralization of bone is characterized by increased   17.___
    inorganic material and
    A. increased collagen with a decrease in water
    B. decreased collagen and water
    C. little change in collagen or water content
    D. decreased water with little change in collagen content
    E. increased collagen and water

18. In hyaline cartilage, the chondrocytes are surrounded by 18.___
    a capsule which is
    A. a zone of decalcification
    B. an envelope of loose connective tissue
    C. a blister-like extension of the chondrocyte
    D. a calcified layer of intercellular substance
    E. the youngest layer of intercellular substance

19. In the cervical region, preganglionic sympathetic neurons 19.___
    synapse with postganglionic sympathetic neurons in the
    _____ ganglion.
    A. celiac   B. dorsal root
    C. submandibular   D. superior cervical
    E. mandibular

20. The optic disk is an area of the retina consisting of   20.___
    A. optic nerve fibers   B. rods and bipolar cells
    C. cones and bipolar cells D. cones *only*
    E. none of the above

21. Sharpey's fibers consist of   21.___
    A. elastic fibers   B. reticular fibers
    C. collagenous fibers   D. all of the above
    E. none of the above

22. Pancreatic alpha cells secrete   22.___
    A. insulin   B. gastrin
    C. glucagon   D. pancreatic juice
    E. intrinsic factor

23. Bacteria are frequently ingested by   23.___
    A. mast cells   B. fibrocytes
    C. small lymphocytes   D. basophilic leukocytes
    E. neutrophilic leukocytes

24. The nerves lying in close relation to the lateral surfaces 24.___
    of the pericardial sac are the ____ nerves.
    A. vagus   B. phrenic
    C. intercostal   D. lesser splanchnic
    E. greater splanchnic

25. The thyroid gland receives its blood supply from branches 25.___
    of the
    A. external carotid arteries
    B. thyrocervical trunks
    C. inferior labial artery
    D. both A and B above
    E. neither A nor B above

KEY (CORRECT ANSWERS)

1. E   11. A
2. B   12. D
3. D   13. D
4. E   14. D
5. C   15. B

6. A   16. C
7. C   17. D
8. C   18. E
9. D   19. D
10. E   20. A

21. C
22. C
23. E
24. B
25. D

TEST 2

1. The esophagus is subdivided into three portions on the basis of a transition in the   1.___
    A. submucosa   B. adventitia
    C. mucosal layer   D. muscularis externa
    E. none of the above

2. In the embryo, the ductus connects the   2.___
    A. right atrium with the left atrium
    B. umbilical vein with the inferior vena cava
    C. left pulmonary artery to the aortic arch
    D. right pulmonary artery to the aortic arch
    E. left atrium with the aortic arch

3. The lateral part of the middle cranial fossa is separated from the posterior cranial fossa by the   3.___
    A. crista galli
    B. groove for the transverse sinus
    C. lesser wing of sphenoid bone
    D. petrous part of temporal bone
    E. greater wing of sphenoid bone

4. The bifurcation of the trachea lies at the level of the   4.___
    A. sternal angle
    B. xiphisternal junction
    C. second thoracic vertebra
    D. attachment of the fourth costal cartilage to the sternum
    E. third thoracic vertebra

5. Cell bodies of pre-ganglionic parasympathetic neurons to the duodenum are in the   5.___
    A. submucosal and myenteric plexuses
    B. sacral spinal cord lateral gray column
    C. thoracic spinal cord lateral gray column
    D. dorsal motor nucleus of the vagus nerve
    E. mucosa and myenteric plexuses

6. The slightly movable articulations in which the contiguous bony surfaces are either connected by broad, flattened disks of fibrocartilage or are united by interosseous ligaments are known as   6.___
    A. gomphoses   B. enarthroses
    C. diarthroses   D. amphiarthroses
    E. amphythroses

7. Ligamentous remnants of the fetal circulatory system persisting in the adult include the: 7.___
    I. Ligamentum nuchae
   II. Ligamentum venosum
  III. Ligamentum arteriosum
   IV. Ligamentum teres of the liver
    V. Ligamentum teres of the uterus

   The CORRECT answer is:
    A. I, II, III   B. I, II, V
    C. I, IV, V   D. II, III, IV
    E. III, IV, V

8. Examples of types of dense collagenous connective tissues include: 8.___
    I. Tendon   II. Ligament
   III. Aponeurosis   IV. Adipose tissue
    V. Pigment tissue

   The CORRECT answer is:
    A. I, II, III   B. I, II, III, V
    C. I, II, V   D. III, IV
    E. All of the above

9. Which of the following statements concerning skin is CORRECT?   9.___
    A. The dermis contains a wider variety of nerve endings than does the epidermis.
    B. The epidermis is derived from mesenchyme.
    C. Areas without sebaceous glands have no stratum germinativum in the epidermis.
    D. In thick skin, as on the sole of the foot, the basement membrane is lacking.
    E. The dermis contains a narrower variety of nerve endings than does the epidermis.

10. The dermis may be classified as what type of connective tissue?   10.___
    A. Modified elastic tissue
    B. Reticular connective tissue
    C. Dense regular connective tissue
    D. Dense irregular connective tissue
    E. Dense elastic tissue

11. Most of the lymph is returned to the blood at which of the following sites?   11.___
    A. Right brachiocephalic vein
    B. Right external jugular vein
    C. Junction of left internal jugular and subclavian veins
    D. Junction of right internal jugular and subclavian veins
    E. Left brachiocephalic vein

12. Urinary bladder differs from gallbladder in that urinary   12.___
    bladder
       A. is lined with transitional epithelium and gallbladder
          is lined with simple columnar epithelium
       B. has a mucosal layer and gallbladder has no mucosal
          layer
       C. can be stretched and gallbladder cannot be stretched
       D. contains smooth muscle and gallbladder contains no
          smooth muscle
       E. cannot be stretched and gallbladder can be stretched

13. Histologically, the thyroid gland has   13.___
       A. a rather poor vascular supply
       B. clusters of epithelial cells that are packed closely
          together
       C. rings of epithelial cells surrounding a space filled
          with colloid
       D. colloid between rows of epithelial cells, with the
          colloid being formed by connective tissue cells
       E. a rather good vascular supply

14. The outermost portion of a nerve fiber is commonly referred 14.___
    to as the
       A. axolemma   B. neurolemma
       C. perineurium   D. myelin sheath
       E. medullary sheath

15. The vertebral artery on its way to the brain passes through 15.___
    the
       A. foramen magnum   B. foramen lacerum
       C. jugular foramen   D. foramen spinosum
       E. none of the above

16. The female urethra lies   16.___
       A. anterior to the vagina
       B. between the vagina and the rectum
       C. in no direct relation with either the vagina or the
          rectum
       D. all of the above
       E. none of the above

17. Membrane bones are those which   17.___
       A. are composed entirely of spongy bone
       B. retain the exact shape of the membranes which they
          replace
       C. remain thin and, therefore, never have haversian systems
       D. are formed in mesenchyme directly and do not have a
          cartilaginous intermediate state
       E. none of the above

18. Taenia coli characterize the   18.___
       A. ileum   B. stomach
       C. duodenum   D. esophagus
       E. transverse colon

19. Cytoplasmic ribonucleic acid is localized in
    A. lysosomes
    B. mitochondria
    C. Golgi apparatus
    D. granular endoplasmic reticulum
    E. all of the above

19.___

20. Blood in the embryo and fetus is shunted from the pulmonary to the systemic circulation via the
    A. portal vein   B. umbilical vein
    C. ductus venosus   D. ductus arteriosus
    E. all of the above

20.___

21. The thymus is characterized by being
    A. important clinically in immunological reactions
    B. derived embryologically from all three germ layers
    C. a combined exocrine and endocrine gland
    D. constant in size throughout life
    E. of little importance in man

21.___

22. All of the following cell types secrete the substance with which they are paired EXCEPT
    A. Sertoli's cells - testosterone
    B. corpus luteum - progesterone
    C. alpha cells of pancreas - glucagon
    D. chromaffin cells of adrenal - catecholamines
    E. all of the above

22.___

23. All of the following structures can be seen in a histo-logic examination of the adult parotid gland EXCEPT the
    A. striated ducts   B. serous demilunes
    C. intercalated ducts   D. myoepithelial cells
    E. granular serous cells

23.___

24. Each of the following structures is found in the space between the medial pterygoid muscle and the ramus of the mandible EXCEPT the
    A. lingual nerve
    B. lingual artery
    C. inferior alveolar nerve
    D. inferior alveolar artery
    E. none of the above

24.___

25. MOST of the sympathetic postganglionic fibers which extend to the head region have their cell bodies in the
    A. prevertebral ganglia
    B. middle cervical ganglion
    C. cervicothoracic ganglion
    D. superior cervical ganglion
    E. lateral horn of the spinal cord

25.___

KEY (CORRECT ANSWERS)

1.	D	11.	C
2.	C	12.	A
3.	D	13.	C
4.	A	14.	B
5.	D	15.	A
6.	D	16.	A
7.	D	17.	D
8.	A	18.	E
9.	A	19.	D
10.	D	20.	D

21. A
22. A
23. B
24. B
25. D

———

ANATOMIC SCIENCES
EXAMINATION SECTION

TEST 1

DIRECTIONS: Each question or incomplete statement is followed by several suggested answers or completions. Select the one that BEST answers the question or completes the statement. *PRINT THE LETTER OF THE CORRECT ANSWER IN THE SPACE AT THE RIGHT.*

1. The red pulp of the spleen contains
   A. small nodules of lymphoid tissue and lymphatic capillaries
   B. splenic cords, numerous erythrocytes, and blood vascular sinusoids
   C. a reticular fiber stroma, lymphatic sinusoids, and trabkculae of smooth muscle
   D. large nodules of lymphoid cells, vascular channels lined with reticuloendothelial cells, and sheathed arteries
   E. all of the above

1.___

2. Spleen, thymus, and lymph nodes are similar in that they all
   A. filter blood
   B. contain lymphocytes
   C. have a medulla and a cortex
   D. serve as filters for tissue fluid
   E. have afferent and efferent lymphatic vessels

2.___

3. The bony floor of the nasal cavity is formed by the
   A. palatine process of the maxilla and the vertical part of the palatine
   B. palatine process of the temporal and the horizontal part of the palatine
   C. vomer and the vertical part of the palatine
   D. palatine process of the maxilla and the horizontal part of the palatine
   E. none of the above

3.___

4. In proceeding from the bronchus to the respiratory bronchiole, there is a(n)
   A. decrease in cartilage and an increase in elastic fibers
   B. decrease in collagenous fibers and an increase in cilia
   C. decrease in cilia and an increase in cartilage
   D. increase in cilia and a decrease in elastic fibers
   E. decrease in cilia and a decrease in elastic fibers

4.___

5. An important cell organelle related to biochemical break-down and phagocytosis in the oral region is the
   A. lysosome   B. microtubule
   C. mitochondrion   D. Golgi apparatus
   E. endoplasmic reticulum

5.___

2 (#1)

6. The *principal* site of granulocytic hemopoiesis in the
   adult human is
      A. the liver   B. the spleen
      C. lymph nodes   D. red bone marrow
      E. yellow bone marrow   6.___

7. The inguinal ligament runs between the
      A. pubic tubercle and the iliac tubercle
      B. symphysis pubis and the inferior iliac spine
      C. anterior superior iliac spine and the pubic tubercle
      D. anterior and posterior superior iliac spines
      E. symphysis pubis and the pubic tubercle   7.___

8. The parasympathetic preganglionic nerve fibers to the
   urinary bladder have their cell bodies in the
      A. medulla oblongata
      B. submucosal plexus
      C. spinal cord at upper lumbar levels
      D. spinal cord at all thoracic levels
      E. spinal cord at sacral levels 2, 3, and 4   8.___

9. The maxillary sinus normally drains into the
      A. middle meatus   B. inferior meatus
      C. inferior concha   D. superior meatus
      E. superior concha   9.___

10. Sensations of pain and temperature are carried by the
    ____ tract.
       A. corticospinal   B. corticobulbar
       C. lateral spinothalamic   D. ventral spinothalamic
       E. dorsal spinocerebellar   10.___

11. The lesser petrosal nerve carries pre-ganglionic para-
    sympathetic fibers to the ____ ganglion.
       A. otic   B. ciliary
       C. geniculate   D. submandibular
       E. celiac   11.___

12. When a comparison is made among various types of vascular
    channels, the
       A. arteriole has more muscle in its tunica media than
          does a venule, and there are more elastic membranes
          in a large artery than there are in a medium-sized
          artery
       B. endothelial lining of a large artery is thicker than
          it is in a small artery, and the lumen of a small
          vein is larger than it is in a companion small artery
       C. pressure of the blood is greater in a large artery
          than it is in a small artery, and the pressure in a
          small vein is less than it is in a large vein
       D. tunica media is thinner in a small artery than it is
          in a small vein, and the tunica adventitia is generally
          thicker on veins than it is on arteries
       E. none of the above   12.___

13. The sella turcica lies directly above the   13.___
    A. pons   B. foramen ovale
    C. frontal sinus   D. sphenoid sinus
    E. maxillary sinus

14. DNA is found *principally* in   14.___
    A. nucleus
    B. cytoplasm
    C. nucleolus
    D. cell membrane
    E. a diffuse fashion throughout the cell

15. The contractile element of skeletal muscle is in the   15.___
    A. sacrolemma   B. sarcoplasm
    C. myofibril   D. endomysium
    E. adventitia

16. The left coronary artery arises from the   16.___
    A. aorta   B. pulmonary artery
    C. left subclavian artery D. brachiocephalic artery
    E. right pulmonary artery

17. The primary lymph nodes draining the mandible are the: 17.___
       I. Parotid nodes   II. Retropharyngeal nodes
     III. Submandibular nodes   IV. Submental nodes

    The CORRECT answer is:
    A. I, II   B. I, IV
    C. II, III   D. II, IV
    E. III, IV

18. The internal intercostal muscles may be described as: 18.___
       I. 11 in number on both sides
      II. 12 in number on both sides
     III. Having their fibers directed obliquely downward and
          lateralward on the anterior aspect of the chest
      IV. Having their fibers directed obliquely downward and
          medialward on the anterior aspect of the chest

    The CORRECT combination is:
    A. I, III   B. I, IV
    C. II, III   D. II, IV
    E. III *only*

19. The prominent cytoplasmic basophilia in the basal region   19.___
    of serous glandular cells is due to
    A. large amounts of DNA
    B. an abundance of ribosomes
    C. an abundance of mitochondria
    D. the location of zymogen granules
    E. the presence of a prominent Golgi apparatus

20. The salivary, sweat, sebaceous and mammary glands have   20.___
    the common characteristic of being
    A. compound   B. simple
    C. exocrine   D. holocrine
    E. none of the above

21. When cartilage becomes calcified, the chondrocytes *usually*   21. __
    A. die because of the lack of diffusion
    B. proliferate because of the stimulus of calcification
    C. lay down secondary cartilage
    D. transform into chondroblasts
    E. none of the above

22. The posterior cervical triangle is bounded partly by the   22. __
    A. trapezius and subclavius muscles
    B. clavical and longus colli
    C. rhomboids and trapezius muscles
    D. trapezius and sternocleidomastoid muscles
    E. none of the above

23. Infection spreading via lymphatics from the lower lip   23. __
    would FIRST enter the bloodstream at the
    A. brachiocephalic vein   B. inferior labial vein
    C. inferior labial artery   D. pterygoid venous plexus
    E. any of the above

24. Where are zymogenic granules found? In   24. __
    A. chief cells of stomach mucosa
    B. the granular layer of epidermis
    C. pseudostratified columnar ciliated epithelium
    D. goblet cells
    E. none of the above

25. Which of the following are vestigial structures associated   25. __
    with the heart and great vessels?
    A. Ligamentum arteriosum, fossa ovalis
    B. Sulcus terminalis, coronary sinus
    C. Falciform ligament, sinus venarum
    D. Conus arteriosus, ligamentum teres
    E. all of the above

KEY (CORRECT ANSWERS)

1. B		11. A	
2. B		12. A	
3. D		13. D	
4. A		14. A	
5. A		15. C	
6. D		16. A	
7. C		17. E	
8. E		18. A	
9. A		19. B	
10. C		20. C	

21. A
22. D
23. A
24. A
25. A

TEST 2

DIRECTIONS: Each question or incomplete statement is followed by several suggested answers or completions. Select the one that BEST answers the question or completes the statement. *PRINT THE LETTER OF THE CORRECT ANSWER IN THE SPACE AT THE RIGHT.*

1. The ophthalmic artery is a branch of the ____ artery.
   A. lacrimal
   B. vertebral
   C. middle cerebral
   D. internal carotid
   E. anterior meningeal

   1.___

2. Connective tissue is characterized by
   A. being derived from mesenchyme, and by containing more intercellular material than cells
   B. containing amorphous intercellular substance, and by having little tissue fluid
   C. being calcified in some types, and by having sensitivity as its main function
   D. having poor reparative ability, and by containing few lymphatic channels
   E. having good reparative ability, and by containing many lymphatic channels

   2.___

3. Variation of the size of the lumen of the bronchiole during inspiration and expiration is caused *primarily* by
   A. striated muscle and cartilage
   B. smooth muscle and elastic fibers
   C. basement membrane and collagen fibers
   D. areolar connective tissue and cartilage
   E. striated muscle and elastic fibers

   3.___

4. Nerve cell bodies can be seen microscopically
   A. near the sense organs of the skin
   B. in any cross section of a peripheral nerve
   C. in the central nervous system, the autonomic ganglia, and the spinal ganglia
   D. only in the central nervous system
   E. in all of the above

   4.___

5. A node of Ranvier is
   A. one of the supporting cells in brain tissue
   B. a nervous receptor for the sensation of pressure
   C. the point of junction between two neurolemma (Schwann) cells
   D. the point of near-contact between the processes of two neurons (a synapse)
   E. none of the above

   5.___

6. The greater omentum joins the   6.___
    A. stomach to the liver
    B. liver to the duodenum
    C. liver to the transverse colon
    D. transverse colon to the stomach
    E. transverse colon to the duodenum

7. Erythrocytes are characterized by: 7.___
    I. Being round cells, and by functioning best when outside of the bloodstream
    II. Shrinking and becoming crenated in hypertonic saline solution, and by containing heme which is an endogenous pigment
    III. Becoming ghost cells in hypotonic saline solution, and by having no phagocytic ability
    IV. Functioning essentially while within the bloodstream, and by having some ameboid motion

    The CORRECT answer is:
    A. I, II   B. II, III
    C. II, IV   D. III, IV
    E. II, III, IV

8. The unit of striated muscle structure, a sarcomere, is the   8.___
    A. I band plus A band
    B. equivalent of an A band
    C. equivalent of an I band
    D. distance between Z lines
    E. none of the above

9. Slowing of the heart beat and reduction in force are the   9.___
results of stimulation of
    A. cervical sympathetic ganglion
    B. branches from the phrenic nerve
    C. parasympathetic branches from the vagus nerve
    D. postganglionic sympathetic branches from the cardiac plexus
    E. the superior cervical cardiac branch of the left sympathetic trunk

10. At a muscle-tendon junction, the union is made by   10.___
    A. myofibrils connecting with collagenous fibers of the tendon
    B. an overabundance of reticular fibers in the area of the junction
    C. a continuity of connective tissue sheaths of the muscle with those of the tendon
    D. a special thickening of sarcoplasm which unites with the fibrils of collagenous fibers of the tendon
    E. all of the above

11. Veins which connect the venous sinuses of the dura mater   11.___
    with the extracranial veins are
    A. venae comitantes   B. meningeal veins
    C. emissary veins   D. all of the above
    E. none of the above

12. The lining epithelium of the renal pelvis, the ureter,   12.___
    and the bladder is
    A. transitional   B. simple cuboidal
    C. pseudostratified   D. stratified columnar
    E. none of the above

13. The tentorium cerebelli is a duplication of the meningeal   13.___
    layer of the dura mater which separates
    A. pons from the cerebellum
    B. the two cerebellar hemispheres
    C. the fourth ventricle from the cerebellum
    D. the cerebellum from the cerebral hemispheres
    E. none of the above

14. When an individual medium-sized artery is vasodilated, the   14.___
    A. terminal capillary bed has its osmotic pressure
       increased
    B. elastic membranes are stretched and the smooth muscle
       cells are elongated
    C. elastic fibers in the externa aid in holding the lumen
       open in this dilated condition
    D. blood passing through it is flowing at a slower rate,
       thus more tissue fluid passes through its wall
    E. none of the above

15. Cellular cementum and compact bone contain   15.___
    A. Sharpey's fibers and elastic fibers
    B. collagen fibers and blood vessels
    C. canaliculi and incremental lines
    D. lacunae and elastic fibers
    E. none of the above

16. The foramen ovale is located   16.___
    A. in the interatrial septum
    B. in the interventricular septum
    C. only in the interventricular septum of the embryo
    D. in all of the above
    E. in none of the above

17. The Barr body in certain epithelial cells is significant   17.___
    in that it is
    A. diagnostic in differentiating sex
    B. a diagnostic aid indicating pathology
    C. symptomatic of nuclear disintegration
    D. indicative of the onset of mitotic activity
    E. all of the above

18. The root of the lung, containing the bronchus, pulmonary veins and arteries, nerves, and lymphatics, enters the lung at the
    A. apex
    B. base
    C. hilus
    D. mediastinum
    E. pulmonary ligament

19. Superficial lymphatic vessels of the breast are drained *primarily* to the
    A. axillary nodes
    B. cervical nodes
    C. subclavicular nodes
    D. supraclavicular nodes
    E. none of the above

20. Which of the following cranial nerves contains NO parasympathetic component at its origin?
    A. Oculomotor
    B. Trigeminal
    C. Facial
    D. Glossopharyngeal
    E. Vagus

21. In the respiratory system, epithelium of which of the following does NOT normally have cilia?
    A. Primary bronchus
    B. Bronchioles
    C. Alveolar ducts
    D. Trachea
    E. All of the above

22. Which of the following is NOT a cytoplasmic organelle?
    A. DNA
    B. Lysosome
    C. Centriole
    D. Golgi apparatus
    E. Endoplasmic reticulum

23. The platysma is supplied by a branch of which of the following cranial nerves?
    A. V   B. VII   C. IX   D. X   E. XII

24. Each of the following veins have direct or indirect connection with the pterygoid venous plexus EXCEPT the
    A. facial vein
    B. vertebral vein
    C. maxillary vein
    D. cavernous sinus
    E. inferior alveolar vein

25. The sulcular epithelium in man is
    A. not keratinized
    B. heavily keratinized
    C. slightly keratinized
    D. usually keratinized and is composed of many layers of cells forming a thick layer of stratified squamous epithelium
    E. none of the above

KEY (CORRECT ANSWERS)

1. D	11. C	21. C
2. A	12. A	22. A
3. B	13. D	23. B
4. C	14. B	24. B
5. C	15. C	25. A
6. D	16. A	
7. B	17. A	
8. D	18. C	
9. C	19. A	
10. C	20. B	

ANATOMIC SCIENCES
EXAMINATION SECTION
TEST 1

DIRECTIONS: Each question or incomplete statement is followed by several suggested answers or completions. Select the one that BEST answers the question or completes the statement. *PRINT THE LETTER OF THE CORRECT ANSWER IN THE SPACE AT THE RIGHT.*

1. The cell that is MOST capable of mitotic division in the adult is the   1.____

    A. fibroblast   B. odontoblast
    C. nerve cell   D. epithelial cell
    E. smooth muscle cell

2. Movement of the head about its vertical axis (rotation to right or left) occurs at the   2.____
_____ joint.

    A. atlantoaxial
    B. atlanto-occipital
    C. spheno-occipital
    D. third to the seventh cervical vertebrae
    E. all of the above

3. The smooth muscle cell shows no striations because it has no myofilaments in its cyto-   3.____
plasm.

    A. Both statement and reason are correct and related.
    B. Both statement and reason are correct but not related.
    C. The statement is correct but the reason is not.
    D. The statement is not correct but the reason is an accurate statement.
    E. Neither statement nor reason is correct.

4. Abdominal organs supplied by the three unpaired branches of the aorta include all of the   4.____
following EXCEPT the

    A. spleen   B. stomach
    C. pancreas   D. vermiform appendix
    E. suprarenal (adrenal)

5. An osteoclast is a(n)   5.____

    A. cell that forms bone
    B. cell of the endosteum
    C. multinucleated giant cell
    D. osteoblast which has become surrounded by a bony matrix
    E. cell of the periphery of bone which forms from the fibroblasts of the periosteum

6. Which of the following statements apply to DNA?   6.____
      I.   It is found as a component of the nucleoli.
      II. It can be distinguished from RNA by the Feulgen reaction.
      III. In polyploidy, it is a multiple of the normal cell chromosome content.
      IV. It is not confined to the chromosomes.
The CORRECT answer is:

    A. I, II   B. I, III   C. I, IV   D. II, III   E. II, IV

7. The fate of the epithelial rests of Malassez is that they may

    I.   undergo calcification
    II. form into cementicles
    III. become fibrous
    IV. form cartilaginous nodules

The CORRECT answer is:

A. I, II   B. I, II, III
C. II, III   D. II, III, IV
E. III, IV

8. Spleen, thymus, and lymph nodes are SIMILAR in that they all

A. filter blood
B. contain lymphocytes
C. have a medulla and a cortex
D. serve as filters for tissue fluid
E. have afferent and efferent lymphatic vessels

9. Epithelial cells of the small intestine show surface modification known as

A. stereocilia   B. the ciliary border
C. the striated border   D. the cuticular border
E. none of the above

10. The layer of the skin that forms the epithelial root sheaths of the hair follicle is the stratum

A. corneum   B. lucidum
Є. granulosum   D. germinativum
E: lacrimum

11. Which of the following is characteristic of heart muscle?

A. Nodes of Ranvier   B. Rod-shaped nuclei
C. Spindle-shaped fibers   D. Centrally-placed nuclei
E. None of the above

12. Pressure receptors in the carotid sinus are associated with which cranial nerve?

A. Glossopharyngeal   B. Trigeminal
C. Accessory   D. Facial
E. Zygomatic

13. Cell membranes are best described as one layer of

A. charged (polar) lipids
B. protein on the inside and one layer of neutral lipids on the outside
C. protein on either side of a layer of neutral lipids
D. charged (polar) lipids on either side of a layer of neutral lipids
E. neutral lipids

14. The structure that passes through the foramen rotundum is the   14.____

    A. maxillary nerve   B. zygomatic nerve
    C. lacrimal artery   D. maxillary artery
    E. trigeminal nerve

15. Each of the following cell types secretes the substance with which it is paired EXCEPT   15.____

    A. Sertoli's cells - testosterone
    B. corpus luteum - progesterone
    C. alpha cells of the pancreas - glucagon
    D. chromaffin cells of the adrenal - catecholamine
    E. all of the above are correct

16. In H & E stained sections, the large, deeply stained granules found in the cytoplasm of   16.____
epithelial cells in keratinized oral mucosa are *most likely*

    A. glycogen   B. desmosomes
    C. tonofibrils   D. keratohyaline
    E. basophils

17. The diploid number of chromosomes is perpetuated in somatic cells by a process of   17.____

    A. meiosis   B. mitosis
    C. amitosis   D. cytokinesis
    E. pinocytosis

18. The bone that is NOT formed by endochondral ossification is the   18.____

    A. nasal   B. ethmoid
    C. sphenoid   D. temporal
    E. jugular

19. The tentorium cerebelli contains all of the following dural venous sinuses EXCEPT the   19.____

    A. straight   B. transverse
    C. superior petrosal   D. inferior petrosal
    E. superior nasal

20. All of the following are located in the nasopharynx EXCEPT the   20.____

    A. piriform recess   B. eustachian canal
    C. pharyngeal tonsil   D. pharyngeal recess
    E. lacrimal artery

21. An endocrine gland of ectodermal origin in the abdomen is the   21.____

    A. liver
    B. corpus luteum
    C. medulla of the adrenal
    D. cortical portion of the adrenal
    E. interstitial cells of the testis

22. The middle cardiac vein empties into the   22.___

    A. left atrium   B. right atrium
    C. coronary sinus   D. great cardiac vein
    E. anterior cardiac vein

23. Which of the following does NOT occur during contraction of the left ventricle of a normal   23.___
heart?

    A. The aortic similunar valve opens.
    B. Blood enters the coronary arteries.
    C. The pulmonary semilunar valve opens.
    D. The left atrioventricular valve closes.
    E. The right atrioventricular valve closes.

24. The transverse diameter of the pleural cavity is *increased* during inspiration by   24.___

    A. contraction of the diaphragm
    B. relaxation of the scalene muscles
    C. elevation of the arched shaft of the ribs
    D. depression of the anterior ends of the ribs
    E. contraction of the external abdominal oblique muscle

25. The vertical dimension of the thoracic cavity is increased *chiefly* by contraction of the   25.___

    A. diaphragm
    B. quadratus lumborum muscles
    C. external intercostal muscles
    D. serratus posterior inferior muscles
    E. transversus thoracis (sternocostalis) muscle

———

KEY (CORRECT ANSWERS)

1.	D		11.	D
2.	A		12.	A
3.	C		13.	D
4.	E		14.	A
5.	C		15.	A
6.	D		16.	D
7.	A		17.	B
8.	B		18.	A
9.	C		19.	D
10.	D		20.	A

21.	C
22.	C
23.	B
24.	C
25.	A

TEST 2

DIRECTIONS: Each question or incomplete statement is followed by several suggested answers or completions. Select the one that BEST answers the question or completes the statement. *PRINT THE LETTER OF THE CORRECT ANSWER IN THE SPACE AT THE RIGHT.*

1. Progesterone production in the ovary is *primarily* by   1.__

    A. stroma   B. corpora lutea
    C. mature follicles   D. corpora albicans
    E. growing follicles

2. From an anatomic standpoint, an emergency airway may be established MOST readily by an opening into the trachea   2.__

    A. at the level of the jugular notch
    B. through the thyrohyoid membrane
    C. through the median cricothyroid ligament
    D. between the thyroid cartilages
    E. none of the above

3. Systemic arteries and veins DIFFER in that   3.__

    A. veins have more elastic tissue
    B. arteries have a relatively thinner tunica media
    C. valves are often present in veins
    D. arteries have larger endothelial pores
    E. elastic membranes are less pronounced in arteries

4. A small bronchus differs from a bronchiole by possessing   4.__

    A. stratified squamous epithelium and rings or plates of cartilage
    B. stratified squamous epithelium and no rings or plates of cartilage
    C. stratified columnar epithelium and rings or plates of cartilage
    D. pseudostratified columnar epithelium and no rings or plates of cartilage
    E. pseudostratified columnar epithelium and rings or plates of cartilage

5. The basic framework or stroma of ALL lymphoid tissues except thymus consists of   5.__

    A. reticular fibers primarily and a lesser amount of collagen fibers
    B. a combination of epithelioid cells and reticular fibers
    C. a combination of smooth muscle and reticular fibers
    D. some smooth muscle and trabeculae of collagen fibers
    E. collagen fibers primarily and some elastic fibers

6. In a double vertical fracture through the mental foramina, muscle action will cause the small fragment to move   6.__

    A. inferiorly *only*
    B. superiorly *only*
    C. anteriorly and superiorly
    D. posteriorly and inferiorly
    E. posteriorly and superiorly

7. The organelle that binds and releases calcium during relaxation and contraction of skeletal muscle is a

    A. nucleus   B. lysosome
    C. mitochondrion   D. transverse tubule
    E. sarcoplasmic reticulum

7.____

8. The foramen ovale is an embryological opening between

    A. right and left atria
    B. right and left ventricles
    C. right atrium and right ventricle
    D. umbilical vein and inferior vena cava
    E. pulmonary artery and arch of the aorta

8.____

9. A sarcomere is the part of the myofibril enclosed between

    A. two consecutive H bands
    B. two consecutive I bands
    C. two consecutive Z bands
    D. an I band and the next A band
    E. a Z band and the next H band

9.____

10. Mucosa of all parts of the small intestine is characterized by possessing

    A. rugae   B. villi
    C. haustra   D. teniae coli
    E. appendices epiploicae

10.____

11. Ribonucleic acid that is involved in protein synthesis is found *primarily* in the

    A. nucleolus
    B. mitochondria
    C. Golgi complex
    D. fluid ground substance
    E. granular endoplasmic reticulum

11.____

12. The normal percentage of neutrophilic leukocytes in a differential blood count is *approximately* _____ percent.

    A. 0.5-1   B. 2-5
    C. 8-15   D. 20-25
    E. 60-70

12.____

13. The parasympathetic fibers to the pterygopalatine ganglion come from the _____ nerve.

    A. maxillary   B. mandibular
    C. deep petrosal   D. glossopharyngeal
    E. greater petrosal

13.____

14. Production of bile takes place in   14._

    A. the hepatic duct
    B. the gallbladder
    C. von Kupffer's cell
    D. the common bile duct
    E. none of the above

15. The component of bone tissue that gives a bone tensile strength is the   15._

    A. calcified cement substance
    B. interconnecting canaliculi
    C. collagenous fibrils of matrix
    D. periosteal connective tissue
    E. elastic fibers

16. Long bones of the skeleton *increase* in length because of   16._

    A. mitotic division of osteocytes
    B. mitotic division of osteoblasts
    C. resorption of primary bone by osteoclasts
    D. appositional growth on the cartilaginous epiphyseal plate
    E. interstitial growth in the cartilaginous epiphyseal plate

17. In an adult, the site of origin of the thyroid gland is seen as the   17._

    A. copula   B. foramen cecum
    C. eustachian tube   D. palatine tonsil
    E. tuberculum impar

18. In the adult, cerebrospinal fluid can be aspirated most safely by inserting the needle   18._
between the third and the fourth lumbar vertebrae because

    A. there is more space between the laminae of these two vertebrae
    B. the subarachnoid space does not extend below lumbar 4
    C. the spinal cord usually does not extend below lumbar 2
    D. there is less danger of entering the internal vertebral plexus at this level
    E. there are no important nerves in this part of the vertebral canal

19. The visual center of the cerebral cortex is located in the   19._

    A. hypothalamus   B. parietal lobe
    C. occipital lobe   D. indusium griseum
    E. medulla oblongata

20. In normal light microscopy of striated muscle, the dark portion of the striation is caused   20._
by the presence of

    A. actin
    B. myosin
    C. Cohnheim's fields
    D. an intercalated disk
    E. fibers in the endomysium

21. Stereocilia are characteristic of the

    A. epididymis
    B. seminal vesicle
    C. ejaculatory duct
    D. proximal convoluted tubule
    E. ampulla of the ductus deferens

21.____

22. The principal fibrous elements of the periodontal ligament in adults consist *chiefly* of _____ fibers.

    A. elastic
    B. collagen
    C. reticular
    D. a mixture of elastic and collagen
    E. a mixture of elastic and reticular

22.____

23. Mucus-secreting cells are found in the
    I. parotid gland
    II. submandibular gland
    III. mucosa of the trachea
    IV. mucosa of the ureter
    V. glands of the esophagus
    The CORRECT answer is:

    A. I, III   B. I, V
    C. II, III, IV   D. II, III, V
    E. II, IV

23.____

24. Each of the following structures is derived from ectoderm EXCEPT

    A. hair   B. enamel
    C. dentin   D. sweat gland
    E. salivary gland

24.____

25. Testosterone is produced by the

    A. epididymis
    B. Sertoli cells
    C. sustenacular cells
    D. seminiferous tubules
    E. interstitial cells of Leydig

25.____

KEY (CORRECT ANSWERS)

1.	B		11.	E
2.	C		12.	E
3.	C		13.	E
4.	E		14.	E
5.	A		15.	C
6.	D		16.	E
7.	E		17.	B
8.	A		18.	C
9.	C		19.	C
10.	B		20.	B

21.	A
22.	B
23.	D
24.	C
25.	E

BIOCHEMISTRY / PHYSIOLOGY
EXAMINATION SECTION

TEST 1

DIRECTIONS: Each question or incomplete statement is followed by several suggested answers or completions. Select the one that BEST answers the question or completes the statement. *PRINT THE LETTER OF THE CORRECT ANSWER IN THE SPACE AT THE RIGHT.*

1. In helping to control the rhythm of respiration, the vagus nerves in the lungs are stimulated by receptors detecting changes in the   1.___
   A. stretch of the lung parenchyma
   B. PCO_2 and PO_2 of the blood
   C. PCO_2 of the alveolar air
   D. PO_2 of the alveolar air
   E. pH of the blood

2. In third degree heart block, the electrocardiograph shows   2.___
   A. an increased PQ interval
   B. an increase in the height of the R wave
   C. an increase in the height of the QRS complex
   D. the P wave and the QRS complex are dissociated
   E. none of the above

3. The MOST biologically important physicochemical property of connective tissue which is regulated by its mucopoly-saccharide molecules is   3.___
   A. viscosity
   B. buffering capacity
   C. solubility in dilute acids
   D. supersaturation with calcium ions
   E. none of the above

4. A substance that alters the rate of an enzymatic reaction by interacting with the enzyme at a site other than the active site is   4.___
   A. an allosteric modifier
   B. a competitive inhibitor
   C. a non-competitive inhibitor
   D. all of the above
   E. none of the above

5. Homogentisic acid accumulates in the urine in   5.___
   A. ketonuria   B. cystinuria
   C. alkaptonuria   D. phenylketonuria
   E. none of the above

6. An enzyme that is activated by epinephrine is   6.___
   A. hexokinase   B. glucokinase
   C. adenyl cyclase   D. phosphofructokinase
   E. none of the above

7. Cyclic 3', 5'-AMP increases the rate of glycogenolysis by 7.___
   A. promoting the formation of a phosphorylated form of glycogen phosphorylase
   B. serving as a substrate for glycogen phosphorylase
   C. serving as a precursor of 5'AMP which is a cofactor for glycogen phosphorylase
   D. furnishing phosphate for the phosphorolysis of glycogen
   E. none of the above

8. A proportionate INCREASE in resistance of afferent and efferent arterioles of the kidney would result in a DECREASE in 8.___
   A. both filtration fraction and glomerular filtration rate
   B. renal blood flow with no change in glomerular filtration rate
   C. glomerular filtration rate with no change in renal blood flow
   D. urine output
   E. none of the above

9. The depolarization of the skeletal muscle cell membrane by motor nerves is *directly* produced by the 9.___
   A. shift of Na ions out of the end-plate
   B. activation of muscle contractile proteins
   C. increased concentration of neuromuscular cholinesterase
   D. change in end-plate potential level to a critical value
   E. none of the above

10. Vagal stimulation in the mammalian heart has *primarily* a rate effect because 10.___
    A. acetylcholine has little direct effect on contractility of heart muscle
    B. there are few vagal endings distributed to the mammalian ventricles
    C. acetylcholine is not liberated in effective amounts at vagal endings in the mammalian ventricles
    D. sympathetic effects cancel those of the vagus
    E. none of the above

11. The osmotic pressure of the filtrate at the end of the proximal convoluted tubule is 11.___
    A. *greater* than that of plasma
    B. much *less* than that of plasma
    C. about the *same* as that of plasma
    D. *greater* than that of the filtrate in the descending portion of the loop of Henle
    E. none of the above

12. Osteoblasts form the organic matrix of bone prior to calcification of the tissue. This process requires vitamins 12.___
    A. A and B_{12} B. A and C
    C. A and D   D. C and E
    E. D and E

13. Albinism is caused by a deficiency of an enzyme involved   13.___
    in the metabolism of
       A. tyrosine   B. arginine
       C. histidine   D. methionine
       E. tryptophan

14. The MAIN factors *directly* involved in the maintenance of   14.___
    systemic arterial blood pressure are
       A. cardiac output, blood volume, peripheral resistance
          and respiratory rate
       B. cardiac output, blood volume, blood viscosity and
          peripheral resistance
       C. heart rate, ventricular filling, blood viscosity and
          peripheral resistance
       D. plasma colloid osmotic pressure, capillary blood
          pressure, tissue hydrostatic pressure and tissue
          colloid osmotic pressure
       E. none of the above

15. The buffer system MOST important in maintaining the   15.___
    physiological pH of plasma is
       A. protein/proteinate
       B. acetic acid/acetate
       C. carbonic acid/bicarbonate
       D. phosphoric acid/phosphate
       E. hydroxybutyric acid/hydroxybutyrate

16. Pieces of dog parotid gland and of pancreas are trans-   16.___
    planted under the skin of the donor animal. After
    re-establishment of a circulation, ingestion of food will
    result in secretion from
       A. parotid and pancreatic transplants
       B. the fragment of the parotid only
       C. the fragment of the pancreas only
       D. neither fragment
       E. none of the above

17. The products of hydrolysis of lecithin are   17.___
       A. glycerol, fatty acids, phosphoric acid, serine
       B. glycerol, fatty acids, phosphoric acid, choline
       C. sphingosine, acetic acid, phosphoric acid, inositol
       D. glyceraldehyde, fatty acids, phosphoric acid, choline
       E. glyceraldehyde, fatty acids, phosphoric acid,
          ethanolamine

18. If the anticodon on transfer RNA is ACG, the codon on   18.___
    messenger RNA is
       A. CGT   B. GCA   C. CGA   D. UAG   E. UGC

19. Two hormones which act similarly to increase glycogen and   19.___
    lipid breakdown as well as cyclic AMP synthesis are
       A. insulin and calcitonin
       B. glucagon and epinephrine
       C. aldosterone and testosterone
       D. parathyroid hormone and glucagon
       E. none of the above

20. An injection of epinephrine into the left ventricular   20.___
    wall causes an increase in cardiac output. This is an
    example of
       A. positive inotropic activity
       B. heterometric autoregulation
       C. Starling's Law of the Heart
       D. homeometric autoregulation
       E. none of the above

21. The amino acid composition of a protein having an iso-   21.___
    electric pH of 10 has
       A. no acidic amino acids
       B. no basic amino acids
       C. no neutral amino acids
       D. more basic than acidic amino acids
       E. more acidic than basic amino acids

22. The recommended daily dietary allowances for Ca and P   22.___
    provide a Ca/P intake of *approximately*
       A. 0.5   B. 1.0   C. 2.0   D. 3.0   E. 4.0

23. Other factors being equal, one should expect N_2O-O_2 23.___
    sedation to be induced *more slowly* than normal in a person
    having a
       A. tidal volume larger than normal
       B. vital capacity smaller than normal
       C. residual volume smaller than normal
       D. functional residual capacity larger than normal
       E. none of the above

24. Capillary diameter is *directly* influenced by   24.___
       A. parasympathetic nerve impulses
       B. byproducts of metabolism
       C. sympathetic nerve impulses
       D. axon reflexes
       E. none of the above

25. Coenzymes used in pyruvate dehydrogenase reactions are   25.___
         I. thiamine pyrophosphate   II. pyridoxal phosphate
       III. lipoic acid   IV. biotin
         V. NAD^+

    The CORRECT answer is:
       A. I, II   B. I, II, V
       C. I, III, V   D. II, IV
       E. III, IV   ___

KEY (CORRECT ANSWERS)

1. A	11. C	21. D
2. D	12. B	22. B
3. A	13. A	23. D
4. A	14. B	24. B
5. C	15. C	25. C
6. C	16. C	
7. A	17. B	
8. B	18. E	
9. D	19. B	
10. B	20. A	

TEST 2

DIRECTIONS: Each question or incomplete statement is followed by several suggested answers or completions. Select the one that BEST answers the question or completes the statement. *PRINT THE LETTER OF THE CORRECT ANSWER IN THE SPACE AT THE RIGHT.*

1. A person injured in an automobile accident has lost two pints of blood and is now in shock. Which of the following are *likely* to occur? A decrease in
    I. glomerular filtration rate
   II. the reabsorption of H_2O in the distal convoluted tubule
  III. urine formation
   IV. the release of an antidiuretic hormone

   The CORRECT answer is:
    A. I, III   B. I, IV
    C. II, III   D. II, IV
    E. III, IV

   1.___

2. Which of the following is an essential fatty acid?
    A. Acetic   B. Stearic
    C. Myristic   D. Palmitic
    E. Arachidonic

   2.___

3. Which of the following functions of bone could be considered the MOST prominent?
    A. Buffering   B. Phosphate source
    C. Sodium reservoir   D. Fluoride reservoir
    E. Calcium reservoir

   3.___

4. A number of substances yield energy to the body when a phosphate group is transferred to a suitable acceptor. Which of the following compounds yields the MOST energy per mole?
    A. Creatine
    B. Pyruvic acid
    C. Glucose-1-phosphate
    D. Adenosine triphosphate
    E. Fructose-1, 6-diphosphate

   4.___

5. Which of the following is the DIRECT precursor of urea?
    A. Glutamic acid   B. Citrulline
    C. Ornithine   D. Glutamide
    E. Arginine

   5.___

6. Which of the following enzymes is involved in the termination of neuromuscular transmission?
    A. Acetylcholine esterase   B. Methyltransferase
    C. Monoamine oxidase   D. Choline acetylase
    E. Adenyl cyclase

   6.___

7. To which of the following avitaminoses is the gingiva   7.____
   MOST susceptible?
   A. A   B. B_2
   C. B_6 D. C
   E. Niacin

8. Which of the following ions is *especially* required in the   8.____
   blood clotting process?
   A. Fe^{++} B. Na^+ C. Ca^{++} D. Mg^{++} E. K^+

9. In the metabolic conversion of glycogen to lactic acid,   9.____
   which of the following is an intermediate?
   A. Maltose   B. Glycerol
   C. Phosphocreatine   D. Acetoacetic acid
   E. Glucose-1-phosphate

10. Which of the following is *most likely* to promote depoly-   10.____
    merization of the ground substance?
    A. Cortisone   B. Collagenase
    C. Chymotrypsin   D. Hyaluronidase
    E. Ammonium phosphate

11. Where in the cell does MOST protein synthesis occur?   11.____
    A. In the nucleus
    B. Within lysosomes
    C. Within the mitochondria
    D. On polyribosomes
    E. In soluble cytoplasm

12. What changes in the extracellular fluid compartment are   12.____
    caused by prolonged sweating? A(n) ____ in volume and
    a(n) ____ in osmotic pressure.
    A. decrease, increase   B. decrease, decrease
    C. increase, increase   D. increase, decrease
    E. none of the above

13. Which of the following statements concerning salivary   13.____
    gland function or its control is CORRECT?
    A. Epinephrine inhibits parotid amylase secretion by
       decreasing cyclic AMP levels.
    B. Salivary flow is inhibited by the presence of dry
       food in the mouth.
    C. Some chemicals, such as potassium iodide and mercury,
       are excreted in part by the saliva.
    D. Mucoproteins are the most important buffers in the
       saliva.
    E. None of the above

14. Which of the situations below characterizes the exchange   14.____
    of chloride and bicarbonate ion between the red cell and
    plasma in the lungs? The passage of chloride ion
    A. into the cell from the plasma and the passage of
       bicarbonate ion from the cell into the plasma
    B. into the plasma from the cell and the passage of
       bicarbonate ion from the plasma into the cell

C. and bicarbonate ion into the cell from the plasma
so that carbon dioxide can escape
D. and bicarbonate ion from the cell into the plasma
E. none of the above

15. Which of the following amino acids is a thio-ether?   15.___
   A. Leucine   B. Threonine
   C. Isoleucine   D. Methionine
   E. Thiolhistidine

16. Which of the following processes is MOST important in   16.___
    preventing a DECREASE of more than 0.2 units in the pH of
    the blood when CO_2 enters?
   A. Urea formation following amino acid deamination
   B. NH_4^+ formation in the kidney
   C. Formation of ketone bodies
   D. Excretion of acidic urine
   E. Conversion of HbO_2 to Hb

17. Which of the following is MOST commonly associated with   17.___
    transport of free fatty acids in human blood?
   A. Albumin   B. Globulin
   C. Cholesterol   D. Sphingolipid
   E. Mucopolysaccharide

18. Which of the following reflexes is monosynaptic?   18.___
   A. Stretch reflex
   B. Withdrawal reflex
   C. Crossed extensor reflex
   D. Positive supporting reaction
   E. Labyrinthine righting reflex

19. In which of the following combinations is the name of the 19.___
    hormone, its chemical type and its tissue of origin
    correctly matched?
   A. Aldosterone-peptide-pancreas
   B. Glucagon-peptide-adrenal cortex
   C. Epinephrine-steroid-adrenal medulla
   D. ACTH-polypeptide-adrenal cortex
   E. Vasopressin-peptide-posterior pituitary

20. Which of the following is considered to be the LEAST   20.___
    important in producing enamel hypoplasia in developing teeth?
   A. Rickets
   B. Prolonged vitamin A deficiency
   C. Prolonged vitamin D deficiency
   D. Fluoride intake of less than 0.2 ppm in the water
   E. Inadequate calcium intake for a prolonged period

21. Which of the following is NOT a type of connective tissue 21.___
    fiber?
   A. Chitin   B. Elastin
   C. Collagen   D. Reticulin
   E. None of the above

22. Which of the following digestive enzymes is NOT derived   22.____
from an inactive zymogen precursor?
    A. Pepsin   B. Trypsin
    C. Amylase   D. Chymotrypsin
    E. None of the above

23. The hypothalamus-pituitary complex does NOT control   23.____
hormonal secretions of the
    A. thyroid
    B. parathyroids
    C. corpora lutea
    D. ovarian follicles
    E. interstitial cells of the testes

24. An enzyme which is found in the succus entericus but NOT   24.____
in the pancreatic juice is
    A. lipase   B. trypsin
    C. chymotrypsin   D. enterokinase
    E. none of the above

25. Proprioceptors are found in each of the following EXCEPT   25.____
the
    A. gingiva   B. skeletal muscles
    C. pulp of the tooth   D. periodontal ligament
    E. temporomandibular joint

KEY (CORRECT ANSWERS)

1. A	11. D	21. A
2. E	12. A	22. C
3. E	13. C	23. B
4. D	14. A	24. D
5. E	15. D	25. C
6. A	16. E	
7. D	17. A	
8. C	18. A	
9. E	19. E	
10. D	20. D	

BIOCHEMISTRY / PHYSIOLOGY
EXAMINATION SECTION
TEST 1

DIRECTIONS: Each question or incomplete statement is followed by several suggested answers or completions. Select the one that BEST answers the question or completes the statement. *PRINT THE LETTER OF THE CORRECT ANSWER IN THE SPACE AT THE RIGHT.*

1.   Mechanical difficulty of muscular contraction is the   1._____

   A.   ratio between initial heat and total heat
   B.   load under which the muscle does the greatest amount of work
   C.   ratio between amount of work done and total energy expended
   D.   ratio between number of activated motor units and total number of motor units
   E.   none of the above

2.   Aldosterone causes   2._____

   A.   *decreased* renal excretion of potassium
   B.   *decreased* reabsorption of chloride
   C.   *increased* transfer of potassium into the cell
   D.   *increased* renal tubular reabsorption of sodium
   E.   none of the above

3.   The organ *chiefly* responsible for resistance to change in the pH of blood is the   3._____

   A.   liver ⌐   B.   heart
   C.   kidney-   D.   spleen
   E.   gallbladder

4.   Acetylcholine is released at all of the following junctions EXCEPT   4._____

   A.   sympathetic ganglia
   B.   parasympathetic ganglia
   C.   somatic efferents to skeletal muscles
   D.   terminal sympathetic fibers to the heart
   E.   terminal sympathetic fibers to the adrenal medulla

5.   Each of the following is found in pancreatic juice EXCEPT   5._____

   A.   lipase   B.   amylase
   C.   pepsinogen   D.   trypsinogen
   E.   chymotrypsinogen

6.   Triglyceride absorbed into the lymphatic system is transported to the liver as   6._____

   A.   chylomicrons
   B.   very low density lipoprotein
   C.   low density lipoprotein
   D.   high density lipoprotein
   E.   very high density lipoprotein

7. After functioning in the small intestines, the LARGEST portion of bile salts are 7.

   A. excreted in the feces
   B. reabsorbed into the central lacteal
   C. destroyed by bacteria in the large intestines
   D. reabsorbed into the portal circulation and reused
   E. removed from the circulation by the kidneys and excreted in the urine

8. The consequence of appreciable conversion of hemoglobin to methemoglobin is 8.

   A. a significant increase in carbon dioxide combining power
   B. a significant decrease in carbon dioxide combining power
   C. no effect on the ability of blood to pick up oxygen
   D. a noticeable increase in the ability of blood to pick up oxygen
   E. a noticeable decrease in the ability of blood to transport oxygen

9. The MOST susceptible sites in the nervous system for the effects of acute anoxia are the 9.

   A. motor end-plates
   B. sensory receptors
   C. synapses in autonomic ganglia
   D. synapses in the central nervous system
   E. none of the above

10. The MOST significant immediate result of lowered serum calcium is 10

   A. weakened heart action
   B. decalcification of bones
   C. decalcification of teeth
   D. hyperirritability of nerves and muscles
   E. none of the above

11. Enzymes concerned with the citric acid cycle are found in the 11

   A. nucleus   B. ribosomes
   C. mitochondria   D. nonparticulate cytoplasm
   E. none of the above

12. In man, α-amylase ptyalin is secreted by the _____ glands. 12

   A. facial   B. parotid
   C. sublingual   D. submaxillary
   E. none of the above

13. The extracellular polysaccharides synthesized by cariogenic streptococci in the presence of excess sucrose are BEST described as 13

   A. amylase   B. amylopectin
   C. mucopolysaccharide   D. glycogen-like glucan
   E. dextran-like glucan

14. Neutralization of acids by saliva results *mainly* from its content of 14

   A. mucin   B. ammonia
   C. carbonate   D. amino acids
   E. bicarbonate

15. The antidiuretic hormone is released from the posterior pituitary gland and acts to   15.____

    A. *decrease* renal filtration fraction
    B. *increase* storage capacity of the bladder
    C. *decrease* permeability of collecting ducts to water
    D. *increase* permeability of collecting ducts to water
    E. none of the above

16. During a normal cardiac cycle, the isometric contraction phase of ventricular systole   16.____
occurs

    A. following closure of the A-V valves
    B. following opening of the A-V valves
    C. following closure of the aortic valves
    D. following opening of the aortic valves
    E. immediately upon excitation of the atria

17. When a membrane is depolarized, it becomes MORE   17.____

    A. sensitive to a stimulus
    B. permeable to the passage of ions
    C. positively charged on the outside
    D. resistant to the flow of an electric current
    E. none of the above

18. Breathing ceases upon destruction of the   18.____

    A. thalamus   B. cerebrum
    C. cerebellum   D. hypothalamus
    E. medulla oblongata

19. Keratosulfate occurs primarily in   19.____

    A. bile   B. blood
    C. liver   D. urine
    E. cartilage

20. Proteins obtained from corn are "poor" in nutritional value for man because these pro-   20.____
teins are

    A. *low* in glycine
    B. *low* in histidine
    C. *high* in tryptophan
    D. *high* in methionine
    E. *low* in lysine and low in tryptophan

21. The blood glucose level in diabetes mellitus is DECREASED by removal of the   21.____

    A. gonads   B. thyroid
    C. parathyroids   D. anterior pituitary
    E. posterior pituitary

22. Reflex after-discharge can be explained in terms of the properties of   22.____

    A. anterior horn cells   B. afferent nerve fibers
    C. neuromuscular junctions   D. internuncial pool circuits
    E. none of the above

23. The reabsorption of sodium chloride is controlled in the kidney tubules by   23

 A. thyrotropic hormone
 B. antidiuretic hormone
 C. an adrenal cortical hormone
 D. an adrenal medullary hormone
 E. none of the above

24. The *most likely* cause of essential hypertension is   24

 A. *increased* blood volume
 B. *increased* cardiac output
 C. *increased* blood viscosity
 D. *decreased* peripheral resistance
 E. generalized constriction of arterioles

25. The process by which motor neurons to extensor muscles acting at a particular joint are   25
inhibited by stretch of the flexor muscles acting at the same joint is

 A. myotatic reflex   B. spatial summation
 C. monosynaptic reflex   D. reciprocal innervation
 E. none of the above

KEY (CORRECT ANSWERS)

1.	C		11.	C
2.	D		12.	B
3.	C		13.	E
4.	D		14.	E
5.	C		15.	D
6.	A		16.	A
7.	D		17.	B
8.	E		18.	E
9.	D		19.	E
10.	D		20.	E

21. D
22. D
23. C
24. E
25. D

TEST 2

DIRECTIONS: Each question or incomplete statement is followed by several suggested answers or completions. Select the one that BEST answers the question or completes the statement. *PRINT THE LETTER OF THE CORRECT ANSWER IN THE SPACE AT THE RIGHT.*

1. The chorda tympani nerve contains   1.____

   A. postganglionic fibers *only*
   B. preganglionic sympathetic secretory nerves
   C. preganglionic parasympathetic secretory fibers
   D. only fibers that innervate the sublingual gland
   E. none of the above

2. The MAXIMUM frequency of effective nerve stimulation is limited by the length of the   2.____

   A. chronaxie
   B. negative after-potential
   C. relative refractory period
   D. absolute refractory period
   E. utilization time of stimulus

3. Ketosis may be produced experimentally by   3.____

   A. fasting
   B. feeding a low fat diet
   C. feeding a low salt diet
   D. feeding a high protein diet
   E. feeding a high carbohydrate diet

4. A marked reduction in the serum calcium ion concentration in man will result in   4.____

   A. renal failure
   B. loss of equilibrium
   C. spontaneous hemorrhage
   D. increased muscular relaxation
   E. increased muscular irritability

5. The degenerate nature of the genetic code implies   5.____

   A. a common tRNA for at least two amino acids
   B. the existence of multiple codons for each amino acid
   C. that a remarkable degree of inaccuracy occurs in transcription
   D. the existence of multiple species of ribosomes for control of messenger translation
   E. none of the above

6. An EKG showing a consistent rhythmical ratio of three P waves to each QRST complex   6.____
   indicates

   A. idioventricular beat
   B. a bundle-branch block
   C. a complete bundle block
   D. an A-V node partial block
   E. an abnormal S-A node rhythm

7. Countercurrent multiplier activity of the kidney is dependent upon the   7.

    A.   presence of ADH
    B.   reabsorption of water from collecting ducts
    C.   intensity of vasoconstriction of efferent arterioles
    D.   active reabsorption of water in the ascending limb of the loop of Henle
    E.   active reabsorption of sodium ions in the ascending limb of the loop of Henle

8. The DECREASE in osmolarity of plasma that occurs after drinking large amounts of   8.
water results in

    A.   an *increase* in secretion of ADH
    B.   *no change* in osmolarity of urine
    C.   a *decrease* in the ADH level in blood
    D.   an *increase* in reabsorption of NaCl by tubules
    E.   a marked *increase* in glomerular filtration due to a *decrease* in colloid osmotic
       pressure

9. The normal blood bicarbonate-carbonic acid ratio is 20:1.   9.
A patient with a 10:1 ratio is in

    A.   compensated alkalosis
    B.   compensated acidosis
    C.   uncompensated alkalosis
    D.   uncompensated acidosis
    E.   none of the above

10. The mobilization of blood sugar from liver glycogen occurs by way of a series of enzy-   10
matic reactions. The LAST step in this sequence is catalyzed by

    A.   aldolase   B.   glucokinase
    C.   glucose-6-phosphatase   D.   fructose-6-phosphatase
    E.   glycogen phosphorylase

11. Iron-porphyrin protein structures are components of   11

    A.   myoglobin   B.   B vitamins
    C.   hemoglobin   D.   cytochromes
    E.   pyridine dinucleotides

12. The lipotropic effect of lecithin upon fatty livers may also be produced by   12

    A.   choline   B.   lipoic acid
    C.   ethanolamine   D.   B-hydroxybutyric acid
    E.   none of the above

13. Lipid is required in the average diet because it   13

    A.   has a high caloric value
    B.   provides essential fatty acids
    C.   aids in absorption of carbohydrates
    D.   is necessary for storage of carbohydrates
    E.   none of the above

14. The generator potential of a receptor is characterized by being 14.____

    A. an all-or-none response
    B. propagated in a nondecremental manner
    C. universally present in all nerve tissue
    D. graded according to strength of the stimulus
    E. none of the above

15. The physiologic importance of hemoglobin lies in its ability to combine 15.____

    A. *irreversibly* with oxygen and CO_2
    B. *reversibly* with oxygen at the ferric heme prosthetic group
    C. *irreversibly* with oxygen at the ferrous heme prosthetic group
    D. *reversibly* with oxygen at the ferrous heme prosthetic group
    E. none of the above

16. Much of the body sodium content is readily "exchangeable" EXCEPT for that portion found in 16.____

    A. bone
    B. skeletal muscle
    C. potential spaces
    D. cerebrospinal fluid
    E. gastrointestinal secretions

17. Blood leaving the lungs is saturated with O_2 to the extent of *approximately* _____ percent. 17.____

    A. 5   B. 25   C. 50   D. 75   E. 98

18. CO_2 is transported in the blood *predominantly* in the form of 18.____

    A. carbonic acid
    B. carbaminohemoglobin
    C. bicarbonate in plasma
    D. bicarbonate in erythrocytes
    E. CO_2 physically dissolved in plasma

19. The K_m value of an enzyme is *numerically* equal to 19.____

    A. half the maximum velocity expressed in moles/liter
    B. the ratio of velocity of reaction divided by the substrate concentration
    C. the substrate concentration in moles/liter necessary to achieve half the maximum velocity of a reaction
    D. the maximum velocity divided by half the substrate concentration in moles necessary to achieve maximum velocity
    E. none of the above

20. Stimulation of a carotid sinus nerve results in 20.____

    A. *increased* heart rate, *decreased* arterial blood pressure and *decreased* venous return
    B. *increased* heart rate, *increased* arterial blood pressure and *decreased* venous return

C. *decreased* heart rate, *decreased* arterial blood pressure and *decreased* venous return

D. *decreased* heart rate, *decreased* arterial blood pressure and *no effect* on venous return

E. *decreased* arterial blood pressure and *no effect* on heart rate or venous return

21. The general reaction for the transfer of a "one-carbon fragment" requires the coenzyme   21.

A. pyridoxal phosphate
B. tetrahydrofolic acid
C. thiamine pyrophosphate
D. flavin adenine dinucleotide
E. diphosphopyridine nucleotide

22. An IMMEDIATE effect of diminished oxygen tension in the myocardium is   22

A. vasodilatation of coronary vessels
B. vasoconstriction of coronary vessels
C. stimulation of chemoreceptors and, therefore, an increase in coronary blood flow
D. stimulation of chemoreceptors and, therefore, a decrease in coronary blood flow
E. none of the above

23. A vitamin derivative concerned with conversion of glucose to lactic acid is   23

A. thiamine (as cocarboxylase)
B. pantothenic acid (as coenzyme A)
C. pyridoxal (as pyridoxal phosphate)
D. nicotinamide (as nicotinamide adenine dinucleotide)
E. none of the above

24. The adequate stimulus for the Hering-Breuer reflex is the   24

A. stretching of alveoli
B. pressure of blood in the left atrium
C. pressure of blood in the right atrium
D. oxygen content of blood bathing the carotid bodies
E. carbon dioxide content of blood bathing the respiratory center

25. The *most likely* cause of an increase in filtration fraction is   2

A. elevation of ureteral pressure
B. efferent arteriolar constriction
C. afferent arteriolar constriction
D. elevation of renal vein pressure
E. elevation of plasma protein concentration

KEY (CORRECT ANSWERS)

1.	C	11.	D
2.	D	12.	A
3.	A	13.	B
4.	E	14.	D
5.	B	15.	D
6.	D	16.	A
7.	E	17.	E
8.	C	18.	C
9.	D	19.	C
10.	C	20.	C

21.	B
22.	A
23.	D
24.	A
25.	B

———

BIOCHEMISTRY / PHYSIOLOGY
EXAMINATION SECTION
TEST 1

DIRECTIONS: Each question or incomplete statement is followed by several suggested answers or completions. Select the one that BEST answers the question or completes the statement. *PRINT THE LETTER OF THE CORRECT ANSWER IN THE SPACE AT THE RIGHT.*

1. Positive nitrogen balance is *likely* to take place following administration of   1.____

    A. adrenaline   B. aldosterone
    C. growth hormone   D. enterogastrone
    E. thyroid hormone

2. Right-sided lesions of the spinal cord result in loss of motor activity   2.____

    A. and pain and temperature sensations on the same side
    B. on the same side and pain and temperature sensations on the opposite side
    C. and pain and temperature sensations on the opposite side
    D. on the opposite side and pain and temperature sensations on the same side
    E. none of the above

3. Sodium fluoride inhibits glycolysis by affecting   3.____

    A. amylase   B. enolase
    C. phosphatase   D. phosphorylase
    E. none of the above

4. The level of nonprotein nitrogen in the blood is due *principally* to the level of   4.____

    A. urea   B. ammonia
    C. creatine   D. arginine
    E. uric acid

5. Under normal conditions, the MOST important secretory mechanism for conservation of Na^+ by the kidney is   5.____

    A. H^+ secretion for the reabsorption of both Na^+ and HCO_3
    B. H^+ secretion to react with Na_2HPO_4 producing NaH_2PO_4 for excretion
    C. H^+ secretion and NH_3 production to reabsorb Na^+ from $NaCl$ and excrete NH_4Cl
    D. H^+ secretion to react with sodium salts or organic acids like lactate
    E. sodium exchange with potassium where potassium is secreted by the tubule cells for excretion

6. The hyperglycemic effect of glucagon is mediated *primarily* through   6.____

    A. the growth hormone
    B. muscle glycolysis
    C. liver glycogenolysis
    D. inhibition of cortisol action
    E. enhanced glucose reabsorption by renal tubules

7. The plasma protein that transports ferrous iron is   7.___

    A. ferritin   B. myoglobin
    C. hemoglobin   D. transferrin
    E. cytochrome-c

8. The coenzyme for glutamic-pyruvic transaminase is   8.___

    A. zinc   B. copper
    C. vitamin C   D. cytochrome
    E. pyridoxal phosphate

9. Upon complete hydrogenation, oleic, linoleic and linolenic acids yield   9.___

    A. stearic acid
    B. myristic acid
    C. palmitoleic acid
    D. arachidonic acid
    E. multiple acetate fragments

10. The chief constituents of biologic membranes are   10.___

    A. chitin and lecithin
    B. proteins and lipids
    C. lipids and carbohydrates
    D. nucleic acids and histones
    E. proteins and carbohydrates

11. Precocious sexual development in young boys and girls, or masculinization in the adult female, is due to   11.___

    A. excessive production of FSH by the neurohypophysis
    B. hyperplasia of the beta cells of the islets of Langerhans
    C. an excess of the androgenic hormone from the adrenal cortex
    D. a deficiency of the thyrotrophic hormone of the adenohypophysis
    E. destruction of the hypothalamus and a resulting lack of aldosterone supply

12. If two vessels are connected in parallel, their total resistance to blood flow is   12.___

    A. *the sum* of their individual resistances
    B. *the average* of their individual resistances
    C. *greater* than if they were connected in series
    D. *equal* to the resistance of the smaller vessel
    E. *less* than the resistance of either vessel alone

13. When injected, epinephrine causes   13.___

    A. a decrease in blood sugar
    B. an increase in blood sugar
    C. retention of sodium chloride
    D. an increase in blood calcium
    E. a decrease in the metabolic rate

14. Temperature-regulating mechanisms that increase heat *production* include   14.____
     I. shivering
     II. cutaneous vasodilation
     III. increased voluntary activity
     IV. cutaneous vasoconstriction
     V. increased secretion of epinephrine from the adrenal medulla
     The CORRECT answer is:

     A. I, II, III   B. I, II, V
     C. I, III, IV   D. I, III, V
     E. III, IV, V

15. Which of the following dietary components are *specifically* involved in the synthesis of   15.____
hemoglobin?
     I. Sodium
     II. Potassium
     III. Iron
     IV. Copper
     V. Phosphate
     VI. Selenium
     The CORRECT answer is:

     A. I, II   B. II, IV
     C. III, IV   D. III, VI
     E. IV, V

16. In severe degenerative disease of the liver, such as advanced alcoholic cirrhosis, a   16.____
marked deficiency of which of the following factors essential to blood coagulating mechanisms is *likely*?
     I. Prothromboplastin
     II. Prothrombin
     III. Thrombin
     IV. Vitamin K
     V. Fibrinogen
     The CORRECT answer is:

     A. I, V   B. II, III
     C. II, V   D. III, IV
     E. III, V

17. Which of the following are associated with hypothyroidism?   17.____
     I. High blood cholesterol
     II. Positive nitrogen balance
     III. Increased oxygen consumption
     IV. Decreased protein bound iodine
     V. Decreased iodine uptake by the thyroid gland
     The CORRECT answer is:

     A. I, II, III   B. I, II, IV, V
     C. I, III, IV   D. II, IV, V
     E. III, IV, V

18. Ingestion of which of the following MOST markedly affects the rate of gastric emptying?   18.___

    A. Fats   B. Minerals
    C. Proteins   D. Carbohydrates
    E. none of the above

19. In a normal individual, regardless of activity, how does intrapulmonary pressure relate to   19.___
intrapleural pressure?

    A. Intrapleural pressure is always positive.
    B. Intrapulmonary pressure is always positive.
    C. Intrapulmonary pressure is always greater than intrapleural pressure.
    D. Intrapleural pressure is always greater than intrapulmonary pressure.
    E. None of the above

20. Which of the following reactions is the *immediate* source of energy for muscular contrac-   20.___
tion?

    A. Creatine $\rightarrow$ creatinine
    B. Creatine phosphate + ADP $\rightarrow$ ATP + creatine
    C. Creatine phosphate $\rightarrow$ creatine + phosphoric acid
    D. Adenosine triphosphate $\rightarrow$ adenosine diphosphate + phosphoric acid
    E. None of the above

21. In respiratory acidosis, arterial CO_2 content _____ and pH _____.   21.___

    A. decreases, increases   B. decreases, decreases
    C. increases, increases   D. increases, decreases
    E. none of the above

22. Beriberi is associated with a deficiency in   22.___

    A. vitamin B   B. vitamin D
    C. vitamin K   D. thiamine
    E. ascorbic acid

23. Which of the following ions is involved in blood clotting?   23.___

    A. Iron   B. Sodium
    C. Calcium   D. Potassium
    E. None of the above

24. Which of the following combinations of enzymes contains *only* enzymes secreted as   24.___
zymogens?

    A. Lipase, nuclease, pepsin
    B. Pepsin, trypsin, chymotrypsin
    C. Enterokinase, pepsin, trypsin
    D. Enterokinase, pepsin, chymotrypsin
    E. Chymotrypsin, trypsin, enterokinase

25. What type of protein is albumin?   25.___

    A. Nucleoprotein   B. Chromoprotein
    C. Phosphoprotein   D. Simple protein
    E. None of the above

KEY (CORRECT ANSWERS)

1.	C		11.	C
2.	B		12.	E
3.	B		13.	B
4.	A		14.	D
5.	A		15.	C
6.	C		16.	C
7.	D		17.	B
8.	E		18.	A
9.	A		19.	C
10.	B		20.	D

21.	D
22.	D
23.	C
24.	B
25.	D

TEST 2

DIRECTIONS: Each question or incomplete statement is followed by several suggested answers or completions. Select the one that BEST answers the question or completes the statement. *PRINT THE LETTER OF THE CORRECT ANSWER IN THE SPACE AT THE RIGHT.*

1. Which of the following is an aid to the kidney in the elimination of hydrogen ion?

   1.___

   A. Secretion of sodium
   B. Secretion of ammonia
   C. Reabsorption of urea
   D. Secretion of potassium
   E. Reabsorption of bicarbonate

2. Which of the following statements applies to hemoglobin in sickle-cell anemia patients?

   2.___

   A. Hemoglobin cannot bind iron.
   B. Both alpha and beta chains are abnormal.
   C. Valine replaces serine in the alpha chain.
   D. Valine replaces glutamic acid in the beta chain.
   E. The abnormality is caused by methylation of a tryptophan residue in the beta chain.

3. As a result of a damaged tricuspid valve, blood would leak from the

   3.___

   A. right atrium to the vena cava
   B. left atrium to pulmonary veins
   C. right ventricle to right atrium
   D. left ventricle to left atrium
   E. none of the above

4. Which of the following enzymes catalyzes the conversion of 2-phosphoglyceric acid to phosphoenol pyruvate?

   4.___

   A. Enolase   B. Aldolase
   C. Pyruvate kinase   D. Phosphoglycerol kinase
   E. none of the above

5. In which of the following might the arterial blood pressure be abnormally high?

   5.___

   A. Cardiac shock   B. Heart failure
   C. Anaphylactic shock   D. Cerebrovascular accident
   E. Ventricular fibrillation

6. Which of the following minerals are MOST frequently in short supply in the American diet?

   6.___

   A. Calcium and iron
   B. Calcium and iodine
   C. Sulfur and potassium
   D. Iodine, magnesium and iron
   E. None of the above

7. Which of the following compounds is an intermediate in the biosynthesis of cholesterol?   7.____

   A. Squalene   B. Hexosamine
   C. Cholic acid   D. Pregnanediol
   E. Deoxycholic acid

8. Which of the following hormones is a polypeptide?   8.____

   A. Epinephrine
   B. Testosterone
   C. Progesterone
   D. Triiodotyronine
   E. Follicle-stimulating hormone

9. Energy for ATP synthesis is derived from the electron transport system by   9.____

   A. transamination   B. aldolization
   C. reductive synthesis   D. oxidative deamination
   E. oxidative phosphorylation

10. Avidin is an important dietary component because of its influence on   10.____

    A. niacin   B. biotin
    C. thiamine   D. tocopherol
    E. phylloquinone

11. The proportion of collagenous tissue in meat can be estimated by measuring   11.____

    A. glycine   B. nitrogen
    C. disulfide   D. hydroxyproline
    E. none of the above

12. Which of the following vitamins is *least* likely to be involved in tooth development and cal-   12.____
    cification?

    A. A   B. B_1
    C. C   D. D
    E. All of the above

13. In which of the following situations is diffusion LEAST important?   13.____

    A. Formation of glomerular filtrate
    B. Movement of Na^+ into nerve fiber
    C. Movement of lipid-soluble solute through cell membrane
    D. Exchange of CO_2 between pulmonary capillary blood and alveolar air
    E. Exchange of CO_2 between interstitial fluid and capillary blood of skeletal muscle

14. Which of the following is NOT a theory of the effect of parathyroid hormone on bone?   14.____
    The

    A. hormone influences the rate of bone resorption
    B. hormone causes a decrease in new bone formation
    C. action on bone is related to its action on phosphate excretion
    D. effect of parathyroid extract is to influence osteoclastic activity
    E. none of the above

15. Which of the following is NOT a part of the hemoglobin molecule?   15.___

    A. Iron   B. Protein
    C. Magnesium   D. Histidine
    E. Pyrrole ring

16. Which of the following conditions does NOT cause an increase in glomerular filtration   16.___
rate?

    A. Increased plasma oncotic pressure
    B. Decreased plasma oncotic pressure
    C. Vasodilation of afferent arterioles
    D. Decreased pressure in Bowman's capsule
    E. Moderate vasoconstriction of efferent arterioles

17. The free fatty acid level of blood is NOT *primarily* affected by   17.___

    A. serum albumin levels
    B. action of calcitonin
    C. anti-lipolytic action of insulin
    D. intestinal absorption of fatty acids
    E. none of the above

18. Glomerular filtrate contains everything contained in plasma EXCEPT   18.___

    A. urea   B. glucose
    C. plasma protein   D. sodium chloride
    E. none of the above

19. Excessive utilization of fats by the body as a source of energy during disturbances in car-   19.___
bohydrate metabolism can lead to all of the following conditions EXCEPT

    A. ketosis   B. acidosis
    C. ketonuria   D. alkalosis
    E. none of the above

20. Denaturation usually destroys all of the following bonds in protein EXCEPT _____   20.___
bonds.

    A. hydrogen   B. covalent
    C. hydrophobic   D. electrostatic
    E. magnesium

KEY (CORRECT ANSWERS)

1.	B	11.	D
2.	D	12.	B
3.	C	13.	A
4.	A	14.	B
5.	D	15.	C
6.	A	16.	A
7.	A	17.	B
8.	E	18.	C
9.	E	19.	D
10.	B	20.	B

BIOCHEMISTRY / PHYSIOLOGY
EXAMINATION SECTION
TEST 1

DIRECTIONS: Each question or incomplete statement is followed by several suggested
answers or completions. Select the one that BEST answers the question or
completes the statement. *PRINT THE LETTER OF THE CORRECT ANSWER
IN THE SPACE AT THE RIGHT.*

1. The vitamin which functions in coenzymes specifically involved in the transfer and utiliza-   1.____
   tion of the single carbon moiety is

   A. niacin   B. thiamine   C. vitamin K
   D. vitamin A   E. folic acid

2. The fibers in connective tissue consist of   2.____

   A. fibrin   B. mucoid   C. gelatin
   D. collagen   E. glycolipid

3. The oxidative degradation of pyruvic acid is facilitated by the repeated regeneration of   3.____
   _____ acid.

   A. malic   B. fumaric   C. succinic
   D. isocitric   E. oxaloacetic

4. The heteropolysaccharide known to prevent the formation of active thrombin is   4.____

   A. heparin   B. keratosulfate   C. hyaluronic acid
   D. dermatan sulfate   E. chondroitin sulfate

5. The basal metabolic rate is usually expressed as a function of the   5.____

   A. body surface area
   B. amount of exercise being performed
   C. amount of food consumed
   D. rate at which water is consumed
   E. area of the lung surface because that is where most of the CO_2 is produced

6. Hypersecretion of growth hormones in humans results in   6.____

   A. acromegaly in the young; gigantism in the adult
   B. gigantism in the young; acromegaly in the adult
   C. gigantism in both young and adults
   D. acromegaly in both young and adults

7. In sickle cell anemia, a variation in an amino acid of the hemoglobin is detected.   7.____
   This substitution of valine for glutamic acid

   A. results in no change in solubility
   B. results in no change in isoelectric pH
   C. is a result of change in DNA coding
   D. has no noticeable effect on the O_2 transport behavior of the erythocyte

8. *All* of the following amino acids are involved in urea synthesis EXCEPT

    A. arginine   B. histidine   C. ornithine
    D. citrulline   E. aspartic acid

9. The principal function of the cardiac sphincter is to

    A. facilitate the storage of food in the lower esophagus
    B. prevent the reflux of gastric contents
    C. mix the food particles entering the stomach
    D. control the rate of entry of food into the stomach
    E. None of the above

10. Proteins serve as each of the following EXCEPT

    A. hormones   B. oxygen carriers   C. storage materials
    D. structural elements E. carriers of genetic information

11. Moderate exercise in the normal individual will increase heart rate and will tend to

    A. decrease coronary blood flow
    B. have little effect on coronary blood flow
    C. increase coronary blood flow
    D. All of the above
    E. None of the above

12. Progressive organ changes are observed in progressive stages of shock.
    They include *all* of the following EXCEPT

    A. metabolic acidosis
    B. decreased blood supply to the brain
    C. decreased kidney function (decreased glomerular filteration leading to tubular damage)
    D. damage to liver due to hypoxia (pyruvates and lactates are not metabolized; possible passage of bacterial endotoxins through the liver into the systemic circulation)

13. An anemic man with 7.5 grams of hemoglobin per 100 cc blood has no respiratory impairment and is breathing room air.
    His hemoglobin saturation is _____ percent.

    A. 33   B. 50   C. 66
    D. 75   E. 100

14. Digitalis is prescribed to persons with atrial fibrillation.
    Though pathogenesis of atrial fibrillation remains unsettled, the reason digitalis is used is that it

    A. depresses A-V conduction
    B. ameliorates A-V conduction
    C. increases number of discharges from S-A node
    D. decreases number of discharges from S-A node

15. Oxygen removal from the alveoli of the lung may be facilitated by   15.____

    A. low PO_2 of pulmonary artery blood
    B. increased total alveolar surface area
    C. increased blood flow through alveolar capillaries
    D. all of the above
    E. none of the above

16. Passage of water through a selectively permeable membrane is   16.____

    A. osmosis
    B. dialysis
    C. ionization
    D. active transport
    E. Donnan membrane equilibrium

17. In third degree heart block, the electrocardiograph shows   17.____

    A. an increased PQ interval
    B. an increase in the QRS complex
    C. an increase in the height of the R wave
    D. one QRS complex for every three P waves
    E. the P wave and the QRS complex are dissociated

18. In a compensation acidosis, the pH of blood plasma is normal but the total carbon dioxide content is low. The compensation is achieved by   18.____

    A. excretion of an alkaline urine
    B. decreasing the volume of respiration per minute
    C. increasing the volume of respiration per minute
    D. excretion of an acid urine
    E. increasing the carbon dioxide production per minute

19. The first heart sound begins during the   19.____

    A. PR segment   B. PR interval   C. R wave
    D. QRS complex   E. ST segment

20. The affinity of hemoglobin for oxygen   20.____

    A. is unaffected by pH
    B. increases as pH decreases
    C. is reduced by presence of 2,3-diphosphoglycerate
    D. is unaffected by presence of 2,3-diphosphoglycerate except in the fetus

21. The sinoatrial (S-A) node is the normal pacemaker for the cardiac impulse because it   21.

    A. is specialized nervous tissue
    B. is richly supplied with nerve endings
    C. possesses a high frequency of rhythmic discharge
    D. contains the cell bodies of the conductile fibers

22. Administration of heparin to a human results in symptoms similar to vitamin K deficiency   22.
in that both conditions result in

    A. release of lipoprotein lipase to the blood and rapid clearance of chylomicrons
    B. an increase in bleeding time due to lack of thrombin formation
    C. retardation of fibrinogen synthesis by the liver
    D. elevated non-esterified fatty acids which chelate serum calcium, thus retarding
    blood clotting

23. Ingestion of sodium lactate leads to an alkalinizing action because   23.

    A. The presence of sodium lactate in the plasma makes it alkaline
    B. the sodium ion is more readily absorbed than the lactate ion
    C. the sodium is conserved and the lactic acid excreted by the kidney
    D. sodium lactate is readily absorbed and the lactate is rapidly metabolized
    E. sodium lactate is slightly alkaline since it is a salt of strong alkali and weak acid

24. Triglyceride absorbed into the lymphatic system is transported to the liver as   24.

    A. chylomicrons
    B. very low density lipoprotein
    C. low density lipoprotein
    D. high density lipoprotein
    E. very high density lipoprotein

25. The kidney compensates for a metabolic alkalosis by increasing   25.

    A. ammonia excretion
    B. bicarbonate excretion
    C. hydrogen ion excretion
    D. bicarbonate reabsorption
    E. More than one but not all of the above

KEY (CORRECT ANSWERS)

1. E	11. C
2. D	12. B
3. E	13. E
4. A	14. A
5. A	15. D
6. B	16. A
7. C	17. E
8. B	18. C
9. B	19. E
10. E	20. C

21. C
22. B
23. D
24. A
25. B

TEST 2

DIRECTIONS: Each question or incomplete statement is followed by several suggested answers or completions. Select the one that BEST answers the question or completes the statement. *PRINT THE LETTER OF THE CORRECT ANSWER IN THE SPACE AT THE RIGHT.*

1. The movement of Na^+ and K^+ ions is believed to be of major importance in development of the action potential in nerve and muscle fibers.
    Activation of the membrane and development of the spike potential most likely relates to the

    A. rapid influx of the K
    B. rapid outflow of the K^+
    C. rapid influx of the Na^+
    D. rapid outflow of the Na^+
    E. sudden equilibration of the K^+ and the Na^+

2. A sudden rise of pressure within the carotid sinus causes

    A. *increased* pulse rate
    B. *decreased* pulse rate
    C. *increased* peripheral resistance
    D. *increased* blood pressure
    E. *increased* cardiac output

3. The condition in the retina that is MOST characteristic of night blindness is that

    A. sufficient NAD (DPN) in not available
    B. the protein opsin is not in adequate supply
    C. isomeric transformation of retinene does not occur
    D. regeneration of rhodopsin does not take place at an adequate rate
    E. riboflavin is not present in sufficient concentration for normal sight

4. If the reaction, hemoglobin->methemoglobin, occurs to an appreciable extent in the body, there is

    A. no effect on the ability of blood to pick up O_2
    B. a noticeable diminution of the ability of the blood to transport O_2
    C. a noticeable increase in the ability of the blood to pick up O_2
    D. a decrease in CO_2 -combining power
    E. an increase in CO_2-combining power

5. Pepsinogen is found in cells of the

    A. colon   B. stomach   C. duodenum
    D. pancreas   E. villi of small intestine

6. In collagen diseases with an increased turnover of breakdown of collagen, the urine is likely to exhibit a(n)

    A. *decrease* in glycine
    B. *increase* in tryptophan
    C. *increase* in phenylalanine
    D. *increase* in hydroxyproline
    E. *increase* in hydroxyapatite

6.___

7. The glomerular filtration rate may be determined by the clearance of

    A. urea   B. water   C. inulin
    D. glucose   E. para-aminohippuric acid (PAH)

7.___

8. Glycogen is stored in the

    A. liver   B. spleen   C. muscles
    D. Both A and B above   E. Both A and C above   F. All of the above

8.___

9. Hyperventilation increases the length of time one can hold his breath. This is PRIMARILY because hyperventilation

    A. significantly increases the O_2 content of the arterial blood
    B. significantly depletes the CO_2 content of the blood
    C. causes a complete saturation of the oxygen stores of the body
    D. All of the above
    E. None of the above

9.___

10. In reciprocal innervation the

    A. muscle and its antagonist are stimulated simultaneously
    B. muscle is stimulated and its antagonist is simultaneously inhibited
    C. muscle and its antagonist are simultaneously inhibited
    D. no relation necessarily exists between innervation of the muscle and its antagonist

10.___

11. Carbonic anhydrase in the erythocyte increases the

    A. permeability of erythrocyte to HCO_3
    B. rate of formation of oxyhemoglobin
    C. formation of carbamino compounds with hemoglobin
    D. rate of hydration of CO_2 and rate of dehydration of H_2CO_3

11.___

12. The carbohydrate in highest concentration in resting muscle is

    A. glucose   B. lactose   C. sucrose
    D. glycogen   E. inositol

12.___

13. Total body water can be estimated using the dilution principle with   13.__

    A. inulin   B. antipyrine
    C. radioactive iron   D. sodium thiocyanate
    E. radioactive potassium

14. The *only* avenue of heat loss at an environmental (air and wall) temperature above body   14.__
temperature is

    A. sweating   B. conduction   C. convection   D. radiation

15. Starling factors influencing the exchange of fluid across the capillary membranes in the   15.__
liver differ from those of other tissues in that

    A. hydrostatic pressure is lower
    B. hydrostatic pressure is higher
    C. plasma oncotic pressure is lower
    D. interstitial fluid oncotic pressure is lower
    E. interstitial fluid oncotic pressure is higher

16. Active transport systems generally involve specific binding molecules which are   16.__

    A. lipids   B. proteins   C. carbohydrates
    D. nucleic acids   E. polyphosphates

17. Parathyroid hormone acts in the body by   17.__

    A. decreasing absorption of calcium in the intestinal tract
    B. accelerating the removal of calcium and phosphate from the skeleton but not the
        teeth
    C. stimulating gluconeogenesis in the liver
    D. decreasing the excretion of sodium and chloride
    E. all of the above

18. The PRIMARY location of the translation of the genetic message in the cell is the   18.__

    A. nucleus   B. ribosome   C. lysosome
    D. nucleolus   E. mitochondrion

19. The mechanism of fluoride action in reducing dental decay is *most likely* the result of a(n)   19.__

    A. increase in the hardness of the tooth
    B. increase in remineralization of enamel
    C. reduction of solubility of the enamel as the fluoride content increases
    D. influence on exchange of ions between body fluids and the hard tissues
    E. decrease in carbohydrate metabolism in the oral cavity as a result of its bacterio-
        static effect

20. The termination of synthesis of a polypeptide is believed to involve   20.__

    A. nonsense codons
    B. anticodon-codon interaction
    C. tRNA which cannot bind, amino acids
    D. hydrolysis of messenger RNA
    E. none of the above

4 (#2)

21. A compound which has been obtained from the nucleus of a cell is found to contain one   21.____
molecule each of a purine, deoxyribose and phosphoric acid, and is called a

    A. nucleotide   B. nucleoside   C. nucleic acid
    D. nucleoprotein   E. polynucleotide

22. Severe chronic vitamin D deficiency results in an inability to absorb calcium from the   22.____
small intestine. The reason for this is that vitamin D or a metabolite

    A. emulsifies the non-esterified fatty acids which would otherwise form insoluble cal-
       cium salts
    B. stimulates the flow of bile acids which inhibit the absorption of calcium
    C. is required for the biosynthesis of a specific protein involved in calcium transport in
       the small intestine
    D. stimulates the synthesis of oxalic acid by the intestinal epitheliunforming calcium
       oxalate which is absorbed

23. The glucose transport mechanism sensitive to insulin is   23.____

    A. active transport   B. simple diffusion
    C. facilitated diffusion   D. single-file diffusion
    E. none of the above

24. Reactions which have unfavorable energetics in metabolic pathways may be driven to   24.____
completion by a process called

    A. coupling   B. allosterism
    C. modification   D. microscopic reversibility

25. If a filtered load of glucose is above its Tm, then the amount of glucose reabsorbed per   25.____
minute would be

    A. independent of the plasma concentration of glucose
    B. in direct proportion to the amount of glucose excreted
    C. in direct proportion to the plasma concentration of glucose
    D. in an inverse proportion to the plasma concentration of glucose

KEY (CORRECT ANSWERS)

1.	C	11.	D
2.	B	12.	D
3.	D	13.	B
4.	B	14.	A
5.	B	15.	E
6.	D	16.	B
7.	C	17.	B
8.	E	18.	B
9.	B	19.	C
10.	B	20.	A

21.	A
22.	C
23.	C
24.	A
25.	A

MICROBIOLOGY / PATHOLOGY

EXAMINATION SECTION
TEST 1

DIRECTIONS: Each question or incomplete statement is followed by several suggested answers or completions. Select the one that BEST answers the question or completes the statement. *PRINT THE LETTER OF THE CORRECT ANSWER IN THE SPACE AT THE RIGHT.*

1. The MOST common primary malignant neoplasm of the lung is   1._____

    A. adenocarcinoma
    B. bronchial adenoma
    C. alveolar cell carcinoma
    D. squamous cell carcinoma
    E. undifferentiated carcinoma

2. A candidate virus for the induction of cervical carcinoma is   2._____

    A. adenovirus
    B. C-type virus
    C. varicella zoster
    D. Epstein-Barr virus
    E. herpes virus hominis Type 2

3. In MOST slow viruses, tissue damage occurs in the   3._____

    A. lung   B. heart
    C. brain   D. spleen
    E. kidney

4. The MOST common causative organism in gram-negative sepsis is   4._____

    A. pneumococcus   B. virus organism
    C. escherichia coli   D. streptococcus viridans
    E. streptococcus pyogenes

5. Fluoride is MOST effective and safe as a prophylactic measure when it is   5._____

    A. in the F_2 state
    B. applied topically
    C. taken intravenously
    D. supplied in sucrose
    E. added to the water supply

6. The MOST common etiologic agent of septic arthritis in adults is   6._____

    A. neisseria gonorrhoeae
    B. hemophilus influenzae
    C. streptococcus pyogenes
    D. streptococcus pneumoniae
    E. herpes hominis

7. The delayed type of hypersensitivity can be transferred by   7.__

    A. lysozyme   B. antibodies
    C. mast cells   D. plasma cells
    E. sensitized lymphocytes

8. The BASIC effect of x-radiation upon living tissues is   8.__

    A. ionization   B. denaturation
    C. agglutination   D. precipitation
    E. cauterization

9. The PRINCIPAL antibody-producing cell is the   9.__

    A. mast cell   B. lymphocyte
    C. macrophage   D. eosinophil
    E. plasma cell

10. The histologic pattern in a renal ischemic infarct is _____ necrosis.   10.__

    A. caseous   B. gummatous
    C. gangrenous   D. coagulation
    E. liquefaction

11. Dextrans are extracellular polysaccharides readily produced by *streptococcus*   11.__

    A. mitis   B. mutans
    C. pyogenes   D. salivarius
    E. acidogenic

12. A bacterial mutation leading to the requirement for a single amino acid is due to   12.__

    A. lack of mRNA
    B. loss of ability to utilize glucose
    C. absence of a single enzyme activity
    D. absence of cell wall polysaccharide
    E. absence of several enzyme activities

13. Transmission of the hepatitis B virus may be through   13.__
      I. parental administration of blood or blood products
      II. use of contaminated instruments or injection equipment
      III. microabrasions in skin and mucous membranes by contact with infected
           materials (blood, saliva, feces)
    The CORRECT answer is:

    A. I *only*   B. II *only*   C. I, III
    D. II, III   E. I, II, III

14. Rickettsiae are similar to bacteria in that they   14.__
      I. multiply by binary fission
      II. can be cultured on enriched blood agar
      III. are capable of producing heat-resistant endospores
      IV. possess an energy-yielding, autonomous enzyme metabolism
      V. are susceptible to the lethal effects of certain antibiotics
    The CORRECT answer is:

    A. I, II, III   B. I, III, IV   C. I, IV, V
    D. II, III, V   E. II, IV, V

15. Significant functions of polymorphonuclear leukocytes in inflammation are   15._____
       I.   replication of new cells
      II.   phagocytosis of bacteria
     III.   elaboration of proteolytic enzymes
     IV.   elaboration of antibodies
The CORRECT answer is:

   A. I, II   B. I, III   C. II, III
   D. II, IV   E. III, IV

16. Neonatally thymectomized mice and nude mice exhibit   16._____
       I.   reduced numbers of T-lymphocytes
      II.   inability to reject allografts
     III.   reduced antibody production to most antigens
The CORRECT answer is:

   A. I *only*   B. II *only*   C. I, II
   D. II, III   E. I, II, III

17. The choice that *correctly* shows the following types of cells or tissues in DECREASING   17._____
order of radiosensitivity from MOST sensitive to LEAST sensitive is:
       I.   Osteocyte
      II.   Endothelium
     III.   Smooth muscle
     IV.   Spermatogonium
      V.   Intestinal mucosa
The CORRECT answer is:

   A. II, III, I, V, IV   B. III, I, II, IV, V   C. IV, II, III, I, V
   D. IV, V, II, III, I   -   E. V, IV, III, I, II

18. Cells of which of the following retain a latent capacity for mitotic division?   18._____
       I.   Liver
      II.   Bone marrow
     III.   Cardiac muscle
     IV.   Salivary glands
      V.   Neurons
The CORRECT answer is:

   A. I, II, III   B. I, II, IV   C. I, III, IV
   D. II, III, V   E. II, IV, V

19. Which of the following statements explain the advantageous effects of fibrin formation?   19._____
Fibrin
       I.   transforms into fibroblasts serving in repair
      II.   generates hyaluronidase to dissolve exudates
     III.   serves as scaffolding for fibroblasts to proliferate in repair
     IV.   serves to wall off attacking agents to prevent further spread
The CORRECT answer is:

   A. I, II   B. I, III   C. I, IV
   D. II, III   E. III, IV

20. Which of the following are possible sequelae to acute appendicitis?   20.__
    I.   Generalized peritonitis
    II. Periappendiceal abscess formation
    III. Pylephlebitis
    IV. Hepatic abscess
    The CORRECT answer is:

    A. I, II, III   B. I, II, IV
    C. I, III, IV   D. II, III, IV
    E. I, II, III, IV

21. Which of the following are related to streptococcal cross-antigenicity?   21.__
    I.   Sympathetic opthalmia
    II. Milroy's disease
    III. Systemic lupus erythematosus
    IV. Rheumatic fever
    V.   Acute glomerulonephritis
    The CORRECT answer is:

    A. I, III   B. II, III
    C. II, V   D. III, V
    E. IV, V

22. Which of the following hormones has the GREATEST effect on granulation tissue in heal-   22._
    ing wounds?

    A. Thyroxin   B. Estrogen
    C. Cortisone   D. Parathormone
    E. Antidiuretic hormone

23. When horse serum is injected intravenously into a rabbit and again into the skin two or   23._
    three weeks later, what is the necrotizing reaction that occurs at the site of the second
    injection?

    A. Atopy
    B. Anaphylaxis
    C. Serum sickness
    D. Arthus phenomenon
    E. Prausnitz-Kustner reaction

24. Recurring attacks of bronchial asthma may predispose to   24._

    A. empyema   B. emphysema
    C. tuberculosis   D. cor pulmonale
    E. none of the above

25. The one of the following that is classified as a hemolytic anemia is _____ anemia.   25._

    A. aplastic   B. pernicious
    C. sickle-cell   D. iron deficiency
    E. none of the above

KEY (CORRECT ANSWERS)

1.	D	11.	B
2.	E	12.	C
3.	C	13.	E
4.	C	14.	C
5.	E	15.	C
6.	A	16.	D
7.	E	17.	D
8.	A	18.	B
9.	E	19.	E
10.	D	20.	E

21.	E
22.	C
23.	D
24.	B
25.	C

———

TEST 2

DIRECTIONS: Each question or incomplete statement is followed by several suggested answers or completions. Select the one that BEST answers the question or completes the statement. *PRINT THE LETTER OF THE CORRECT ANSWER IN THE SPACE AT THE RIGHT.*

1.   Increased functional demand on the heart produces increased size of the myocardium by   1.__

   A.   hyperplasia
   B.   hypertrophy
   C.   calcification
   D.   fatty infiltration
   E.   increased amounts of fibrous connective tissue

2.   An infectious disease with low morbidity and which is constantly present in a given com-   2.__
   munity is considered to be

   A.   endemic   B.   epidemic
   C.   pandemic   D.   epizootic
   E.   polyzygotic

3.   A tumor composed of multiple tissues in which there may be representatives of all three   3.__
   embryonal layers is a(n)

   A.   teratoma   B.   adenoma
   C.   carcinoma   D.   sarcoma
   E.   hamartoma

4.   Shock is a circulatory disturbance characterized by   4.__

   A.   *increased* blood pressure
   B.   *elevated* body temperature
   C.   *increased* atmospheric pressure
   D.   *decreased* volume of circulating blood
   E.   *decreased* volume of interstitial fluid

5.   Diphtheria, pertussis, smallpox, poliomyelitis and tetanus have in common the fact that   5.__
   all are

   A.   air-borne diseases
   B.   vector-borne diseases
   C.   characterized by toxemia
   D.   primarily diseases of infants
   E.   prevented by active immunization

6.   The three general classes of vaccines are   6.__

   A.   killed organisms, virulent bacteria and attenuated viruses
   B.   toxoids, antitoxins and attenuated organisms
   C.   killed organisms, toxoids and attenuated organisms
   D.   killed organisms, antitoxins and gamma globulins
   E.   none of the above

7. Adjuvants are nonspecific, mildly irritating substances which are used to   7._____

     A. enhance antibody response
     B. depress antibody response
     C. desensitize to a given antigen
     D. remove antibodies from circulation
     E. none of the above

8. Hemorrhage might be difficult to curb in patients with liver disorders because of   8._____

     A. anemia which invariably accompanies liver dysfunction
     B. vitamin C shortage caused by impaired fat absorption
     C. deficiency of vitamin B_{12}
     D. hypoprothrombinemia
     E. lack of bile pigments

9. The MOST common complication of chronic peptic ulcer is   9._____

     A. hemorrhage
     B. malabsorption syndrome
     C. development of carcinoma
     D. development of hypoacidity
     E. development of obstruction during healing

10. Acute glomerulonephritis is *most commonly* a sequela of   10._____

     A. measles
     B. diphtheria
     C. upper respiratory infections due to hemolytic streptococci
     D. upper respiratory infections due to nonhemolytic streptococci
     E. mumps

11. When a thrombotic embolus originates in a femoral vein, it *usually* becomes arrested in   11._____
the

     A. right heart   B. renal circulation
     C. portal circulation   D. hepatic circulation
     E. pulmonary circulation

12. Ribonucleic acid is considered to be the chemical basis for heredity in poliomyelitis virus   12._____
because

     A. it is the only nucleic acid present
     B. ultraviolet light induces mutations
     C. DNA is infective under appropriate conditions
     D. viral infectivity is destroyed by deoxyribonuclease
     E. none of the above

13. Transfer of inheritable characteristics among bacteria is dependent on   13._____

     A. ATP   B. DPT   C. DNA   D. RNA   E. FDS

14. Enzymes responsible for suppuration in an abscess are derived *mainly* from   14.__

    A. serum
    B. lymph
    C. lymphocytes
    D. polymorphonuclear leukocytes
    E. hemoglobin

15. Heat sensitive materials may be sterilized without destruction by means of   15.__

    A. dry heat
    B. boiling water
    C. ethylene oxide
    D. quaternary ammonium compounds
    E. laser sterilization

16. Orchitis is a serious complication in adults with   16.__

    A. mumps
    B. measles
    C. nongonococcal urethritis
    D. ECHO virus meningoencephalitis
    E. parainfluenza virus nasopharyngitis

17. Rickettsia are distinguishable from viruses because viruses contain   17.__

    A. DNA; rickettsia contain RNA
    B. RNA; rickettsia contain DNA
    C. either RNA or DNA; rickettsia contain both RNA and DNA
    D. both RNA and DNA; rickettsia contain either RNA or DNA
    E. either RNA or DNA; rickettsia contain neither RNA nor DNA

18. Organisms which exhibit dimorphism, are gram-positive, and grow on Sabouraud's   18.__
medium are

    A. fungi   B. bacteria
    C. mycoplasma   D. rickettsia
    E. spirochetes

19. The genus bacillus is distinguished from the genus clostridium chiefly in that the strains   19.__
of bacillus are

    A. aerobic   B. anaerobic
    C. parasitic   D. sporebearers
    E. none of the above

20. Striated muscle, smooth muscle and cardiac muscle have in common the fact that   20.__

    A. hyperplasia of these elements is common
    B. hypertrophy is a common response to injury
    C. they have a limited capacity to regenerate
    D. they need a constant high O_2 concentration to function
    E. none of the above

21. The cell MOST important in the production of antibody is the

    A. mast cell
    B. histiocyte
    C. lymphocyte
    D. plasma cell
    E. polymorphonuclear leukocyte

21.____

22. Osteomyelitis is MOST commonly caused by

    A. nocardia asteroides
    B. borrelia vincentii
    C. actinomyces bovis
    D. staphylococcus aureus
    E. mycobacterium tuberculosis

22.____

23. Histamine released by mast cells is responsible for the principal symptoms of

    A. anaphylaxis
    B. serum sickness
    C. macroglobulinemia
    D. immune-complex diseases
    E. delayed hypersensitivity

23.____

24. The BASIC difference between gram-positive and gram-negative bacteria is

    A. cell wall structure
    B. chromosome structure
    C. that gram-negative bacteria are motile
    D. that gram-positive bacteria have capsules
    E. there is no basic difference

24.____

25. A benign mushroom-like neoplasm of bone showing a peripheral cartilage cap in the metaphyseal area of a young person is *most likely* a(n)

    A. exostosis   B. osteosarcoma
    C. chondrosarcoma   D. osteochondroma
    E. metaphyseal defect

25.____

KEY (CORRECT ANSWERS)

1.	B	11.	E
2.	A	12.	A
3.	A	13.	C
4.	D	14.	D
5.	E	15.	C
6.	C	16.	A
7.	A	17.	C
8.	D	18.	A
9.	A	19.	A
10.	C	20.	C

21.	D
22.	D
23.	A
24.	A
25.	D

———

MICROBIOLOGY / PATHOLOGY
EXAMINATION SECTION
TEST 1

DIRECTIONS: Each question or incomplete statement is followed by several suggested answers or completions. Select the one that BEST answers the question or completes the statement. *PRINT THE LETTER OF THE CORRECT ANSWER IN THE SPACE AT THE RIGHT.*

1. The early bronchial mucosal alteration *most likely* to be observed in cigarette smokers is   1.____

    A. dysplasia   B. neoplasia
    C. metaplasia   D. hypoplasia
    E. hyperplasia

2. A 65-year-old male who demonstrates urinary retention or difficulty in voiding his bladder   2.____
    most likely has

    A. carcinoma of the prostate
    B. benign prostatic hyperplasia
    C. malignant neoplasm of the ureter
    D. bladder metastasis of bronchogenic carcinoma
    E. polyps

3. Interstitial pulmonary inflammation is MOST characteristic of   3.____

    A. lobar pneumonia   B. viral pneumonia
    C. bronchial asthma   D. bronchopneumonia
    E. pleurisy

4. Aerobic organotrophic (or heterotrophic) bacteria which oxidize a substrate to CO_2 and   4.____
    H_2O use, in the final electron transport, enzymes containing

    A. cytochromes   B. coenzyme A
    C. ribose nucleic acid   D. pyridine nucleotides
    E. flavin adenine dinucleotide

5. The etiology of acute diffuse glomerulonephritis seems to be   5.____

    A. circulatory deficiency associated with prolonged shock
    B. bacteremia with localization of organisms in kidney tissue
    C. injury of glomeruli by exogenous inorganic toxins
    D. degenerative changes induced by sclerotic alterations of blood vessels
    E. allergic reaction of glomerular and vascular tissue to beta-hemolytic streptococcal products

6. Following the initial transient vasoconstriction, the NEXT vascular reaction to injury in the   6.____
    sequence of events in inflammation is

    A. margination of leukocytes
    B. dilation of blood vessels
    C. increased capillary permeability
    D. movement of leukocytes toward the irritant
    E. phagocytosis of bacteria and other particles

7. Recurrent aphthae resemble recurrent herpes in that

    A. symptoms are similar
    B. life-long immunity results
    C. vesicles occur with both diseases
    D. intranuclear inclusion bodies are present
    E. circulating antibodies to the etiologic agents may be demonstrated

8. The BEST evidence for a causal relationship between a nasal carrier of staphylococci and a staphylococcal infection in a hospital patient is the demonstration that the organisms from both individuals

    A. are coagulase-positive
    B. are penicillin resistant
    C. are of the same phage type
    D. are aureus-type staphylococci
    E. produce hemolysis, liquefy gelation and ferment mannitol

9. For the MAJORITY of individuals, the INITIAL infection with herpes simplex virus results in

    A. encephalitis as a young adult
    B. a dermal rash in childhood
    C. herpes labialis in puberty
    D. a subclinical disease
    E. genital herpes

10. The radiosensitivity of tissue is MOST closely related to the

    A. mitotic rate
    B. nuclear cytoplasmic ratio
    C. RNA content of the cytoplasm
    D. size of the cells that make up the tissue
    E. ionization density of the primary irradiation

11. The MOST conspicuous clinical sign of right-sided heart failure is

    A. hypertension
    B. mitral stenosis
    C. pulmonary edema
    D. systemic venous congestion
    E. brown induration of the lung

12. An example of hypoplasia is the

    A. absence of an organ
    B. underdevelopment of an organ
    C. acquired reduction in size of an organ
    D. increase in number of cells of an organ
    E. none of the above

13. The renal disease *most commonly* related to hypertension is   13.____

    A. renal atresia   B. nephrosclerosis
    C. acute pyelonephritis   D. chronic pyelonephritis
    E. none of the above

14. Myxedema is an endocrine disturbance resulting from   14.____

    A. secondary hyperparathyroidism in children
    B. primary hyperparathyroidism in adults
    C. hyperpituitarism in adults
    D. hypothyroidism in children
    E. hypothyroidism in adults

15. Some investigators believe streptococci are predominant in the etiology of caries because streptococci   15.____

    A. produce caries in germ-free rats when introduced as monocontaminants
    B. are predominant in saliva
    C. are beta-hemolytic
    D. contain M protein
    E. all of the above

16. Detergents kill bacteria by interfering with the function of the cell   16.____

    A. wall   B. nucleus
    C. capsule   D. membrane
    E. cytoplasm

17. Massive necrotizing lesions of the palate in a patient with poorly-controlled diabetes mellitus are *frequently* related to   17.____

    A. phycomycosis   B. blastomycosis
    C. histoplasmosis   D. cryptococcosis
    E. coccidoidomycosis

18. An example of an endogenous bacterial infection is   18.____

    A. trachoma   B. Weil's disease
    C. leptospirosis   D. salmonellosis
    E. actinomycosis

19. MOST forms of lung cancer arise from the   19.____

    A. peribronchial lymph nodes
    B. lining epithelium of the alveoli
    C. lining epithelium of the tracheobronchial tree
    D. submucosal glands of the tracheobronchial tree
    E. pleural sacs

20. Rheumatic fever, scleroderma and rheumatoid arthritis exhibit _____ degeneration.   20.____

    A. fatty   B. amyloid
    C. hyaline   D. fibrinoid
    E. epithelial

21. A bacterium well known for its large polysaccharide capsule is   21.

    A. clostridium tetani
    B. staphylococcus aureus
    C. hemophilus influenzae
    D. streptococcus pneumoniae
    E. mycobacterium tuberculosis

22. Recurrent herpes labialis occurs in those people who   22.

    A. have had no previous contact with herpesvirus
    B. have been infected with herpesvirus but who fail to produce antibodies against the virus
    C. have been infected with herpesvirus and who have antibodies against the virus
    D. are hypersensitive to herpesvirus
    E. have little resistance

23. Cellular swelling is one of the MOST common changes observed in tissues obtained at   23.
autopsy. Its occurrence

    A. proves only that the circulation was deficient
    B. is useful only in identifying certain infections
    C. usually indicates the action of specific etiologic agents
    D. assists in evaluating the nutritional status of the organ involved
    E. is of little practical diagnostic importance

24. IgG antibodies have a half-life of *approximately*   24.

    A. 20 minutes   B. 1 hour
    C. 1 day   D. 1 week
    E. 1 month

25. The MOST reliable finding in the serodiagnosis of an acute infectious disease is   25.

    A. high antibody titer
    B. rising antibody titer
    C. falling antibody titer
    D. positive complement-fixation test
    E. positive tuberculin-type skin test

KEY (CORRECT ANSWERS)

1.	C		11.	D
2.	B		12.	B
3.	B		13.	B
4.	A		14.	E
5.	E		15.	A
6.	B		16.	D
7.	A		17.	A
8.	C		18.	E
9.	D		19.	C
10.	A		20.	D

21.	D
22.	C
23.	E
24.	E
25.	B

———

TEST 2

DIRECTIONS: Each question or incomplete statement is followed by several suggested answers or completions. Select the one that BEST answers the question or completes the Statement. *PRINT THE LETTER OF THE CORRECT ANSWER IN THE SPACE AT THE RIGHT.*

1.   The end-product of glucose metabolism by streptococcus mutans is   1.

   A.   lactate
   B.   pyruvate
   C.   citric acid
   D.   a combination of carbon dioxide and water
   E.   none of the above

2.   Myocardial infarction results in   2.

   A.   coagulation necrosis   B.   liquefaction necrosis
   C.   amyloid degeneration   D.   Zenker's degeneration
   E.   mucinous degeneration

3.   The cellular infiltrate in a fully-developed delayed hypersensitivity reaction consists   3.
     mainly of

   A.   mast cells and erythrocytes
   B.   macrophages and lymphocytes
   C.   macrophages and polymorphonuclear leukocytes
   D.   plasma cells and polymorphonuclear leukocytes
   E.   none of the above

4.   Active passage of leukocytes through capillary walls is accomplished by means of   4.

   A.   desmosome lysis
   B.   endothelial pores
   C.   pinocytotic vesicles
   D.   loosened interendothelial junctions
   E.   none of the above

5.   The chemotactic accumulation at the site of immune complex deposition is a result of   5.

   A.   steroids   B.   histamine
   C.   complement   D.   antihistamines
   E.   analgesics

6.   The *primary* value of soap lies in its   6.

   A.   sporocidal action
   B.   bactericidal action
   C.   bacteriostatic action
   D.   removal of microbes from skin surfaces
   E.   detergent properties

7. The epithelial change MOST predictive of cancer is   7.____

    A. acanthosis   B. dysplasia
    C. metaplasia   D. parakeratosis
    E. hyperkeratosis

8. The MOST reliable postmortem indicator of left ventricular cardiac failure is   8.____

    A. ascites
    B. venous congestion
    C. enlargement of the spleen
    D. peripheral edema of the ankles
    E. chronic passive congestion of the lungs

9. Histoplasmosis is a highly infectious mycotic disease that is characterized microscopi-   9.____
cally by

    A. intranuclear inclusion bodies
    B. flask-shaped ulcers of the ileum
    C. intracytoplasmic microorganisms in the R-E system
    D. focal abscesses of the liver and the intestinal tract
    E. none of the above

10. "Late" proteins synthesized in viral replication include   10.____

    A. DNA polymerases
    B. virus structural proteins
    C. proteins that inhibit host cell protein synthesis
    D. proteins that cause cessation of host cell RNA synthesis
    E. none of the above

11. A thymectomized animal or a person with an inborn deficiency of thymus *usually* has   11.____

    A. no lymph nodes
    B. no phagocytic cells
    C. a selective deficiency of IgE
    D. total absence of circulating antibodies
    E. decreased or absent delayed-type hypersensitivity

12. In transduction, DNA is transferred from donor cell to recipient cell by   12.____

    A. a plasmid   B. an episome
    C. a bacteriophage   D. purified nucleic acid
    E. none of the above

13. The MOST common cause of hepatomegaly without other distinctive signs and symp-   13.____
toms is

    A. ascites   B. hematoma
    C. hepatitis   D. neoplasia
    E. fatty change

14. Arguments against indiscriminate use of antibiotics as chemotherapeutic agents include   14._
     I.   toxic effects of the antibiotics
     II.   allergic reactions induced in patients
     III.   development of drug resistance by an infectious agent
     IV.   secondary effects experienced due to creation of an imbalance in the normal body flora
     V.   alteration of the immune response
The CORRECT answer is:

A. I, II, III   B. I, II, IV, V
C. II, IV, V   D. III, IV, V
E. I, II, III, IV, V

15. Irreversible pathologic changes include   15._
     I.   fatty degeneration
     II.   hydropic degeneration
     III.   autolysis
     IV.   coagulative necrosis
The CORRECT answer is:

A. I, III   B. I, III, IV
C. II, III   D. II, IV
E. III, IV

16. Seeding or transplantation metastasis would be *likely* in carcinomas of the   16._
     I.   tongue
     II.   stomach
     III.   ovary
     IV.   skin
     V.   large bowel
The CORRECT answer is:

A. I, II, III   B. I, IV, V
C. II, III, IV   D. II, III, V
E. II, IV, V

17. Which of the following therapeutic agents are classed as broad-spectrum antibiotics?   17._
     I.   Tetracycline
     II.   Chloromycetin
     III.   Dihydrostreptomycin
     IV.   Penicillin
     V.   Isoniazid
The CORRECT answer is:

A. I, II   B. I, II, IV, V
C. I, III, V   D. I, V
E. II, III, IV

18. Oversecretion of which of the following hormones causes phosphate diuresis and results   18._
in elevated serum calcium?

A. Thyroxin   B. Cortisone
C. Pituitrin   D. Parathormone
E. Guanine

19. Of the following bone diseases, which is of endocrine etiology?   19.____

    A.   Myeloma
    B.   Acromegaly
    C.   Osteopetrosis
    D.   Paget's disease
    E.   Monostotic fibrous dysplasia

20. A Ghon focus (tubercle) is a   20.____

    A.   primary lung lesion in the periphery
    B.   lesion occurring only in the bronchi
    C.   fibrous lesion in 50 percent of the bronchi
    D.   secondary lung lesion in over 90 percent of adults
    E.   none of the above

21. Which of the following antibiotics is effective in treating candidiasis?   21.____

    A.   Nystatin   B.   Bacitracin
    C.   Penicillin   D.   Tetracycline
    E.   Griseofulvin

22. The presence of which of the following factors in viruses makes protective vaccines a   22.____
possibility?

    A.   Lipids   B.   Enzymes
    C.   Protein coat   D.   Polysaccharide
    E.   Methylcytosine

23. Which of the following statements is CORRECT regarding a patient recovered from hep-   23.____
atitis type B infection?

    A.   The virus will be excreted in the feces.
    B.   The patient is a good candidate for blood donation.
    C.   The patient will have protective immunity to all viral hepatitides.
    D.   Detection of hepatitis B antigen in serum is indicative of the carrier state.
    E.   None of the above

24. Infectious mononucleosis is caused by the _____ virus.   24.____

    A.   verruca   B.   rubella
    C.   rubeola   D.   Epstein-Barr
    E.   varicella-zoster

25. Which of the following viruses is suspect in cervical cancer?   25.____

    A.   HVH-1   B.   HVH-2
    C.   EBV   D.   C-type particles
    E.   ADP

KEY (CORRECT ANSWERS)

1.	A		11.	E
2.	A		12.	C
3.	B		13.	E
4.	B		14.	E
5.	C		15.	E
6.	D		16.	D
7.	B		17.	A
8.	E		18.	D
9.	C		19.	B
10.	B		20.	A

21.	A
22.	C
23.	D
24.	D
25.	B

———

EXAMINATION SECTION

TEST 1

DIRECTIONS: Each question or incomplete statement is followed by
several suggested answers or completions. Select the
one that BEST answers the question or completes the
statement. *PRINT THE LETTER OF THE CORRECT ANSWER IN
THE SPACE AT THE RIGHT*.

1. An increase in the size of an organ caused by an increase   1.___
    in the number of cells describes
        A. atrophy   B. metaplasia
        C. hypertrophy   D. hyperplasia
        E. regeneration

2. The chemical constituents of bacteria and viruses that are   2.___
    MOST sensitive to ultraviolet irradiation are
        A. lipids   B. proteins
        C. carbohydrates   D. nucleic acids
        E. inorganic salts

3. In leukemia, prolongation of bleeding time is caused by   3.___
        A. anemia
        B. neutropenia
        C. thrombocytopenia
        D. the presence of leukemic cells in circulating blood
        E. erythroblastosis

4. Increase in the size of the heart in an athlete is an   4.___
    example of
        A. anaplasia   B. metaplasia
        C. hyperplasia   D. hypertrophy
        E. none of the above

5. Denaturation of protein and dissolution of lipid are   5.___
    antiseptic properties associated with
        A. soaps   B. alcohols
        C. cresols   D. glutaraldehydes
        E. mercuric chloride

6. An antibacterial substance found in saliva, tears and egg   6.___
    white is
        A. albumin   B. isozyme
        C. amylase   D. lysozyme
        E. betalysin

7. Squamous cell carcinoma *usually* metastasizes by way of   7.___
        A. the venous system   B. the arterial system
        C. the lymphatic system   D. aspiration into the lung
        E. none of the above

8. The appearance of HB$_s$ antigen in the plasma is associated with   8.___
   A. Q fever   B. influenza
   C. German measles   D. serum hepatitis
   E. lupus erythematosus

9. The fluid that leaks out of vessels in noninflammatory conditions, such as cardiac failure, is   9.___
   A. exudate   B. effluvium
   C. ecchymosis   D. metachysis
   E. transudate

10. A benign neoplasm of the myometrium of the uterus is a   10.___
   A. myeloma   B. fibroma
   C. leiomyoma   D. myoblastoma
   E. rhabdomyoma

11. The spores of bacillus anthracis are destroyed by   11.___
   A. refrigerating (-7° C. for 48 hours)
   B. autoclaving (121° C. for 20 minutes)
   C. pasteurizing (61.7^O C. for 30 minutes)
   D. immersing in boiling water (100° C. for 10 minutes)
   E. placing in a hot air oven (121° C. for 20 minutes)

12. Anoxia MOST seriously affects the brain and the   12.___
   A. lung   B. heart
   C. liver   D. spleen
   E. kidney

13. Deposition of calcium in dying or dead tissue is described as   13.___
   A. calcium soap formation   B. embolic calcification
   C. metastatic calcification   D. dystrophic calcification
   E. none of the above

14. Viruses may cause disease by   14.___
   A. lysing many cells of the host
   B. transforming cells to malignant cells
   C. making vital target cells nonfunctional
   D. disrupting the normal defense mechanisms of the host
   E. all of the above

15. Epithelial pearls and intercellular bridges observed in an infiltrating malignancy are diagnostic of   15.___
   A. adenocarcinoma
   B. anaplastic carcinoma
   C. squamous cell carcinoma
   D. undifferentiated carcinoma
   E. transitional cell carcinoma

16. The MOST common organism producing subacute bacterial endocarditis is   16.___
   A. staphylococcus
   B. alpha-hemolytic streptococcus
   C. beta-hemolytic streptococcus
   D. gamma-hemolytic streptococcus
   E. gonococcus

17. Metachromatic granules are characteristically observed   17.___
    in properly stained smears of
    A. salmonella typhi
    B. escherichia coli
    C. brucella melitensis
    D. bordetella pertussis
    E. corynebacterium diphtheriae

18. Resistance of staphylococcus aureus to penicillin is   18.___
    caused by
    A. pleomorphism
    B. an enzyme that attacks penicillin
    C. production of a penicillin analogue
    D. a lack of mycolic acid in the cell wall
    E. the presence of a tough lipopolysaccharide capsule

19. Transformation is BEST described as   19.___
    A. DNA coding for RNA synthesis
    B. RNA coding for protein synthesis
    C. acquisition of an inheritable trait by bacteria
       mediated by DNA
    D. acquisition of an inheritable trait by bacteria
       mediated by RNA
    E. ATP transference

20. Elevation of serum acid phosphatase levels is likely to   20.___
    be seen in patients with carcinoma of the
    A. colon   B. breast
    C. cervix   D. uterus
    E. prostate gland

21. The MOST common cause of esophageal varices is   21.___
    A. thrombosis   B. coarctation
    C. cor pulmonale   D. portal hypertension
    E. ageing changes in the vessels

22. The leading cause of cardiac death in the United States is 22.___
    A. mitral stenosis
    B. congenital anomalies
    C. coronary heart disease
    D. myocarditis (all causes)
    E. hypertensive cardiovascular disease

23. An infection following a serious skin burn that is   23.___
    characterized by the production of greenish pus and is
    generally resistant to antibiotic therapy is *probably*
    caused by
    A. proteus vulgaris
    B. streptococcus mitis
    C. streptococcus mutans
    D. staphylococcus aureus
    E. pseudomonas aeruginosa

24. When horse serum is injected intravenously into a rabbit,   24.___
    and again into the skin two or three weeks later, a
    necrotizing reaction occurs at the site of the second
    injection. This is
       A. atopy
       B. anaphylaxis
       C. serum sickness
       D. an Arthus reaction
       E. a Prausnitz-Kustner reaction

25. The *primary* result of bacterial carbohydrate metabolism   25.___
    is production of
       A. heat   B. energy
       C. alcohol   D. acetone
       E. fat

KEY (CORRECT ANSWERS)

1. D		11. B
2. D		12. B
3. C		13. D
4. D		14. E
5. B		15. C
6. D		16. B
7. C		17. E
8. D		18. B
9. E		19. C
10. C		20. E

21. D
22. C
23. E
24. D
25. B

TEST 2

DIRECTIONS: Each question or incomplete statement is followed by several suggested answers or completions. Select the one that BEST answers the question or completes the statement. *PRINT THE LETTER OF THE CORRECT ANSWER IN THE SPACE AT THE RIGHT.*

1. Certain staphylococci, pseudomonas aeruginosa, escherichia   1.___
   coli and streptococci share as a property the fact that they
   A. are gram-positive
   B. fail to ferment glucose
   C. do not grow on nutrient agar
   D. are common in hospital-acquired infections
   E. are anaerobic

2. The class of immunoglobulin responsible for atopic allergy   2.___
   is
   A. IgA   B. IgD   C. IgE   D. IgG   E. IgM

3. Passive congestion occurs when increased amounts of blood   3.___
   in the tissues collect secondary to
   A. hyperplasia   B. hypertension
   C. inflammation   D. arterial dilatation
   E. venous obstruction

4. A 56-year-old diabetic man had atrial fibrillation for   4.___
   two years following a myocardial infarct. He experienced
   right flank pain and hematuria, paralysis of the right
   side of the body and sharply demarcated ischemia in the
   left foot.
   These signs and symptoms were *most likely* due to
   A. septicemia   B. lymphangitis
   C. venous thrombi   D. arterial emboli
   E. venous emboli

5. In skin graft rejection, the MAJOR host response is   5.___
   A. an Arthus reaction
   B. delayed hypersensitivity
   C. a Shwartzman reaction
   D. passive cutaneous anaphylaxis
   E. none of the above

6. Vegetations on the heart valves in acute bacterial endo-   6.___
   carditis *usually* consist of
   A. swellings caused by inflammatory edema
   B. scar tissue containing masses of bacteria
   C. fused platelets, fibrin and masses of bacteria
   D. areas where healing and calcification have occurred
   E. none of the above

7. The etiologic agent of actinomycosis in man is   7.___
   A. exogenous and is found in infected meat
   B. exogenous and requires contact with a vector
   C. exogenous and requires inhalation of spores
   D. endogenous and is found in healthy mouths
   E. endogenous and is carried in the lower gastro-
      intestinal tract

8. Actinomycosis is characterized by a ____ exudate.   8.___
   A. serous   B. purulent
   C. hemorrhagic   D. pseudomembranous
   E. fibrinous, nonpurulent

9. A lysogenic bacterium is one that   9.___
   A. lyses red cells
   B. produces properdin
   C. harbors a temperate bacteriophage
   D. produces lecithinase when incubated anaerobically
   E. produces spheroplasts when incubated anaerobically

10. A complete blood cell count in a patient with severe   10.___
    emphysema is *most likely* to show
    A. anemia   B. leukopenia
    C. polycythemia   D. leukocytosis
    E. macrocythemia

11. The pulmonary neoplasm to which the endocrine effect of   11.___
    hyperparathyroidism is attributed is
    A. adenocarcinoma   B. oat cell carcinoma
    C. pheochromocytoma   D. medullary carcinoma
    E. squamous cell carcinoma

12. Of the following, the MOST common site of a basal cell   12.___
    carcinoma is the
    A. tongue   B. gingiva
    C. lower lip   D. upper face
    E. oral mucosa

13. Immune serums showing high agglutination titers often fail   13.___
    to agglutinate homologous bacteria in low dilution. This
    is designated as
    A. the prozone
    B. the opsonic index
    C. an Arthus reaction
    D. agglutination adsorption
    E. the Bordet-Gengou phenomenon

14. As opposed to lobar pneumonia, bronchopneumonia is   14.___
    characterized grossly and microscopically by
    A. inflammation of a bronchus
    B. organization of alveolar exudate
    C. a patchy, inflammatory distribution
    D. a diffuse, inflammatory distribution
    E. pleural inflammation

15. The MOST common malignancy found in bones of the human skeleton is   15.___
    A. osteosarcoma   B. chondrosarcoma
    C. multiple myeloma   D. giant cell tumor
    E. metastatic carcinoma

16. The MOST common cause of acute purulent meningitis between ages 3 months and 2 years is   16.___
    A. myxovirus   B. hemophilus influenzae
    C. mycoplasma pneumoniae   D. streptococcus pneumoniae
    E. smallpox

17. The two genera MOST frequently associated with bacterial cystitis are   17.___
    A. salmonella and shigella
    B. brucella and hemophilus
    C. pseudomonas and escherichia
    D. escherichia and proteus
    E. proteus and pseudomonas

18. The active mechanism *directly* responsible for damage to blood vessels in an immune complex disorder is the   18.___
    A. activation of the complement system
    B. formation of small, soluble, immune complexes
    C. formation of large, insoluble, immune complexes
    D. phagocytosis of immune complexes by the RE system
    E. release of histamine from mast cells causing a vasomotor response

19. Vitamin K is necessary for   19.___
    A. ossification of osteoid
    B. formation of fibrinogen (Factor I)
    C. formation of prothrombin (Factor II)
    D. maturation of megakaryocytes to platelets
    E. maturation of collagen from tropocollagen

20. MOST viral antigens of diagnostic importance are   20.___
    A. lipids   B. proteins
    C. nucleic acids   D. polysaccharides
    E. lipopolysaccharides

21. The MOST common cause for megaloblastic anemia is   21.___
    A. gastric bleeding
    B. lack of dietary iron
    C. lack of dietary folic acid
    D. lack of dietary pyridoxine
    E. lack of absorption of vitamin B_{12}

22. Vitamin A functions to   22.___
    A. prevent pellagra
    B. promote absorption of calcium
    C. promote differentiation of epithelial cells
    D. maintain the integrity of connective tissues
    E. maintain skin hue

23. Glutaraldehyde, betapropiolactone, formaldehyde and   23.___
    ethylene oxide share the common characteristic of being
       A. unstable   B. explosive
       C. cidal agents   D. static agents
       E. carcinogens

24. The normal form of bacterial gene transfer that is LEAST   24.___
    susceptible to DNAase and does NOT require cell-to-cell
    contact is
       A. transition   B. conjugation
       C. transduction   D. transformation
       E. incubation

25. Which of the following is NOT characteristic of plasmids?   25.___
       A. Confer conjugal fertility
       B. Carry genetic information
       C. Exist as circular RNA molecules
       D. Exist as extrachromosomal elements in bacteria
       E. None of the above

KEY (CORRECT ANSWERS)

1. D		11. B	
2. C		12. D	
3. E		13. A	
4. D		14. C	
5. B		15. E	
6. C		16. B	
7. D		17. D	
8. B		18. D	
9. C		19. C	
10. C		20. B	

21. C
22. C
23. C
24. C
25. C

MICROBIOLOGY / PATHOLOGY

EXAMINATION SECTION
TEST 1

DIRECTIONS: Each question or incomplete statement is followed by several suggested answers or completions. Select the one that *BEST* answers the question or completes the statement. *PRINT THE LETTER OF THE CORRECT ANSWER IN THE SPACE AT THE RIGHT.*

1.   True bacteria multiply by   1.____

    A.   budding   B.   sexual fusion
    C.   binary fission   D.   fragmentation of mycelia
    E.   formation of sexual spores

2.   Primary infection with coccidioidomycosis generally affects the   2.____

    A.   liver   B.   spleen   C.   brain
    D.   lungs   E.   lymph nodes

3.   The antiviral action of interferon is due to   3.____

    A.   interference with replication of virus
    B.   interference with adsorption of virus to cells
    C.   production of antibody against theinvading virus
    D.   prevention of viral penetration
    E.   destruction of antibody against the invading virus

4.   The *MOST* conspicuous clinical sign of right-sided heart failure is   4.____

    A.   hypertension   B.   mitral stenosis
    C.   pulmonary edema   D.   systemic venous congestion
    E.   brown induration of the lung

5.   The capacity to grow in either filamentous or yeast form is termed   5.____

    A.   dimorphism   B.   eumorphism
    C.   parthenogenesis   D.   hermaphroditism
    E.   allomorphism

6.   In antibody synthesis, the *predominant* cell-type is the   6.____

    A.   mast cell   B.   giant cell
    C.   lymphocyte   D.   macrophage
    E.   plasma cell

7.   With respect to its histologic appearance, biologic behavior, and pre-invasive states, oral   7.____
    cancer *MOST* closely resembles the *most common* form of

    A.   carcinoma of the colon   B.   carcinoma of the lung
    C.   Hodgkin's disease   D.   cervical cancer
    E.   breast cancer

8. Hypothyroidism in children results in   8._

    A. myxedema   B. gigantism   C. cretinism
    D. acromegaly   E. diabetes insipidus

9. A transudate differs from an exudate in that the transudate has   9._

    A. a cloudy appearance
    B. a higher specific gravity
    C. a lower protein concentration
    D. numerous erythrocytes
    E. a characteristic cellular component

10. In hematology, a "shift to the left" infers an increase in circulating   10._

    A. monocytes   B. erythrocytes
    C. thromboeytes   D. immature neutrophils
    E. segmented neutrophils

11. Interstitial pulmonary inflammation is *MOST* characteristic of   11._

    A. lobar pneumonia   B. viral pneumonia
    C. bronchial asthma   D. bronchopneumonia
    E. streptococcal pneumonia

12. Granulation tissue usually contains all of the following   12._
    EXCEPT

    A. lymphocytes   B. fibroblasts   C. giant cells
    D. macrophages   E. capillary buds

13. Osteoporosis may be associated with each of the following EXCEPT   13._

    A. prolonged corticosteroid administration
    B. prolonged immobilization
    C. chronic malnutrition
    D. hypervitaminosis D
    E. advanced ag

14. Jaundice is usually a result of each of the following   14_
    EXCEPT

    A. gallstones   B. hemolytic anemia
    C. infectious hepatitis   D. vitamin K deficiency
    E. carcinomatous involvement of the common bile duct

15. The form of bacterial gene transfer which is *least* susceptible to DNAase and does *NOT* 15_
    require cell-to-cell contact is

    A. transition   B. conjugation   C. transduction
    D. transformation   E. induction

16. The predominant bacteria found in saliva are   1_

    A. vibrios   B. spirochetes   C. lactobacilli
    D. streptococci   E. fusiform bacilli

17. The mechanism of fibrin formation in damaged tissue is initiated by the   17._____

    A. release of thromboplastin from damaged cells
    B. release of calcium from damaged cells
    C. formation of thrombin from the interaction of prothrombin and fibrinogen
    D. interaction of thrombin and calcium
    E. release of lymphocytes from undamaged cells

18. A neoplasm composed of either blood vessels or lymph vessels is designated as   18._____

    A. angioma   B. hematoma   C. papilloma
    D. blue nevus   E. lymphosarcoma

19. An endocrine disease characterized by increased susceptibility to infection, increased   19._____
    fatigability, recessive inheritance, and polyuria is

    A. acromegaly   B. Graves' disease
    C. diabetes mellitus   D. Cushing's disease
    E. Hashimoto's disease

20. Rickettsial diseases can be diagnosed in the laboratory using certain strains of *Proteus*   20._____
    vulgaris because the rickettsia and these bacteria

    A. are morphologically similar
    B. have certain antigens in common
    C. produce similar pathogenic changes
    D. have similar physiologic characteristics
    E. are morphologically different

21. When a thrombotic embolus originates in a femoral vein, it usually becomes arrested in   21._____
    the

    A. right heart   B. renal circulation
    C. portal circulation   D. hepatic circulation
    E. pulmonary circulation

22. Which of the following malignancies has the *BEST* prognosis?   22._____

    A. Osteosarcoma   B. Multiple myeloma
    C. Basal cell carcinoma   D. Carcinoma of the breast
    E. Carcinoma of the esophagus

23. Which of the following neoplasms is *PRIMARY* in the adrenal medulla?   23._____

    A. Pheoehromocytoma   B. Arrhenoblastema
    C. Eosinophilic adenoma   D. Hürthle cell tumor
    E. None of the above

24. In *which* of the following bacterial infections is there a lysogenic virus that may be   24._____
    responsible for toxin production?

    A. Syphilis   B. Gonorrhea   C. Diphtheria
    D. Candidiasis   E. None of the above

25. Which of the following is formed in large quantities during the degradation of glucose by   25.__
    homofermentative *Streptococcus mutans?*

  A. Marinitol   B. Lactic acid
  C. Acetic acid   D. Butyric acid
  E. Propionic acid

KEY (CORRECT ANSWERS)

1.	C		11.	B
2.	D		12.	C
3.	A		13.	D
4.	D		14.	D
5.	A		15.	C
6.	E		16.	D
7.	D		17.	A
8.	C		18.	A
9.	C		19.	C
10.	D		20.	B

21. E
22. C
23. A
24. C
25. B

TEST 2

DIRECTIONS: Each question or incomplete statement is followed by several suggested answers or completions. Select the one that *BEST* answers the question or completes the statement. *PRINT THE LETTER OF THE CORRECT ANSWER IN THE SPACE AT THE RIGHT.*

1. Bacterial spores are a problem in sterilizing instruments and equipment because   1.____

    A. they are resistant to antibiotics
    B. they are easy to kill, but are usually protected by organic matter
    C. they are resistant to physical and chemical agents
    D. most pathogenic bacteria are spore-formers
    E. few pathogenic bacteria are spore-formers

2. Koplik's spots on the buccal mucosa are pathognomonic for   2.____

    A. rubella   B. rubeola   C. roseola
    D. varicella   E. Coxsackie virus A

3. Splenic infarcts *MOST* commonly result from emboli from the   3.____

    A. lungs   B. deep leg veins
    C. left side of the heart   D. right side of the heart
    E. left side of the brain

4. A 59-year-old male who demonstrates urinary retention or difficulty in voiding his bladder   4.____
   most likely has

    A. carcinoma of the prostate
    B. malignant neoplasm of the ureter
    C. benign prostatic hyperplasia (hypertrophy)
    D. bladder metastasis of bronchogenic carcinoma
    E. carcinoma of the colon

5. The change of a more specialized cell-type to a less specialized cell-type is   5.____

    A. dysplasia   B. neoplasia   C. metaplasia
    D. hyperplasia   E. hypoplasia

6. Osteoporosis, metastatic calcification, renal stones, giant cell granulomas, and increased   6.____
   serum calcium levels are manifestations of

    A. hypothyroidism   B. hyperthyroidism
    C. hyperadrenalism   D. hypoparathyroidism
    E. hyperparathyroidism

7. An afebrile adult relates a 4-month history of chronic subcutaneous swelling over the   7.____
   angle of the mandible associated with intermittent, purulent drainage. Clinically, sinus
   tracts and scarring are present.
   In the differential diagnosis, one should consider

    A. tuberculosis   B. herpes zoster
    C. actinomycosis   D. histoplasmosis
    E. tertiary syphilis

8. An oral disease characterized by white patches on the buccal mucous membranes which consist largely of pseudo-mycelium and with minimal erosion of the membranes, is caused by   8.

    A. *Candida albicans*   B. *Treponema pallidum*
    C. *Entamoeba histolytlca*   D. *Sporothrichum schenckii*
    E. *Corynebacterium diphtheriae*

9. The *MOST* predominant organisms found in dental plaque are   9.

    A. diplococci   B. streptococci   C. lactobacilli
    D. staphylococci   E. eorynebacteria

10. Red (hemorrhagic) infarcts are *MOST* frequently found in the   10.

    A. lung   B. brain   C. spleen   D. kidney   E. colon

11. The pathogenesis of jaundice in patients with infectious hepatitis is the result of   11.

    A. massive hemolysis
    B. damage to liver cells
    C. massive fibrosis of liver
    D. obstruction of biliary tree
    E. portal hypertension

12. The etiologic agent of rubella is   12

    A. group B streptococcus   B. Coxsackie virus
    C. adenovirus   D. myxovirus
    E. poxvirus

13. The chemical constituents of bacteria and viruses which are *MOST* sensitive to ultraviolet irradiation are   13

    A. lipids   B. proteins   C. carbohydrates
    D. nucleic acids   E. inorganic salts

14. Chronic passive congestion of the lungs is *MOST* often secondary to   1.

    A. malnutrition
    B. massive hemorrhage
    C. cor pulmonale
    D. atherosclerotic heart disease
    E. obesity

15. A benign glandular neoplasm is termed   1.

    A. cyst   B. nevus   C. adenoma   D. papilloma   E. ozena

16. The *initial* lesion of syphilis is a   1

    A. bubo   B. gumma   C. chancre
    D. pustule   E. mucous patch

17. Prolonged anti-bacterial antibiotic therapy may predispose to infectious disease caused   17.____
by the indigenous oral microorganism,

    A. *Fusobacterium fusiforme*   B. *Streptococcus mitis*
    C. *Treponema microdentium*   D. *Actinomyces israelii*
    E. *Candida albicans*

18. Generally, the antibiotic of choice for prophylactic therapy covering dental procedures in   18.____
the patient with a heart valve abnormality is

    A. penicillin   B. lincomycin   C. tetracycline
    D. streptomycin   E. erythromycin

19. Enzymes responsible for suppuration are derived *CHIEFLY* from   19.____

    A. serum   B. tissue   C. neutrophils
    D. lymphocytes   E. plasma cells

20. Ethylene oxide is an agent that   20.____

    A. reversibly inhibits growth   B. is antiseptic
    C. disinfects   D. sterilizes
    E. cleanses

21. Which genus is *most likely* involved in bacillary dysentery?   21.____

    A. *Vibrio*   B. *Proteus*   C. *Shigella*
    D. *Entamoeba*   E. *Salmonella*

22. Which of the following is a form of histiocytosis X?   22.____

    A. Porphyria   B. Acromegaly
    C. Niemann-Pick disease   D. Osteitis fibrosa cystica
    E. Hand-Schuller-Christian disease

23. The requirement for an insect vector in the transmission of human disease is a common   23.____
characteristic of all the infectious agents included in the genus,

    A. *Bedsonia*   B. *Brucella*   C. *Treponema*
    D. *Mycoplasma*   E. *Rickettsia*

24. Which of the following statements is (are) *CORRECT?*   24.____
    I. A decayed tooth is properly termed a carious tooth.
    II. Dental caries or dental decay is a specific disease which brings about the
        dissolution and disintegration of the hard structures of the tooth-enamel,
        cementum, and dentin.
    III. Dental caries is the most widespread disease affecting the human race.
    IV. The incidence of the disease is greatest during childhood and young adult-
        hood.
    V. It attacks deciduous teeth the same as it attacks permanent teeth.
The *CORRECT* answer is:

    A. I *only*   B. I, II   C. I, II, III
    D. I, II, III, IV   E. I, II, III, IV, V

25. Regardless of the method used, sterilization is affected by a number of factors. These   25._
    are or may be among the following factors listed.
    Which are the correct factors?

      I.   Cleanliness of material surface being processed
     II.   Type of organism to be destroyed
    III.   Time the item is exposed to a disinfectant or sterilant
    IV.   Steam pressure and temperature (autoclave) used
     V.   A clear understanding and observation of the procedure by the user
    VI.   Extent of intelligent, painstaking efforts
   VII.   Strictness of professional discipline

The *CORRECT* answer is:

A.   I, II, III, IV   B.   II, IV, V, VI, VII
C.   I, II, IV, VI, VII   D.   II, III, IV, V, VI
E.   I, II, III, IV, V, VI, VII

KEY (CORRECT ANSWERS)

1.	C	11.	B
2.	B	12.	D
3.	C	13.	D
4.	C	14.	D
5.	C	15.	C
6.	E	16.	C
7.	C	17.	E
8.	A	18.	A
9.	B	19.	C
10.	A	20.	D

21.	C
22.	E
23.	E
24.	E
25.	E

BASIC FUNDAMENTALS OF
ANATOMY AND PHYSIOLOGY

CONTENTS

		Page
SECTION I.	Basic Concepts	1
SECTION II.	Anatomical and Medical Terminology	5
SECTION III.	The Skeletal System	9
SECTION IV.	The Skeletal Muscular System	19
SECTION V.	The Skin	23
SECTION VI.	The Circulatory System	25
SECTION VII.	The Respiratory System	35
SECTION VIII.	The Digestive System	37
SECTION IV.	The Urinary System	42
SECTION X.	The Nervous System	44
SECTION XI.	The Endocrine System	54
SECTION XII.	The Reproductive System	56

BASIC FUNDAMENTALS OF

ANATOMY AND PHYSIOLOGY

Section I. BASIC CONCEPTS

1. General

The science of anatomy is the study of the structure of the body, its organs, and the relation of its parts. There are many subdivisions or branches of this science. Physiology is the study of the functions and activities of the parts of the body. This science also has many subdivisions. In this chapter both anatomy and physiology will be presented in the discussion of the structure and function of the various systems of the human body, all of which are closely interrelated and interdependent.

2. Cells

The cell is the basic functioning unit in the composition of the human body, as well as in all other living organisms. The human body is composed of billions of cells which vary in shape and size. Cells are microscopic in size, however, the largest being only about 1/1000 of an inch. Because of this, a special unit of measurement, the micron, is used to determine cell dimensions. (One micron equals 1/1000 millimeter or about 1/25,000 of an inch.) A group of the same type of cells is called a tissue and performs a particular function. The human body is composed of many groups of cells performing a variety of functions.

a. Cells reproduce to replace wornout cells, to build new tissues, and to bring about the growth of the body as a whole. Cells reproduce themselves or increase by dividing, maturing, and dividing again. This process is known as growth by division. It results in a mass of apparently identical cells; however, as cell division continues, differences begin to appear in various groups of cells as they develop the characteristics necessary for them to perform their roles in the development and functions of the body. This development of special characteristics is called *cell differentiation*.

b. Cells are composed of a substance called protoplasm. A typical animal cell (fig. 2–1) is made up of a cell membrane and two main parts—the *nucleus* and the *cytoplasm*, which are types of protoplasm. The *nucleus* controls all activities of the cell, including growth and reproduction. *Cytoplasm* is the matter surrounding the nucleus and is responsible for most of the work done by the cell. The cell membrane incloses the protoplasm and permits the passage of fluid into and out of the cell. This permeable cell membrane is an important structural feature of the cell. It is through the cell membrane that all materials essential to metabolism are received and all products of metabolism are disposed of. The bloodstream and tissue fluid which constantly circulate around the cell transports the materials to and from cells.

(1) *Metabolism* is the ability to carry on all the chemical activities required for cell function. It includes using food and oxygen, producing and eliminating wastes, and manufacturing new materials for growth, repair, and use by other cells.

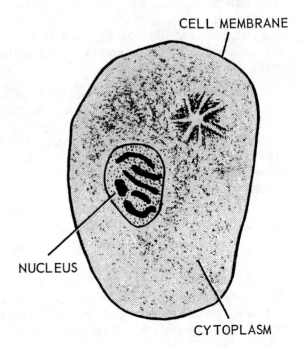

Figure 2–1. Simple cell.

(2) *Tissue fluid* is the body fluid that lies outside blood vessels and outside cells and is therefore also called *extravascular* (outside blood vessels) or *extracellular* (outside cells) fluid. Living body cells contain large amounts of water and must be bathed continuously in a watery solution in order to survive and carry on their functions. The colorless and slightly salty tissue fluid is derived from the circulating blood.

3. Tissues

A tissue is a part of the body made up of similarly specialized cells which work together to perform particular body functions. There are four main types of tissues, each of which has a particular function (fig. 2–2).

a. Epithelial. Epithelial tissue forms the outer layer of skin for the protection of the body. It is also a lining tissue. As *mucous membrane,* it lines the nasal cavity, mouth, larynx, pharynx, trachea, stomach, and intestines. As *serous membrane,* it lines the abdominal, chest, and heart cavities and covers the organs that lie in these cavities. As *endothelium,* it lines the heart and blood vessels. It lines respiratory and digestive organs for the functions of protection and absorption. It helps form organs concerned with the excretion of body wastes, certain glands for the purpose of secretion, and certain sensory organs for the reception of stimuli. Based on the shape of the cells, there are 3 types of epithelial tissue (fig. 2–2Ⓐ). As illustrated, squamous (flat) epithelial cells in a single layer compose such structures as the microscopic air sacs of the lungs; in other places as in the skin, squamous epithelium is in several layers or stratified (not illustrated). Columnar epithelium cells are more important in the formation of ducts.

b. Connective. Connective tissue is distributed throughout the body to form the supporting framework of the body and to bind together and support other tissues. It binds organs to other organs, muscles to bones, and bones to other bones. There are five principal types of connective tissue—

(1) Areolar tissue is a fibrous connective tissue which forms the subcutaneous layer of tissue. It fills many of the small spaces on the body, and it helps to hold organs in place.

(2) Adipose tissue (fig. 2–2Ⓑ) is a fatty connective tissue which is found under the skin and in many other regions of the body. It serves as a padding around and between organs. It insu-

lates the body, reducing heat loss, and it serves as a food reserve in emergencies.

(3) Reticular tissue is a fibrous connective tissue which forms the supporting framework of lymph glands, liver, spleen, bone marrow, and lungs.

(4) Elastic tissue is a fibrous connective tissue composed of elastic fibers and is found in the walls of blood vessels, in the lungs, and in certain ligaments.

(5) Cartilage (fig. 2–2Ⓑ) is a tough, resilient connective tissue found at the ends of the bones, between bones, and in the nose, throat, and ears.

c. Muscular. Muscular tissue is composed of long, slender cells held together by connective tissue. There are three kinds of muscle tissues: striated, smooth, and cardiac (heart muscle). Muscle tissue has the ability to contract (shorten) and, by so doing, to produce movement.

(1) Striated muscle has striations (its fibers are divided by transverse bands) (fig. 2–2Ⓒ) when viewed through a microscope. Because most striated muscle attaches to bones, it is often referred to as skeletal muscle. Skeletal muscle contraction is stimulated by impulses from nerves and, in theory, the nerve impulses can be controlled by voluntary or conscious effort. Skeletal muscle tissue is therefore referred to as striated, voluntary muscle tissue.

(2) Smooth muscle which has no striations when viewed through a microscope (fig. 2–2 Ⓒ), is found in the walls of internal organs (viscera), blood vessels, and internal passages. Contraction of smooth muscle helps propel the contents of internal structures along. Smooth muscle contractions are stimulated by nerve impulses not under conscious control. Smooth muscle is therefore referred to as visceral, nonstriated, involuntary muscle.

(3) Cardiac muscle (fig. 2–2Ⓒ) is found only in the walls of the heart; i.e., myocardium is heart muscle.

d. Nervous. Nervous tissue is composed of cells highly specialized to receive and transmit impulses (messages). These nerve cells, which are called neurons (fig. 2–2Ⓓ), are bound together by a special structure called neuroglia.

4. Organs

An organ is a group of tissues which has combined to perform a specific function. The body is

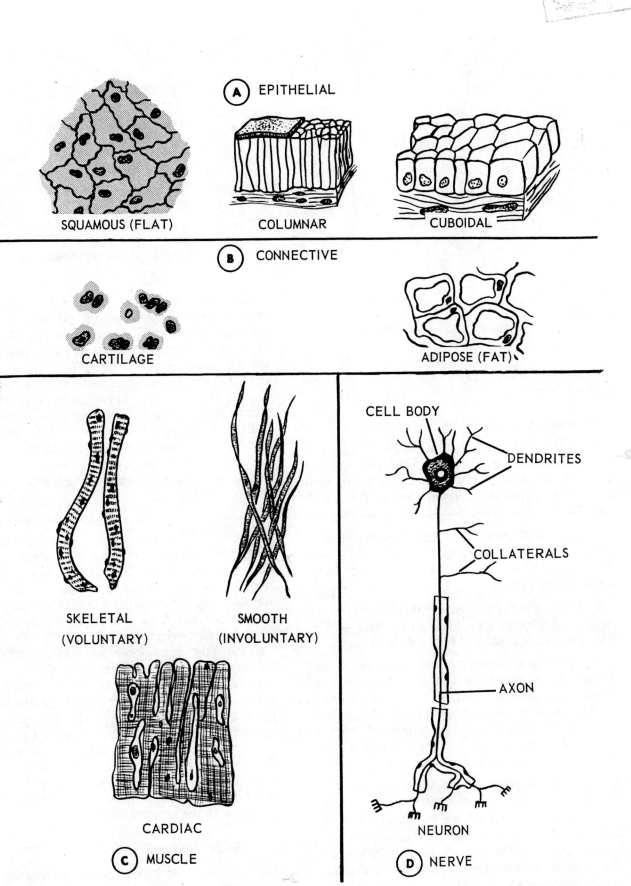

Figure 2-2. Types of tissues.

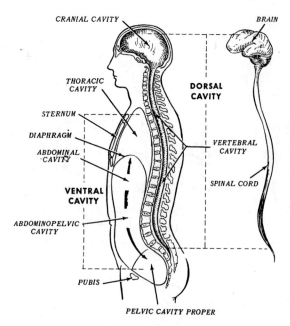

Figure 2-3. Main body cavities.

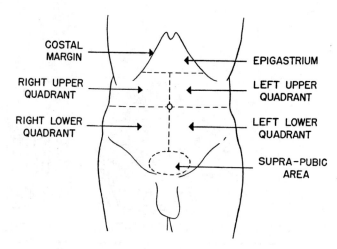

Figure 2-4. Areas of the abdomen.

composed of many organs, each with its own specialized function.

5. Body Cavities

The organs of the body are located in certain cavities, the major ones of which are the dorsal cavity (toward the back part of the body) and the ventral cavity (toward the front part of the body) (fig. 2-3).

  a. Dorsal Cavity. The dorsal cavity has a cranial area, which contains the brain, and a vertebral area, which contains the spinal cord. These areas are continuous.

  b. Ventral Cavity. The ventral cavity has a thoracic cavity and an abdomino pelvic cavity. These areas are separated by the diaphragm.

  (1) In the thoracic cavity are two pleural cavities, each containing a lung. In the space between the pleural cavities is the pericardial cavity, which contains the heart, and the mediastinal region, in which are contained the trachea, esophagus, thymus gland, large blood and lymphatic vessels, lymph nodes, and nerves.

  (2) In the upper part of the abdomino pelvic cavity are the stomach, small intestine, liver, gallbladder, pancreas, spleen, kidneys, adrenal glands, and ureters. The lower part of the cavity (pelvic cavity) contains the urinary bladder, the end of the large intestine (rectum), and parts of the reproductive system.

  c. Anterior Abdominal Surface Area. The large anterior area of the abdomino pelvic cavity is divided into four parts or quadrants (fig. 2-4). Initials that identify quadrants are LUQ (left upper), RUQ (right upper), LLQ (left lower), and RLQ (right lower). These initials are often used to indicate the approximate location of an organ, pain, a wound, or a surgical incision. In addition to identification by quadrants, the upper central abdominal region is referred to as epigastric (over the stomach), and the lower central region as suprapubic (above the pubis). The rib area is called costal.

6. Membranes

Certain membranes are combined layers of tissue that form partitions, linings, envelopes, or capsules. They reinforce and support body organs and cavities. Others are a combination of connective tissues only (*examples:* mucous, pleural, pericardial, and peritoneal membranes). Connective tissue membranes are combinations of connective tissue only (*examples:* meninges, fascia, periosteum, and synovia). Different kinds of membranes are associated with different body systems (*examples:* pleural membranes with the respiratory system; pericardial membranes with the circulatory system; peritoneal membranes with the digestive system; meningeal membranes with the nervous system; fascial membranes with the muscular system; and periosteal and synovial membranes with the skeletal system).

7. Body Systems

The organs of the human body are arranged into major systems, each of which has its specific function to perform and all of which are interdependent. The body systems and their overall functions are—

a. *Skeletal.* This system provides the body framework, supports and protects body organs, and furnishes a place of attachment for muscles.

b. *Muscular.* This system moves and propels the body.

c. *Skin.* The integumentary system, or skin, covers and protects the entire body surface from injury and infection, has functions of sensation (heat, cold, touch, and pain) and assists in regulation of body temperature and excretion of wastes.

d. *Circulatory.* This system transports oxygen and nutrient material in the blood to all parts of the body and carries away the waste products formed by the cells.

e. *Respiratory.* This system takes in air, delivers oxygen from the air to the blood, and removes the waste (carbon dioxide) from the blood.

f. *Digestive.* This system receives, digests, and absorbs food substances and eliminates waste products.

g. *Urinary.* This system filters waste products from blood and excretes waste products in urine.

h. *Nervous.* This system gives the body awareness of its environment, enables it to react to stimuli from the environment, and makes the body work together as a unit.

i. *Endocrine.* This system controls many body activities by the manufacture of hormones which are secreted into the blood.

j. *Reproductive.* This system produces and transports reproductive (sex) cells.

Section II. ANATOMICAL AND MEDICAL TERMINOLOGY

8. Anatomical Terminology

Terms of position, direction, and location that are used in reference to the body and its parts include the following:

a. *Terms of Position.*

(1) Anatomical position—the body standing erect, arms at side, palms of hands facing forward. The anatomical position is the position of reference when terms of direction and location are used.

(2) Supine position—the body lying face up.

(3) Prone position—the body lying face down.

(4) Lateral recumbent—the body lying on the left or right side.

b. *Terms of Direction and Location.*

(1) Superior—toward the head (cranial).

(2) Inferior—toward the feet (caudal).

(3) Anterior—toward the front (ventral—the belly side).

(4) Posterior—toward the back (dorsal—the backbone side).

(5) Medial—toward the midline.

(6) Lateral—to right or left of midline.

(7) Proximal—near point of reference.

(8) Distal—far away from point of reference.

c. *Body Regions.* Terms of location in relation to body regions are shown in figure 2–5 Ⓐ and Ⓑ.

d. *Anatomical Planes.* Imaginary straight line divisions of the body are called planes. Medical illustrations and diagrams that indicate internal body structure relationships are labeled to indicate the plane division as—

(1) Sagittal—a lengthwise division, producing right and left sections.

(2) Transverse—a crosswise division, producing top and bottom sections.

(3) Frontal—a side-to-side division, producing front and back sections.

9. Medical Terminology

To understand most medical words, all that is necessary is to break the words into their parts and to know the meaning of these parts. Many medical words contain a stem or root to which is affixed either a prefix, a suffix, or both. A prefix is a group of letters combined with the beginning of a word to modify its meaning. A suffix is a group of letters added to the end of a word to modify its meaning. *For example,* the word "myocarditis"

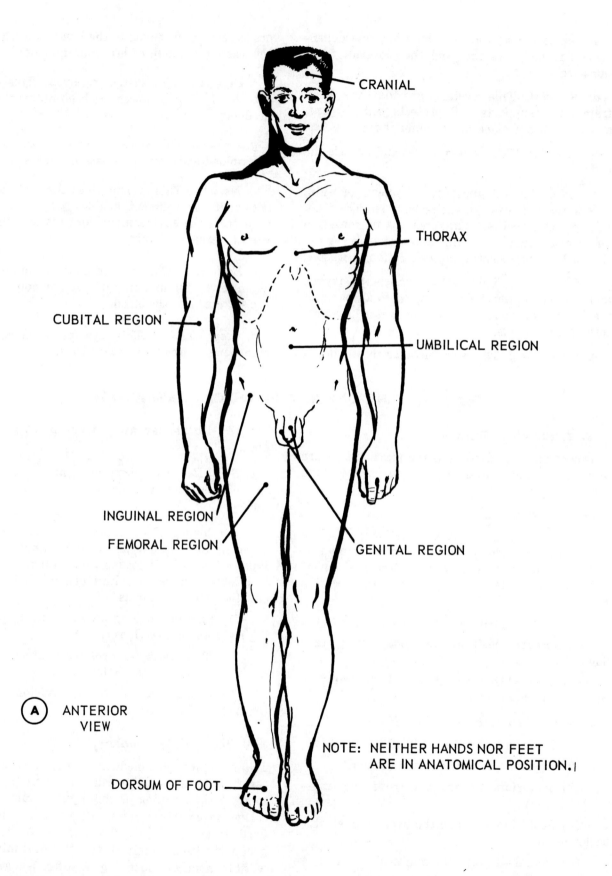

CRANIAL

THORAX

CUBITAL REGION

UMBILICAL REGION

INGUINAL REGION

FEMORAL REGION

GENITAL REGION

(A) ANTERIOR VIEW

NOTE: NEITHER HANDS NOR FEET ARE IN ANATOMICAL POSITION.

DORSUM OF FOOT

Figure 2–5.   Names of body regions.

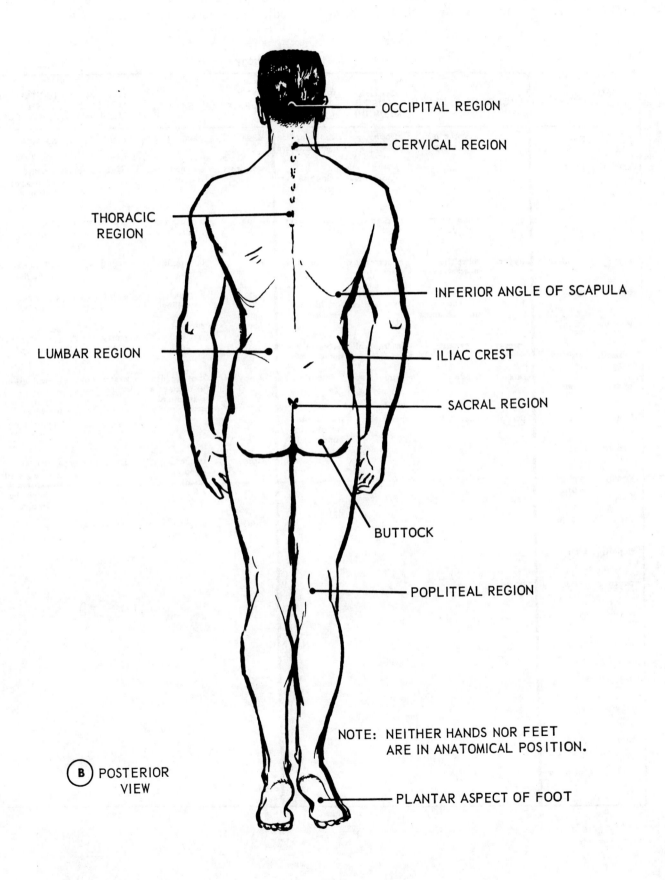

OCCIPITAL REGION

CERVICAL REGION

THORACIC
REGION

INFERIOR ANGLE OF SCAPULA

LUMBAR REGION

ILIAC CREST

SACRAL REGION

BUTTOCK

POPLITEAL REGION

NOTE: NEITHER HANDS NOR FEET
ARE IN ANATOMICAL POSITION.

B POSTERIOR
VIEW

PLANTAR ASPECT OF FOOT

Figure 2-5—Continued.

consists of the prefix "myo," the stem "card," and the suffix "itis." Myo means "muscle." Card means "cardiac" or "heart." Itis means "inflammation." Thus, myocarditis means inflammation of muscles of the heart. Table 2–1 gives combining forms that are commonly used in medical terminology. These must be learned to understand medical references that will occur from now on.

Table 2-1. Medical Terminology

STEM WORDS	MEANING	PREFIX	MEANING	EXAMPLE OF USE IN MEDICINE	DEFINITION OF EXAMPLE	SUFFIX	MEANING	EXAMPLE OF USE IN MEDICINE	DEFINITION OF EXAMPLE
adeno	gland	a-, an-	absence of, deficiency	atrophy	shrinking, wasting away	-algia	pain	otalgia	ear ache
arthro	joint	endo-	inner, inside	endocardial	inside the heart	-ectomy	surgical removal	nephrectomy	surgical removal of a kidney
cardio	heart								
cephalo	head	epi-	upon, on the outside	epidermis	outside layer of skin	-emia	a condition of the blood	septicemia	blood poisoning
cysto	bladder	hyper-	more than normal, over	hypertrophy	enlargement	-itis	inflammation	hepatitis	inflammation of the liver
cyto	cell	hypo-	less than normal, under	hypotension	low blood pressure	-oma	a tumor, a swelling	adenoma	a glandular tissue tumor
dermo	skin					-plasty	surgical repair	thoraco-plasty	surgical repair of the chest wall
entero	intestine	inter-	between	interneural	between nerves				
gastro	stomach	intra-	inside	intraocular	inside the eye	-scopy	looking into or through an instrument	cystoscopy	examination of the urinary bladder through a cystoscope
hemo	blood	peri-	surrounding	periosteum	membrane surrounding bone				
hepato	liver								
myelo	*spinal cord					-stomy	surgical opening creating a hole	gastrostomy	artificial opening into the stomach through the abdomen
myo	muscle					-tomy	surgical incision	arthrotomy	incision into a joint
nephro	kidney								
neuro	nerve								
oculo	eye								
osteo	bone								
oto	ear								
procto	rectum								
thoraco	chest								
	*or bone marrow								

Section III. THE SKELETAL SYSTEM

10. Functions and Divisions
(fig. 2–6 Ⓐ and Ⓑ)

The skeletal system includes the bones and the joints (articulations), where separate bones come together. The skeletal system has several important functions, in addition to providing the bony framework of the body.

a. Skeletal System Function.

(1) To give support and shape the body.
(2) To protect internal organs.
(3) To provide movement when acted upon by muscles.
(4) To manufacture blood cells.
(5) To store mineral salts.

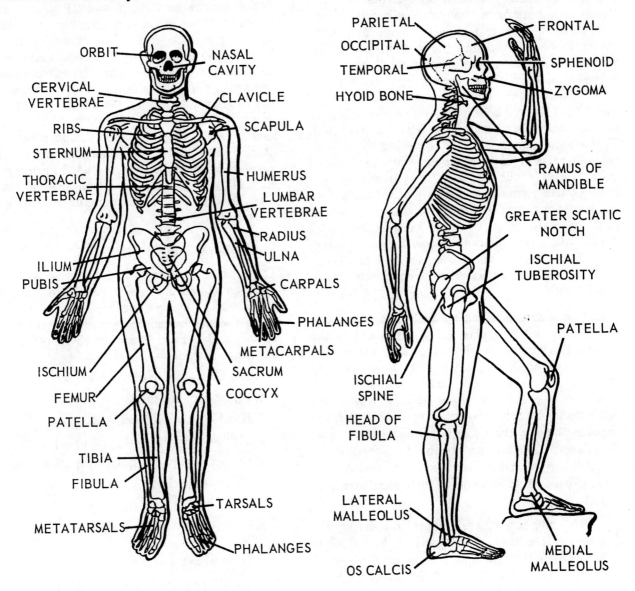

Ⓐ ANTERIOR VIEW

Ⓑ LATERAL VIEW

NOTE: THE ANATOMICAL POSITION IS ILLUSTRATED IN Ⓐ

Figure 2–6. Human skeleton.

b. Divisions of the Skeleton. For study purposes, the 206 bones of the adult are divided into the bones of the axial skeleton (80 bones) and the appendicular skeleton (126 bones). The axial skeleton includes the skull, vertebral column, ribs, and sternum. The appendicular skeleton includes bones of the shoulder girdle, upper limb, the pelvic girdle, and lower limb.

11. Bone Structure and Shape of Bones

a. Bone is living tissue, containing blood vessels and nerves within the hard bone structures. The living cells that form bones are osteocytes. Bone cells have the ability to select calcium and other minerals from blood and tissue fluid and to deposit the calcium in the connective tissue fibers between cells. With increasing age, from childhood to adulthood, bones become harder; in old age, bones become brittle because there are higher proportions of minerals and fewer active cells. Periosteum, the membrane covering bone surfaces, carries blood vessels and nerves to the bone cells. Bone-producing cells in periosteum are active during growth and repair of injuries. Two kinds of bone are formed by the bone cells—compact and cancellous. Compact bone is hard and dense, while cancellous bone has a porous structure. The combination of compact and cancellous bone cells produces maximum strength with minimum weight.

b. Bones are classified by their shape as long, short, flat, and irregular. Long bones are in the extremities and act as levers to produce motion when acted on by muscles. Short bones, strong and compact, are in the wrist and ankle. Flat bones form protective plates and provide broad surfaces for muscle attachments; *for example,* the shoulder blades. Irregular bones have many surfaces and fit into many locations; *for example,* the facial bones, vertebral, and pelvic bones. A long bone is used as an example of bone structure (fig. 2–7).

(1) Long bones have a shaft (the diaphysis) and two extremities (the epiphyses). The shaft is a heavy cylinder of compact bone with a central medullary (marrow) cavity. This cavity contains bone marrow, blood vessels, and nerves. Cancellous bone is located toward the epiphyses and is covered by a protecting layer of compact bone.

(2) Articular cartilage covers the joint surfaces at the ends of a long bone. The cartilage provides a smooth contact surface in joint formation and gives some resilience for shock absorption.

(3) Periosteum, the membrane covering the bone surface, is anchored to the bone by connective tissue fibers. It is essential for bone nourishment and repair. In severe bone injuries, the periosteum may be torn away or damaged, inhibiting repair of the bone.

12. Bone Marrow

Two kinds of marrow, yellow and red, are found in the marrow cavities of bones. Red bone marrow is active blood cell manufacturing material, producing red blood cells and many of the white blood cells. Deposits of red bone marrow in an adult are in cancellous portions of some bones—the skull, ribs, and sternum, for example. Yellow bone marrow is mostly fat and is found in marrow cavities of mature long bones. The examination of red marrow deposits is important for diagnostic tests when the condition of developing blood cells must be determined. For microscopic examination, the doctor obtains a small amount through a special needle puncture, usually in the sternum.

13. Bone Landmarks

The special markings and projections on bones are used as points of reference. Each marking has a function; *for example,* in joint formation, for muscle attachments, or as passageways for blood vessels and nerves. Terms used to refer to bone markings include—

a. Foramen—an opening, a hole.

b. Sinus—an air space.

c. Head—a rounded ball end.

d. Neck—a constricted portion.

e. Condyle—a projection fitting into a joint.

f. Fossa—a socket.

g. Crest—a ridge.

h. Spine—a sharp projection.

14. The Skull

The skull forms the framework of the head. It has 29 bones—8 cranial, 14 facial, 6 ossicles (3 tiny bones in each ear), and 1 hyoid (a single bone between the skull and neck area).

a. Cranial Bones. The cranial bones support and protect the brain. They fuse together after birth in firmly united joints called sutures. The eight

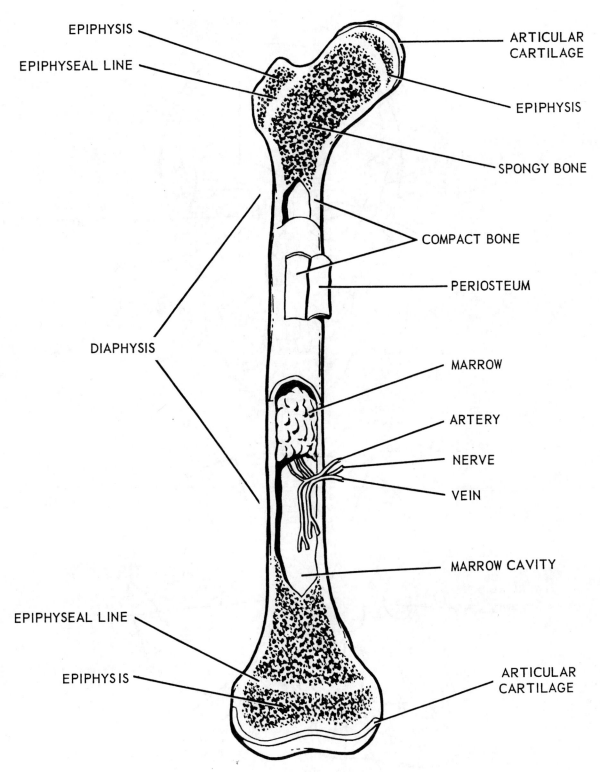

EPIPHYSIS

EPIPHYSEAL LINE

ARTICULAR CARTILAGE

EPIPHYSIS

SPONGY BONE

COMPACT BONE

PERIOSTEUM

DIAPHYSIS

MARROW

ARTERY

NERVE

VEIN

MARROW CAVITY

EPIPHYSEAL LINE

EPIPHYSIS

ARTICULAR CARTILAGE

Figure 2-7.   A long bone (femur).

cranial bones include one frontal, two parietal, one occipital, two temporal, one ethmoid, and one sphenoid (fig. 2–8 Ⓐ). The frontal bone forms the forehead, part of the eye socket, and part of the nose. The parietal bones form the dome of the skull and the upper side walls. The occipital bone forms the back and base of the skull. (The foramen magnum, the large hole in the lower part of the occipital bone, is the passageway for the spinal cord.) The temporal bones form the lower part of each side of the skull and contain the essential organs of hearing and of balance in the middle and

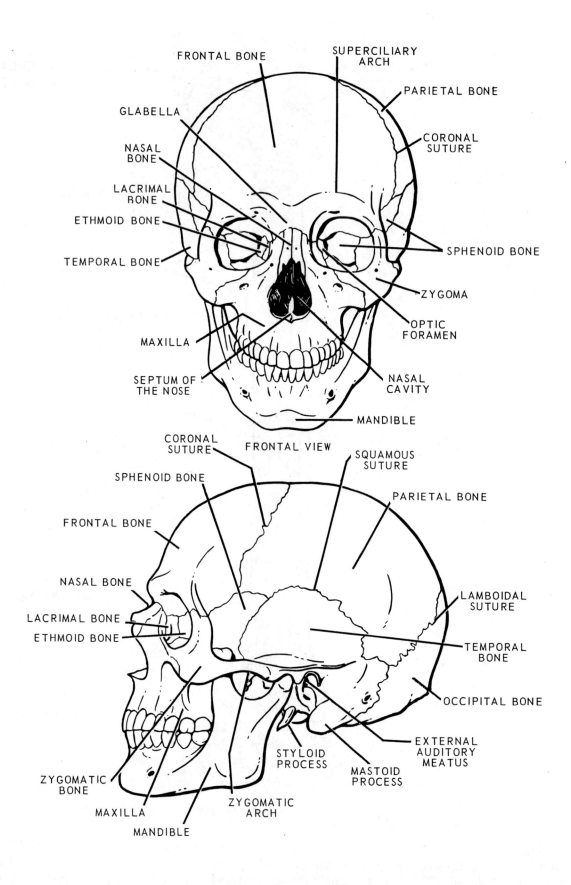

FRONTAL BONE

SUPERCILIARY ARCH

PARIETAL BONE

GLABELLA

CORONAL SUTURE

NASAL BONE

LACRIMAL BONE

ETHMOID BONE

SPHENOID BONE

TEMPORAL BONE

ZYGOMA

OPTIC FORAMEN

MAXILLA

SEPTUM OF THE NOSE

NASAL CAVITY

MANDIBLE

FRONTAL VIEW

CORONAL SUTURE

SPHENOID BONE

SQUAMOUS SUTURE

FRONTAL BONE

PARIETAL BONE

NASAL BONE

LAMBOIDAL SUTURE

LACRIMAL BONE

ETHMOID BONE

TEMPORAL BONE

OCCIPITAL BONE

EXTERNAL AUDITORY MEATUS

ZYGOMATIC BONE

STYLOID PROCESS

MASTOID PROCESS

MAXILLA

ZYGOMATIC ARCH

MANDIBLE

Figure 2–8. The skull.

inner parts of the ear. The ethmoid and sphenoid bones complete the floor of the cranium, the ethmoid toward the front and the sphenoid toward the center. The air spaces in the frontal, ethmoid, and sphenoid bones are sinuses.

b. *Facial Bones.* The 14 facial bones fit together like a very complicated jigsaw puzzle; for example, part of 7 different cranial and facial bones form each eye socket; 2 maxillary bones, the upper jaw; 2 zygomatic, the upper cheeks; and 1 mandible, the lower jaw (fig. 2–8 Ⓑ). The maxillary bones support the upper teeth, and the mandible supports the lower teeth. The joints formed by the mandible and temporal bones permit jaw movement. Nine smaller facial bones complete the nose and roof of the mouth (two nasal, two turbinate, one vomer, two lacrimal, and two maxilla).

15. The Vertebral Column

(fig. 2–9)

The 26 bones of the vertebral column form a flexible structure, supporting the head, thorax, and the upper extremities. The arrangement of the vertebrae provides a protected passageway for the spinal cord. Vertebral bones are classified into four regions—cervical (neck); thoracic (chest); lumbar (lower back); and sacral-coccygeal (pelvic).

a. *Vertebral Structure.*

(1) A typical vertebra has an anterior portion, the body, and a posterior portion, the arch (fig. 2–10). The body and the arch encircle the spinal canal, the opening through which the spinal cord passes. Between vertebral bodies are the intervertebral discs, which are fibrocartilage structures that serve as shock-absorbing connections between vertebrae. The irregular projections from the arches are spinous processes posteriorly (these are the projections you feel when you run your fingers along the midline of the back) and transverse processes laterally. Intervertebral foramena are openings on either side of the arches for passage of spinal nerves to and from the spinal cord.

(2) The movement of casualties suspected of having a spinal injury is always potentially hazardous. Careless movement increases the possibility of damage to the spinal cord. At least three persons are needed to move such a casualty. It is particularly important that the individual directing the movement understand the anatomy and physiology of the vertebral column and its relationship with the spinal cord and nerves.

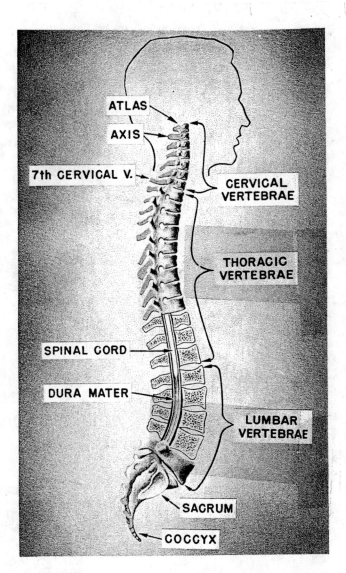

Figure 2–9. *Vertebral column.*

b. *Vertebral Curves.* The vertebral column has four normal curves for strength and balance —cervical and lumbar curves are concave, curving inward; thoracic and sacral curves are convex, curving outward. Abnormal, exaggerated spinal curvatures can be disabling.

c. *Classification of Vertebrae.* Seven cervical vertebrae are in the neck region. The first cervical vertebra is called the atlas, the second vertebra, the axis. These are the only named vertebrae. All other vertebrae are numbered according to region. The prominent knob at the base of the neck is formed by the spinous process of the 7th cervical vertebra. Twelve thoracic vertebrae form the posterior wall of the chest, and each thoracic vertebra articulates with one pair of ribs. The five lumbar vertebrae are in the lower back and support the posterior abdominal wall. The sacrum, a

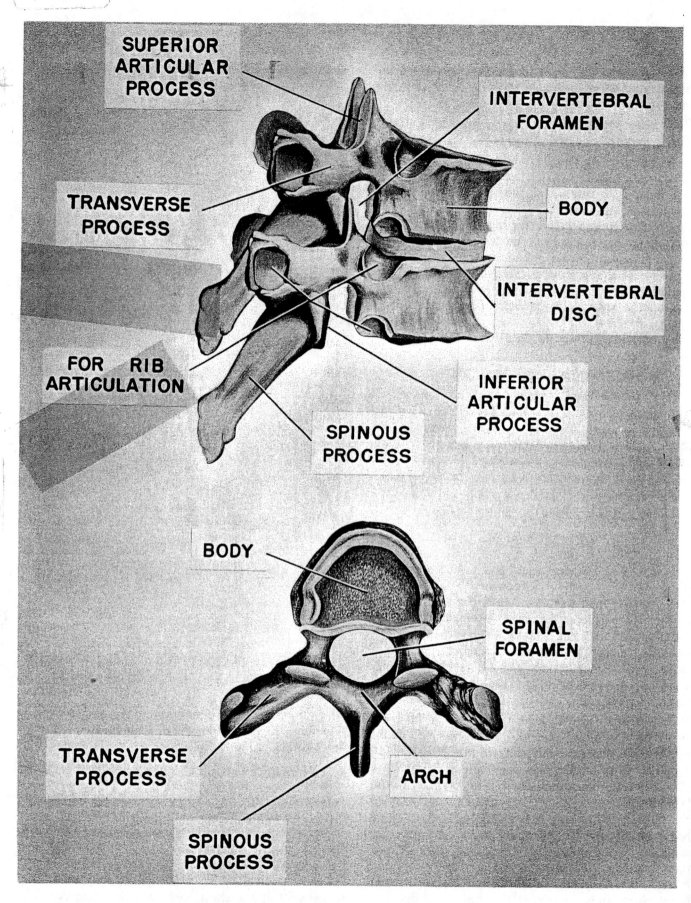

SUPERIOR ARTICULAR PROCESS

INTERVERTEBRAL FORAMEN

TRANSVERSE PROCESS

BODY

INTERVERTEBRAL DISC

FOR RIB ARTICULATION

INFERIOR ARTICULAR PROCESS

SPINOUS PROCESS

BODY

SPINAL FORAMEN

TRANSVERSE PROCESS

ARCH

SPINOUS PROCESS

Figure 2–10. Typical vertebrae.

flat, spade-shaped bone, forms the posterior part of the pelvic girdle. The coccyx is the "tail bone," the thin, curving end of the vertebral column. In the adult, five sacral bones have fused to form one sacrum, and four coccygeal bones have fused to form one coccyx.

16. The Thorax

The thorax, or chest cage, is formed by 25 bones: 12 thoracic vertebrae, 2 pairs of ribs, and 1 sternum. Rib cartilages (costal cartilages) complete the chest cage. The thorax contains and protects the heart, lungs, and related structures of circulation and respiration. The ribs curve outward, forward, and downward from their posterior attachments to the vertebrae. The first seven pairs of ribs are joined directly to the sternum by their costal cartilages. The next three pairs (numbered 8, 9, 10), are attached to the sternum indirectly—each cartilage attaches to the one above —while the last two pairs, "the floating ribs," are not attached to the sternum. The sternum is the anterior flat breastbone and the ribs form the expandable chest cage wall.

17. The Shoulder Girdle and Upper Limbs

(fig. 2–11)

The shoulder girdle is a flexible yoke that suspends and supports the arms. Held in place by muscles, it has only one point of attachment to the axial skeleton—the joint between the clavicle and sternum. The shoulder girdle is formed by two scapulae posteriorly and two clavicles anteriorly. The bones of the shoulder and upper limb include the scapula (shoulder blade); clavicle (collar bone); humerus (arm bone); radius and ulna (forearm bones); carpals (wristbones); metacarpals (hand bones); and phalanges (finger bones).

a. The scapula is a large triangular bone extending from the second to the seventh or eighth ribs, posteriorly. The heavy ridge extending across the upper surface of the scapula ends in a process called the acromion, which forms the tip of the shoulder and the joint with the clavicle, anteriorly. A socket for the head of the humerus is on the lateral surface of the scapula. Strong muscles attach to the scapula for shoulder and arm movement.

b. The clavicle is a slender, S-curved bone lying horizontally above the first rib. The lateral end of the clavicle forms a joint with the scapula

(acromio-clavicular joint). The medial end of the clavicle forms a joint with the sternum at the sterno-clavicular joint, which can be felt as the knob on either side of the notch at the base of the throat. The clavicle acts as a shoulder brace, holding the shoulder up and back. When the clavicle is fractured, the shoulder slumps forward.

c. The humerus is a heavy long bone in the arm that extends from the shoulder to the elbow. The rounded proximal end fits into the scapula in a socket, the glenoid fossa. The distal end of the humerus forms the elbow joint, articulating with the ulna and part of the radius. Strong muscles reinforce the shoulder joint and attach to the humerus, protecting the large blood vessels and nerves that extend along the bone.

d. The radius and ulna (fig. 2–12) are the bones of the forearm. The ulna, on the little finger side, forms the major part of the elbow joint with the humerus. A projection of the ulna, the olecranon, is the "funny bone" at the point of the elbow. The radius, on the thumb side, forms the major part of the wrist joint. The action of the radius about the ulna permits hand turning.

e. The wrist (fig. 2–12) has eight small bones (carpal bones) arranged in two rows of four each. They articulate with each other and with the bones of the hand and forearm. Articulating with the carpals are five metacarpals which form the bony structure of the palm of the hand. The metacarpal of the thumb is particularly important—its muscular attachment permits the thumb to meet the other fingers of the hand, an action called opposing. (This opposing thumb enables the human hand to manipulate articles with great dexterity.) The 14 phalanges in each hand are the finger bones, 3 in each finger and 2 in each thumb. The nerves, blood vessels, and tendons in the hand and wrist are close to the surface and, when injured, can cause serious disability. Injuries to the hand require special evaluation and painstaking treatment to prevent deformities and crippling of finger movements.

18. The Pelvis and Lower Limbs

The two hip bones form the pelvic girdle, which provides articulation for the lower limbs. The pelvis, jointed by the hip bones, sacrum, and coccyx, forms a strong bony basin which supports the trunk and protects the contents of the abdomino pelvic cavity. When the upright body is in proper alinement, the pelvis distributes the weight evenly to both lower extremities. The bones of the pelvis

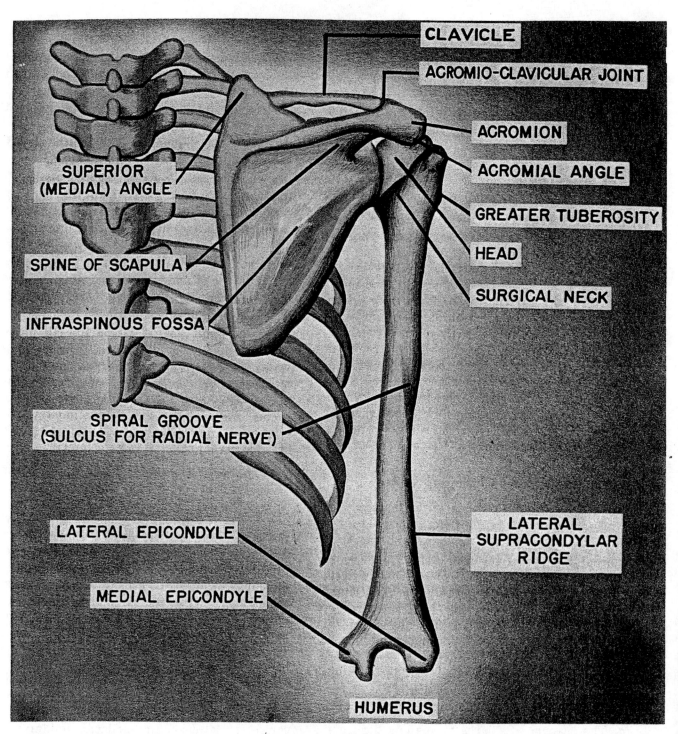

CLAVICLE

ACROMIO-CLAVICULAR JOINT

ACROMION

ACROMIAL ANGLE

GREATER TUBEROSITY

HEAD

SURGICAL NECK

LATERAL
SUPRACONDYLAR
RIDGE

SUPERIOR
(MEDIAL) ANGLE

SPINE OF SCAPULA

INFRASPINOUS FOSSA

SPIRAL GROOVE
(SULCUS FOR RADIAL NERVE)

LATERAL EPICONDYLE

MEDIAL EPICONDYLE

HUMERUS

Figure 2–11. Shoulder girdle.

and lower extremity are the os coxa (hip bone), femur (thigh bone), patella (knee cap), tibia and fibula (leg bones), tarsals (ankle bones), metatarsals (foot bones), and phalanges (toe bones) (fig. 2–6). In contrast to the shoulder girdle, the pelvic girdle is inflexible and very strong (for weight bearing).

a. The hip bone is formed by the fusion of three bones into one massive, irregular bone, the os coxa. The two hip bones are joined together anteriorly in the symphysis pubis. Posteriorly, the hip bones are fused to the sacrum. Each hip bone has three distinctive parts—the ilium, ischium and pubis (fig. 2–13). The ilium is the broad, flaring

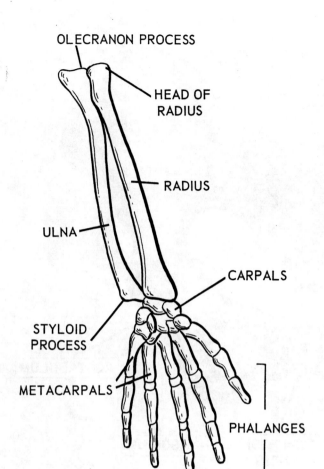

OLECRANON PROCESS

HEAD OF RADIUS

RADIUS

ULNA

CARPALS

STYLOID PROCESS

METACARPALS

PHALANGES

Figure 2–12. Forearm and hand.

upper part of the hip. The iliac crests, the upper ridges of the ilium, are important landmarks. The ischium is the lower, posterior portion on which one sits. The pubis is the anterior portion of the hip. A deep, cup-shaped socket, the acetabulum, is located on the lower lateral surface of each hip bone. The cup shape of the acetabulum fits the head of the femur to form the hip joint.

b. The femur or thigh bone (fig. 2–7) is the longest, strongest bone in the body. The head of the femur fits into the acetabulum of the hip bone. The neck of the femur, just below the head, is the part most frequently fractured, particularly by elderly individuals. The distal end of the femur articulates with the tibia, to form the knee joint. A large prominent projection at the junction of the shaft and neck of the femus is the trochanter, which is an important attachment for strong thigh muscles.

c. The patella, or knee cap, is the bone protecting the front of the knee joint. It is a special kind of bone embedded within the powerful tendon

that extends from the strong anterior thigh muscles. The patella has an oval shape in cross section and is classified as a sesamoid bone (bone embedded in tendons).

d. The tibia and fibula are the two bones in the leg. The tibia, which is thicker and stronger, is the shin bone. It supports body weight and articulates with the femur in the knee joint. The projection at its lower end is the medial malleolus, the inner ankle bone. The fibula, the lateral leg bone, is joined to the tibia at its proximal end, but not to the femur. The projection at the distal end of the fibula is the lateral malleolus, the outer ankle bone.

e. The skeleton of the foot consists of the tarsals, metatarsals, and the phalanges. Seven tarsals form the ankle, heel, and posterior half of the instep. The talus is the largest ankle bone, and the calcaneus is the heel bone. Five metatarsals form the anterior half of the instep. The tarsals and metatarsals together form the arch of the foot, a structure important in weight distribution to the foot. Tendons and ligaments hold the tarsals and metatarsals in their arched position, and when this support is weak, the foot is flat. The 14 phalanges of the toes are similar to finger bones but are less important for foot function than fingers are for hand function.

19. Joints (Articulations)

A joint is a structure which holds together separate bones. Joints are classified according to the amount of movement they permit—immovable, slightly movable, and freely movable (fig. 2–14).

a. Immovable joints have bone surfaces fused together to prevent motion. At one time during skeletal development, these joints had some movement but as the bones matured they grew together for stability. The pelvic girdle, sacral and coccygeal vertebrae, and skull bones are examples of immovable joints.

b. Slightly movable joints have cartilage discs between bones and are held in place by strong ligaments. The cartilage permits some give, and ligaments prevent bone separation. Vertebral bodies and the symphysis pubis are examples of slightly movable joints.

c. Freely movable joints permit maximum motion. These joints have a more complex arrangement since they have joint cavities. The several parts of a joint cavity include the joint capsule, the capsule lining (synovial membrane), and some lubricating fluid within the cavity. Ligaments are

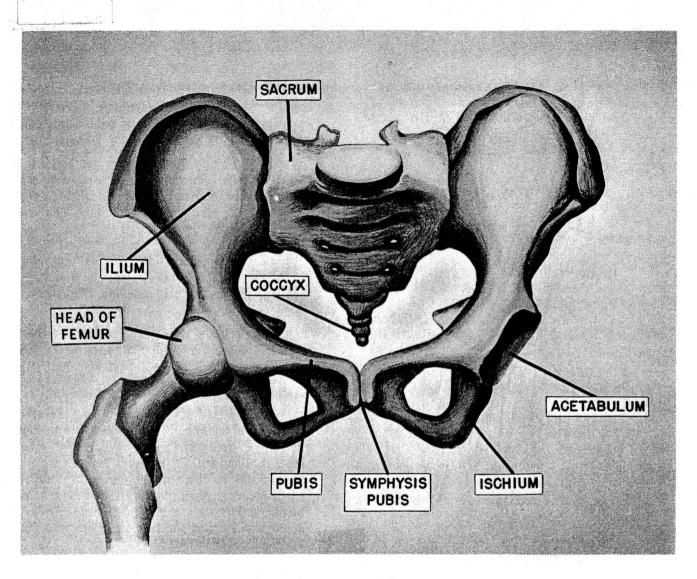

Figure 2–13. Pelvis.

strong fibrous connective tissue bands that hold the bones together at the joint. In some joints, the ligaments enclose the joint, forming the joint capsule.

d. Some joint disorders are mechanical—the parts of the joint are displaced or dislocated. Another term for a type of dislocation is "subluxation," a partial displacement of one bone surface within the joint. When the ligaments holding the joint together are partially torn, but the joint is not displaced, the injury is called a sprain.

20. Joint Movements

a. Movable joints allow change of position and motion. Examples of joint movement (app. B) are flexion (bending), extension (straightening), abduction (movement away from the midline), and adduction (movement toward the midline), prona-

tion (turning the forearm so that the palm of the hand is down), and supination (turning the forearm so that the palm of the hand is up).

b. Attempts to force joints to move beyond their normal limitations can be disastrous. The structure of the joint determines the kind of movement that is possible, since the bone ends reciprocate, or fit into each other, at the joint. Examples of joint structure that permit certain kinds of joint movement include:

(1) Ball and socket joints, as in the shoulder and hip. These joints permit the widest range of motion—flexion, extension, abduction, adduction, and rotation.

(2) Hinge joints, as in the elbow and knee. Hinge joints permit flexion and extension. Elbow joints have forward movement—the anterior bone surfaces approach each other. Knee joints have

backward movement—the posterior bone surfaces approach each other.

(3) Pivot joints, as at the head and neck, at the first and second cervical vertebrae. The distal ends of the radius and ulna also form a pivot joint for rotation of the wrist.

21. Joints and Bursae

At some joint locations, the tendon connecting muscle to bone passes over a joint; *for example,* at the shoulder, elbow, knee, and heel. To reduce pressure, small sacs containing fluid are formed over and around the tendon. The sac is a bursa, and an irritated bursa is bursitis. The knee has four bursae, over and around the patella. When domestic chores included scrubbing floors on hands and knees, inflammation of the knee bursae was called "housemaid's knee." Bursitis can be very painful, and normal movement may be impossible.

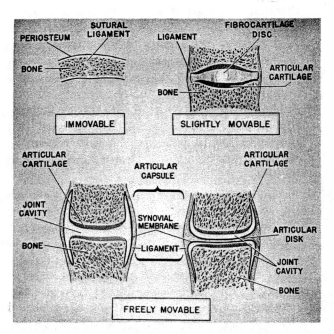

Figure 2–14. Types of joints.

Section IV.   THE SKELETAL MUSCULAR SYSTEM

22. Muscles

The muscles of the body include the smooth muscle in the walls of internal organs, the cardiac muscle in the walls of the heart, and the skeletal muscle attached to and causing movements of bones. Muscles have the ability to contract, and it is this power of muscle contraction that produces body movements. The skeletal muscles and their action and movements on bones and joints will be discussed in this section.

23. Skeletal Muscles

Although skeletal muscles are called voluntary muscles, they require a functioning nerve supply and something to pull against for normal contraction. It is important to think of skeletal muscles as one part of a three-part, neuro-muscular-skeletal unit. *For example,* a functioning nerve supply (a motor nerve from the central nervous system) is needed to stimulate muscle contraction; the muscle itself must be able to contract and to relax; and the power of the muscle contraction must be transmitted to a bone, or other attachment, to produce the desired movement. When any one part of this three-part unit cannot function normally, the other two parts also lose their ability to function normally. When all three parts—nerve, muscle, and bone—are intact, the many movements associated with skeletal muscles are possible. Skeletal muscle movements include loco-

motion, or moving from place to place; rhythmic breathing movements; blinking of eyelids; position changes; chewing and swallowing; coughing; and changes in facial expression. Many of these movements are essential for survival.

24. Muscle Structure and Muscle Movements

Long, slender muscle cells form fibers; muscle fibers are grouped together into bundles; and muscle bundles are grouped together to form an individual skeletal muscle. Each skeletal muscle is wrapped in a connective tissue sheath, a form of fascia. This muscle sheath incloses the blood vessels and nerves that stimulate and nourish the muscle cells. The connective tissue parts are opaque, or whitish, in color, while the muscle bundles are the lean, red-meat part of muscles. Individual muscles differ considerably in size, shape, and arrangement of muscle fibers. The fiber arrangement determines the line of pull of an individual muscle.

a. Muscle Attachments. Extensions of muscle sheath become continuous with tough connective tissue attachments such as tendons or aponeuroses that bind muscles to bones or to adjacent muscles. Tendons are cordlike attachments of connective tissue that unite with the periosteum of bone. Aponeuroses are broad, sheetlike attachments which can unite with muscle sheaths of adjacent muscles. At the midline of the abdomen, where there are no bones for muscles to attach to, abdominal muscles to the left and right of the midline are attached to central aponeuroses.

b. Muscle Movements. When muscle fibers are stimulated to contract by an impulse received from a motor nerve, the muscle shortens and pulls against its connective tissue attachment. One attachment is sometimes a fixed joint or anchor, and the direction of motion is then toward it. The power of the muscle contraction is transmitted to the bone or to an adjacent muscle, and movement occurs.

c. Muscle Tone. Healthy muscle is characterized by active contraction in response to the reaction of the nervous system to the environment. This readiness to act (resulting in firing of motor units) as stimuli from the environment impinge upon the nervous system is called muscle tone. Muscles that have lost their tone through lack of exercise, through primary muscle disease, or through nerve damage become flabby (flaccid). The tone of muscles is due to the constant, steady contraction and relaxation of different muscle fibers in individual muscles, which helps to maintain the "chemical engine" of the muscle cells. Even minor exercise movements help maintain tone by renewing blood supply to muscle cells. Wriggling the toes, flexing and extending the fingers, changing the depth of respirations, turning and repositioning the body are examples of exercises that help restore and maintain muscle tone.

d. Muscle Activity. Muscle contraction consumes food and oxygen and produces acids and heat. Muscle activity is the major source of the body's heat. Acids accumulating as a result of continued activity cause fatigue, which occurs most rapidly when contractions are frequent. It occurs slowly if rest periods are taken between contractions. Exercise causes muscles to become larger, stronger, and better developed. An increase in muscle size is hypertrophy; wasting away of muscles due to inactivity is atrophy. Physical exercise is necessary to keep muscles in good condition.

25. Principles of Skeletal Muscle Action

A few general principles about skeletal muscle action should be understood. The three principles listed will help associate muscle actions with normal body movements and patient care activities.

a. Muscles produce movements by pulling on bones. Since bones move at joints, most muscles attach to bones above and below a joint. One bone is stabilized while the other bone moves.

b. Muscles moving a part usually lie proximal to the part moved. *For example,* muscles moving the humerus are in the shoulder, chest, and back; muscles moving the femur are in the lumbar and pelvic region.

c. Muscles almost always act in groups rather than singly. The coordinated action of several muscles produces movement—while one group contracts, the other group relaxes, and vice versa. The muscle whose contraction produces the movement is the prime mover. The muscle which relaxes is the antagonist. In bending (flexing) and stretching (extending) the forearm, the biceps and triceps in the upper arm are, alternately, prime movers and antagonists.

26. Principal Groups of Skeletal Muscles

Since there are more than 400 individually named skeletal muscles, only a few will be discussed in this manual. In figure 2–15, both Ⓐ and Ⓑ illustrate the general location of the muscles discussed. Muscles are usually named for one or more features such as their location, action, shape, or points of attachment.

a. Head and Face. Muscles of the head and face act in movements of the eye, facial expressions, talking, chewing, and swallowing. The orbicularis oculi closes the eyelid; the orbicularis oris closes the lips; the masseter closes the jaw and clamps the back teeth together.

b. Neck. The muscles of the neck move the head from side to side, forward and backward, and rotate it. Some also assist in respiration, speaking, and swallowing. The sternocleidomastoid bends the head forward and helps turn it to either side.

c. Chest. The strong chest muscles move the arm, brace the shoulder, and compress the chest for effective coughing. The diaphragm, the major muscle of respiration, separates the thoracic and abdominal cavities. (It is not shown in the diagram of superficial skeletal muscles.) The pectoralis major draws the upper arm forward across the chest. The latimus dorsi and trapezius are major muscles of the posterior thorax.

d. Arm. Among the muscles which cause movement of the arms are the deltoid, biceps, and triceps. (The extensors and flexors cause hand and finger movements.)

(1) The deltoid is a triangular-shaped muscle, capping the shoulder and upper arm. The deltoid lifts the arm forward, sideways, and to the rear.

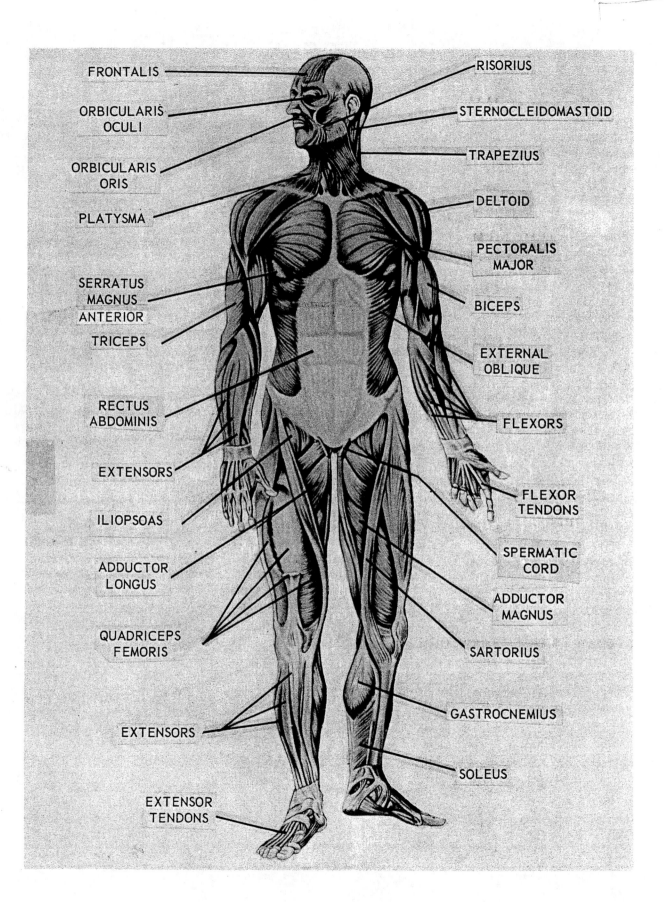

FRONTALIS

ORBICULARIS OCULI

ORBICULARIS ORIS

PLATYSMA

SERRATUS MAGNUS ANTERIOR

TRICEPS

RECTUS ABDOMINIS

EXTENSORS

ILIOPSOAS

ADDUCTOR LONGUS

QUADRICEPS FEMORIS

EXTENSORS

EXTENSOR TENDONS

RISORIUS

STERNOCLEIDOMASTOID

TRAPEZIUS

DELTOID

PECTORALIS MAJOR

BICEPS

EXTERNAL OBLIQUE

FLEXORS

FLEXOR TENDONS

SPERMATIC CORD

ADDUCTOR MAGNUS

SARTORIUS

GASTROCNEMIUS

SOLEUS

Figure 2–15. Superficial muscles.

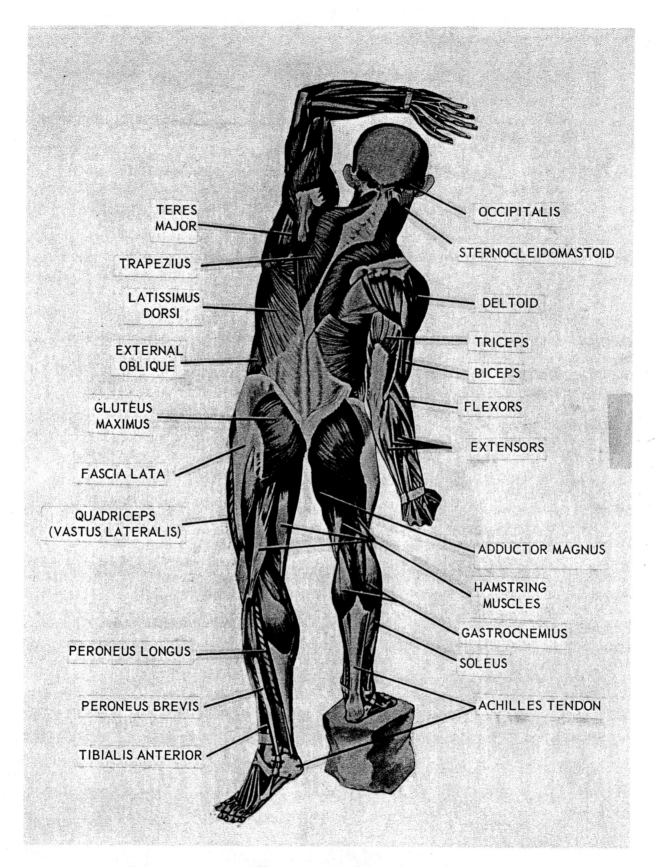

TERES MAJOR

TRAPEZIUS

LATISSIMUS DORSI

EXTERNAL OBLIQUE

GLUTEUS MAXIMUS

FASCIA LATA

QUADRICEPS (VASTUS LATERALIS)

PERONEUS LONGUS

PERONEUS BREVIS

TIBIALIS ANTERIOR

OCCIPITALIS

STERNOCLEIDOMASTOID

DELTOID

TRICEPS

BICEPS

FLEXORS

EXTENSORS

ADDUCTOR MAGNUS

HAMSTRING MUSCLES

GASTROCNEMIUS

SOLEUS

ACHILLES TENDON

Figure 2–15—Continued.

(2) The biceps, a long, two-headed muscle located on the anterior arm, flexes the forearm at the elbow. It also helps to turn the arm palm up in supination.

(3) The triceps, a large three-headed muscle located on the posterior arm, extends the forearm at the elbow.

e. Back. The muscles of the back are large, and some are broad. Attached to vertebrae, the back muscles keep the trunk in an erect posture and aid it in bending and rotating. In the thoracic region, these muscles assist in respiration and in movements of the neck, arm, and trunk. Although the muscles of the midback are very powerful, the thigh and buttock muscles should be used in lifting to avoid straining the bony and ligamentous structures of the back.

f. Abdominal. The abdominal muscles form broad, thin layers which support the internal abdominal organs, assist in respiration, and help in flexion and rotation of the spine. Their names indicate their line of pull—external oblique, rectus abdominis (straight up and down), and transverse. Abdominal muscles also assist in urination and in defecation.

g. Perineal. The muscles of the perineum form the floor of the pelvic cavity and aid in defecation and in urination.

h. Buttocks. The thick, strong muscles of the buttocks help to stabilize the hip, and with the muscles of the posterior thigh, distribute weight to the pelvis in lifting and relieve the strain on the back muscles. This gluteus group includes the gluteus maximus, gluteus medius, and gluteus minimus. These muscles extend and rotate the thigh.

i. Thigh. The muscles located on the anterior and posterior of the thigh cross two joints, the hip and the knee. When they contract, they extend one joint and flex the other. The anterior thigh muscles include the quadriceps femoris and the posterior ones include the biceps femoris.

(1) *Quadriceps femoris.* This four-headed group of muscles located on the anterior of the thigh extends the leg at the knee. Its four muscles are the vastus lateralis, rectus femoris, vastus intermedius, and vastus medialis.

(2) *Biceps femoris (hamstring group).* This muscle group on the posterior of the thigh flexes the knee and extends the thigh.

j. Leg. The anterior muscle group of the leg includes the anterior tibialis, which flexes the foot on the leg, turning the foot upward in dorsiflexion. The largest posterior muscle of the leg is the gastrocnemius, the calf muscle, which attaches to the heel through the Achilles tendon. Contraction of the gastrocnemius causes the foot to turn downward in plantar flexion, or foot drop.

Section V. THE SKIN

27. Integumentary System and Its Functions

The skin is called the integumentary or covering body system and serves the body in many important ways. The most obvious feature of skin is its outward appearance; indeed, the appearance and feel of the skin are important indications of general health and hygiene. Four functions of skin are protection, as a mechanical barrier to the entrance of bacteria; regulation of body temperature, through control of heat loss; sensory perception, through nerve endings that transmit sensations of touch, heat, cold, and pain; and excretion of body wastes, through sweat. Although this is not one of its normal functions, the skin can absorb water and other substances. This property of the skin is used to advantage in prescribing local application of certain drugs. It can be harmful, too, as when toxic agents such as "G" gas, lead salts in gasoline, and insecticides are absorbed and permitted to enter the body through the skin.

28. Structure

The skin has two principal layers, the epidermis, or outer layer, and the dermis, the inner layer or true skin. The epidermis and dermis (fig. 2–16) are supported by a subcutaneous (under-the-skin) layer which connects the skin to underlying muscles.

a. There are no blood vessels or nerve endings in the epidermis, which has two layers, outer and inner. The outer layer has flat, scaly, lifeless cells that are constantly being worn off by surface contacts. As this is happening, rapidly growing inner epidermis cells push up and replace the top layers. Skin pigment, found in the deepest parts of these inner epidermis cells, varies in individuals. It determines the darkness or lightness of skin color. However, the color of the skin is also due to the quantity and state of the blood circulating in the dermis, the inner skin layer. Pinkness, blueness (cyanosis), or pallor (paleness) of the skin surface is due to circulating blood.

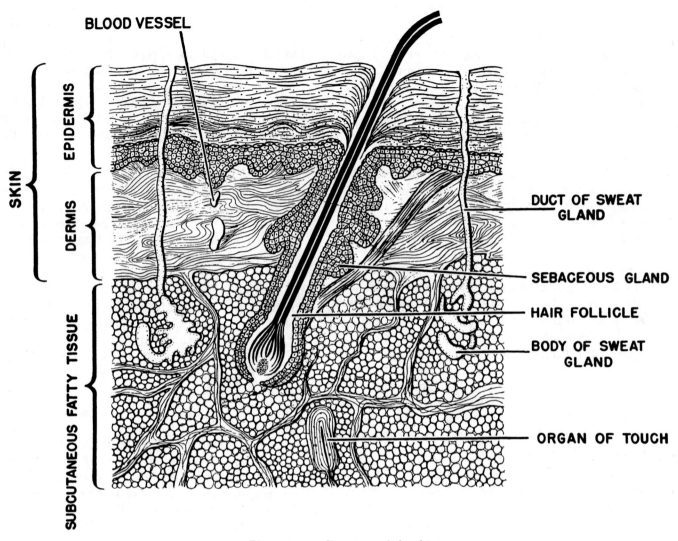

BLOOD VESSEL

SKIN

EPIDERMIS

DERMIS

SUBCUTANEOUS FATTY TISSUE

DUCT OF SWEAT GLAND

SEBACEOUS GLAND

HAIR FOLLICLE

BODY OF SWEAT GLAND

ORGAN OF TOUCH

Figure 2-16. Structure of the skin.

b. The dermis is the deep, true skin layer. Nerves, blood vessels, glands, hair roots, and nail roots are in the dermis, supported by a connective tissue meshwork of elastic fibers. Tiny involuntary muscle fibers in the dermis contract and account for the reactions described as "hair standing on end" and "goose pimples."

c. The subcutaneous layer of tissue beneath the dermis is not skin. It is superficial fascia, a connective tissue. Fat and other connective tissues in the subcutaneous layer round out body surfaces and cushion bony parts. When a hypodermic injection is given, it is given into the subcutaneous tissue, below the skin layers.

29. Skin Accessory Organs

Hair, nails, sebaceous (oil) glands, and sweat glands are skin accessory organs. Each hair grows from a root embedded in the dermis, or

below the dermis. A little tube, the hair follicle, incloses the root. Fingernails and toenails grow from nail beds buried at the proximal ends of the nails. The sebaceous glands secrete an oil called sebum, which lubricates the hair and the skin surface. This oily secretion keeps the skin pliable and helps keep it waterproof. When the openings of the sebaceous glands become plugged with dirt, they form blackheads. Sweat glands manufacture sweat, or perspiration, from fluid drawn from the blood. Sweat contains salts and organic wastes and is about 99 percent water. It is discharged through skin openings called the pores. As sweat evaporates, the body is cooled. Sweat formation and excretion is an important mechanism for losing body heat.

30. Skin as a Temperature Regulator

Skin helps regulate the temperature of the body

by controlling heat loss in two different ways. Blood vessels in the dermis can change size. *For example,* when blood vessels are dilated, warm blood is closer to the skin surface, and heat is lost more rapidly. When blood vessels constrict, the amount of blood at the skin surface is decreased, and heat is conserved. Because the surface of the skin is so large, heat loss by radiation is considerable. Added to this heat loss by radiation is the heat loss by evaporation of sweat. In very humid weather, evaporation of sweat from the skin and from saturated clothing decreases.

Section VI.   THE CIRCULATORY SYSTEM

31. Introduction

The circulatory system has two major fluid transportation systems, the cardiovascular and the lymphatic.

a. Cardiovascular System. This system, which contains the heart and blood vessels, is a closed system, transporting blood to all parts of the body. Blood flowing through the circuit formed by the heart and blood vessels (fig. 2–17) brings oxygen, food, and other chemical elements to tissue cells and removes carbon dioxide and other waste products resulting from cell activity.

b. Lymphatic System. This system, which provides drainage for tissue fluid, is an auxiliary part of the circulatory system, returning an important amount of tissue fluid to the blood stream through its own system of lymphatic vessels.

32. The Heart

The heart, designed to be a highly efficient pump, is a four-chambered muscular organ, lying within the chest, with about 2/3 of its mass to the left of the midline (fig. 2–18). It lies in the pericardial space in the thoracic cavity between the two lungs. In size and shape, it resembles a man's closed fist. Its lower point, the apex, lies just above the left diaphragm.

a. Heart Covering. The pericardium is a double-walled sac inclosing the heart. The outer fibrous surface gives support, and the inner lining prevents friction as the heart moves within its protecting jacket. The lining surfaces of the pericardial sac produce a small amount of pericardial fluid needed for lubrication to facilitate the normal movements of the heart.

b. Heart Wall. This muscular wall is made up of cardiac muscle called myocardium.

c. Heart Chambers. There are four chambers in the heart. These chambers are essentially the same size. The upper chambers, called the atria, are seemingly smaller than the lower chambers, the ventricles. The apparent difference in total size is due to the thickness of the myocardial layer. The right atrium communicates with the right ventricle; the left atrium communicates with the left ventricle. The septum (partition), dividing the interior of the heart into right and left sides, prevents direct communication of blood flow from right to left chambers or left to right chambers. This is important, because the right side of the heart receives deoxygenated blood returning from the systemic (body) circulation. The left side of the heart receives oxygenated blood returning from the pulmonary (lung) circulation. The special structure of the heart keeps the blood flowing in its proper direction to and from the heart chambers.

d. Heart Valves. The four chambers of the heart are lined with endocardium. At each opening from the chambers this lining folds on itself and extends into the opening to form valves. These valves allow the blood to pass from a chamber but prevent its return. The atrioventricular valves, between the upper and lower chambers, are within the heart itself. The semilunar valves are within arteries arising from the right and left ventricles.

(1) *Atrioventricular valves.* The tricuspid valve is located between the right atrium and right ventricle. It has three flaps or cusps. The bicuspid valve or mitral valve is located between the left atrium and left ventricle. It has two flaps or cusps.

(2) *Semilunar valves.* The pulmonary semilunar (half-moon shaped) valve is located at the opening into the pulmonary artery that arises from the right ventricle. The aortic semilunar valve is located at the opening into the aorta that arises from the left ventricle.

33. Flow of Blood Through the Heart

It is helpful to follow the flow of blood through the heart in order to understand the relationship

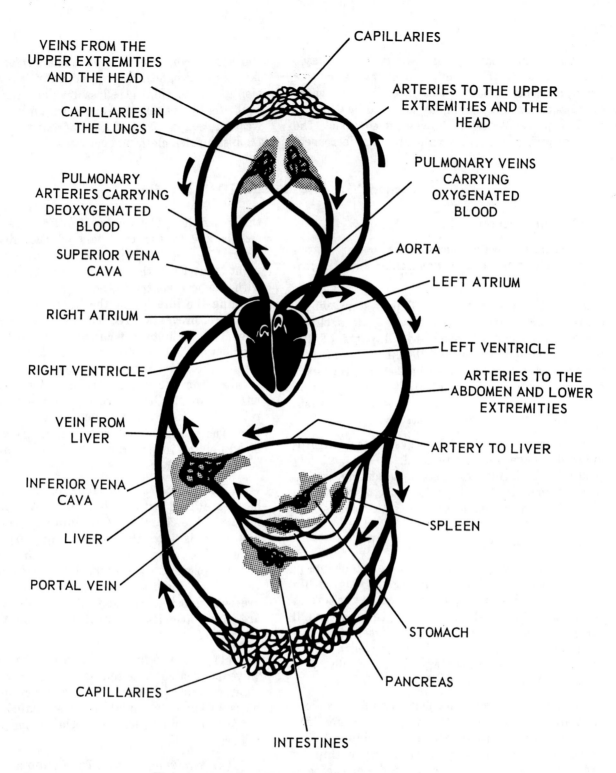

VEINS FROM THE
UPPER EXTREMITIES
AND THE HEAD

CAPILLARIES

CAPILLARIES IN
THE LUNGS

ARTERIES TO THE UPPER
EXTREMITIES AND THE
HEAD

PULMONARY
ARTERIES CARRYING
DEOXYGENATED
BLOOD

PULMONARY VEINS
CARRYING
OXYGENATED
BLOOD

SUPERIOR VENA
CAVA

AORTA

LEFT ATRIUM

RIGHT ATRIUM

LEFT VENTRICLE

RIGHT VENTRICLE

ARTERIES TO THE
ABDOMEN AND LOWER
EXTREMITIES

VEIN FROM
LIVER

ARTERY TO LIVER

INFERIOR VENA
CAVA

LIVER

SPLEEN

PORTAL VEIN

STOMACH

CAPILLARIES

PANCREAS

INTESTINES

Figure 2–17. Circulation of the blood (diagrammatic).

of the heart structures. Remember, the heart is the pump and is also the connection between the systemic circulation and pulmonary circulation. All the blood returning from the systemic circulation must flow through the pulmonary circulation for exchange of carbon dioxide for oxygen. Blood from the upper part of the body enters the heart through a large vein, the superior vena cava, and from the lower part of the body by the inferior vena cava (fig. 2–19).

a. Blood from the superior vena cava and inferior vena cava enters the heart at the right

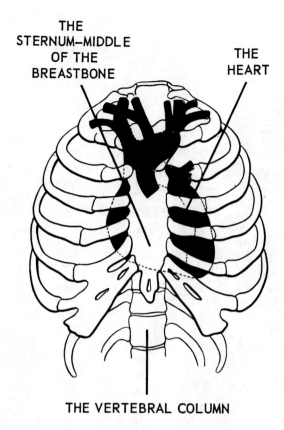

THE STERNUM—MIDDLE OF THE BREASTBONE

THE HEART

THE VERTEBRAL COLUMN

Figure 2–18. Heart and thoracic cage.

atrium. The right atrium contracts, and blood is forced through the open tricuspid valve into the relaxed right ventricle.

b. As the right ventricle contracts, the tricuspid valve is closed, preventing back flow into the atrium. The pulmonary semilunar valve opens as a result of the force and movement of the blood, and the right ventricle pumps the blood into the pulmonary artery.

c. The blood is carried through the lung tissues, exchanging its carbon dioxide for oxygen in the alveoli. This oxygenated blood is collected from the main pulmonary veins and delivered back to the left side of the heart to the left atrium.

d. As the left atrium contracts, the oxygenated blood flows through the open bicuspid (mitral) valve into the left ventricle.

e. As the left ventricle contracts, the bicuspid valve is closed. The aortic semilunar valve opens as a result of the force and movement of the blood, and the left ventricle pumps oxygenated blood through the aortic semilunar valve into the aorta, the main artery of the body. Oxygenated blood now starts its flow to all of the body cells and tissues. The systemic circulation starts from

the left ventricle, the pulmonary circulation from the right ventricle.

34. Blood and Nerve Supply of the Heart

a. Coronary Arteries. The heart gets its blood supply from the right and left coronary arteries. These arteries branch off the aorta just above the heart, then subdivide into many smaller branches within the heart muscle. If any part of the heart muscle is deprived of its blood supply through interruption of blood flow through the coronary arteries and their branches, the muscle tissue deprived of blood cannot function and will die. This is called myocardial infarction. Blood from the heart tissue is returned by coronary veins to the right atrium.

b. Nerve Supply. The nerve supply to the heart is from two sets of nerves originating in the medulla of the brain. The nerves are part of the involuntary (autonomic) nervous system. One set, the branches from the vagus nerve, keeps the heart beating at a slow, regular rate. The other set, the cardiac accelerator nerves, speeds up the heart. Heart muscle has a special ability; it contracts automatically, but the nerve supply is needed to provide an effective contraction for blood circulation. Within the heart muscle itself, there are special groups of nerve fibers that conduct impulses for contraction. These groups make up the conduction system of the heart. When the conduction system does not operate properly, the heart muscle contractions are uncoordinated and ineffective. The impulses within the heart muscle are minute electric currents, which can be picked up and recorded by the electrocardiogram, the ECG.

35. The Heartbeat and Heart Sounds

a. Heartbeat. This is a complete cycle of heart action—contraction, or systole, and relaxation, or diastole. During systole, blood is forced from the chambers. During diastole, blood refills the chambers. The term cardiac cycle means the complete heart beat. The cardiac cycle, repeated continuously at a regular rhythm, occurs 70–80 times per minute. Each complete cycle takes less than one second—in this brief time, all of the heart action needed to move blood must take place, and the heart must be ready to repeat its cycle.

b. Heart Sounds. When heard through a stethoscope, heart sounds are described as "lubb-dup." The first sound, "lubb," is interpreted as the sound, or vibration, of the ventricles contracting

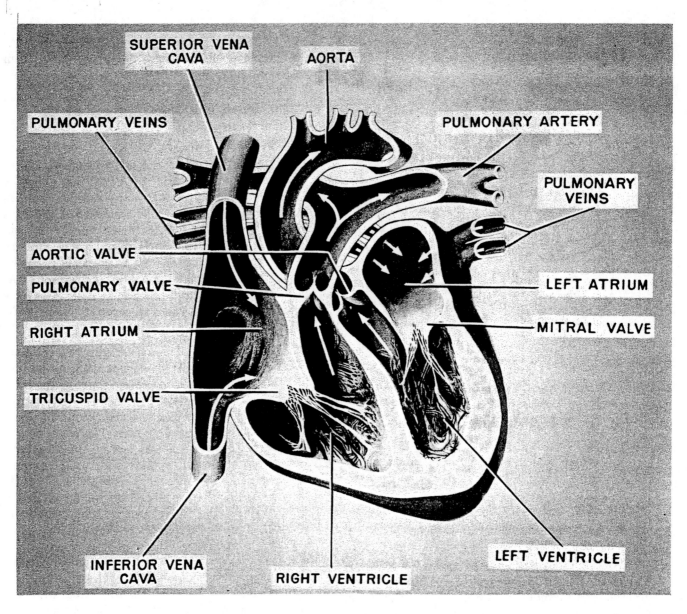

Figure 2–19. The heart, chambers, and flow of blood.

and atrioventricular valves closing. The second, higher-pitched sound, "dup," is interpreted as the sound of the semilunar valves closing. The doctor listening to the heart sounds can detect alterations of normal sounds; the interpretation of these heart sounds is part of the diagnosis of heart disease.

36. Blood Vessels

The blood vessels are the closed system of tubes through which the blood flows. The arteries and arterioles are distributors. The capillaries are the vessels through which all exchange of fluid, oxygen, and carbon dioxide take place between the blood and tissue cells. The venules and veins are collectors, carrying blood back to the heart. The capillaries are the smallest of these vessels but are of greatest importance functionally in the circulatory system.

a. The Arteries and Arterioles. The system of arteries (fig. 2–20) and arterioles is like a tree, with the large trunk, the aorta, giving off branches which repeatedly divide and subdivide. Arterioles are very small arteries, about the diameter of a hair. By way of comparison, the aorta is more than 1 inch in diameter.) An artery wall has a layer of elastic, muscular tissue which allows it to expand and recoil. When an artery is cut, this wall does not collapse, and bright red blood escapes from the artery in spurts. Arterial bleeding

28

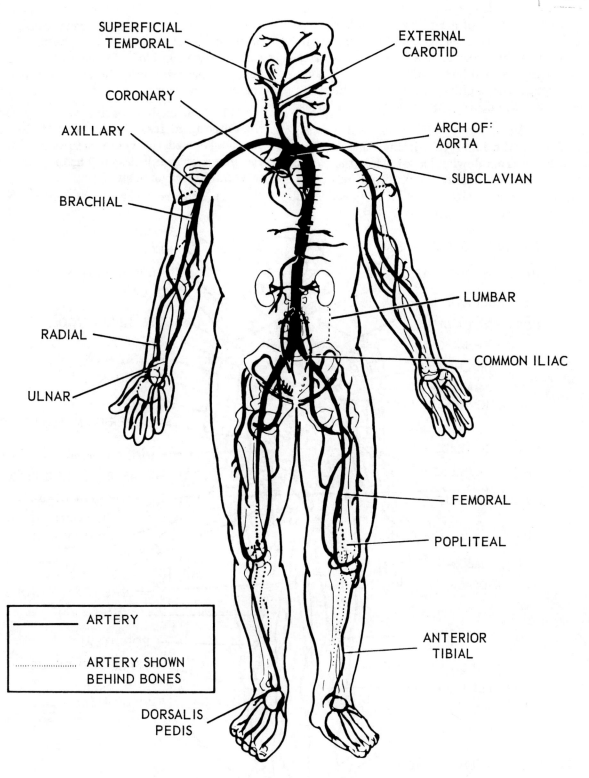

SUPERFICIAL TEMPORAL

EXTERNAL CAROTID

CORONARY

AXILLARY

ARCH OF AORTA

SUBCLAVIAN

BRACHIAL

RADIAL

LUMBAR

COMMON ILIAC

ULNAR

FEMORAL

POPLITEAL

ANTERIOR TIBIAL

ARTERY

ARTERY SHOWN BEHIND BONES

DORSALIS PEDIS

Figure 2–20. Arterial system (diagrammatic).

must often be controlled by clamping and tying off (ligating) the vessel. Some of the principal arteries and the area they supply with blood are—

(1) Carotid arteries, external and internal, supply the neck, head, and brain through their branches.

(2) Subclavian arteries supply the upper extremities.

(3) Femoral arteries supply the lower extremities.

b. *Capillaries.* Microscopic in size, capillaries

are so numerous that there is at least one or more near every living cell. A single layer of endothelial cells forms the walls of a capillary. Capillaries are the essential link between arterial and venous circulation. The vital exchange of substances from the blood in the capillary with tissue cells takes place through the capillary wall. Blood starts its route back to the heart as it leaves the capillaries.

c. *Veins.* Veins have thin walls and valves. Formed from the inner vein lining, these valves prevent blood from flowing back toward the capillaries. Venules, the smallest veins, unite into veins of larger and larger size as the blood is collected to return to the heart. The superior vena cava, collecting blood from all regions above the diaphragm, and the inferior vena cava, collecting blood from all regions below the diaphragm, return the venous blood to the right atrium of the heart. Superficial veins lie close to the surface of the body and can be seen through the skin.

(1) The median basilic vein (fig. 2–21) (at the antecubital fossa in the bend of the elbow) is commonly used for venipuncture to obtain blood specimens or to inject solutions of drugs or parenteral fluid intravenously.

(2) The great saphenous vein is the longest

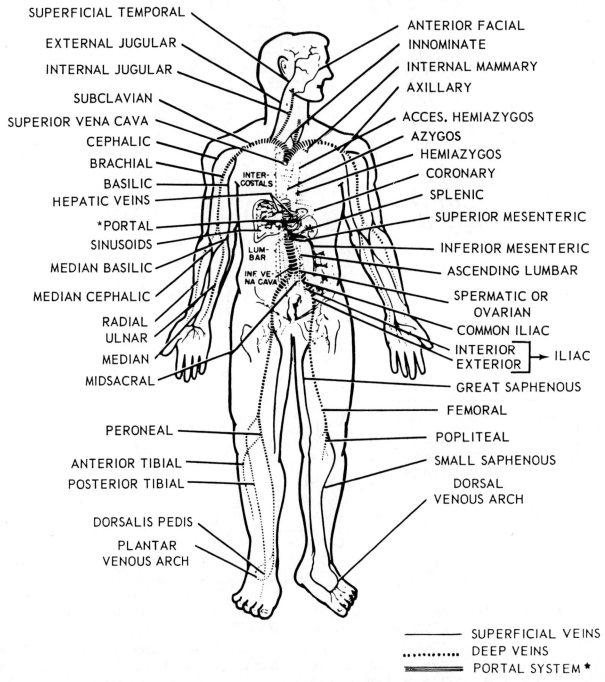

SUPERFICIAL TEMPORAL
EXTERNAL JUGULAR
INTERNAL JUGULAR
SUBCLAVIAN
SUPERIOR VENA CAVA
CEPHALIC
BRACHIAL
BASILIC
HEPATIC VEINS
*PORTAL
SINUSOIDS
MEDIAN BASILIC
MEDIAN CEPHALIC
RADIAL
ULNAR
MEDIAN
MIDSACRAL

PERONEAL
ANTERIOR TIBIAL
POSTERIOR TIBIAL
DORSALIS PEDIS
PLANTAR
VENOUS ARCH

INTER-COSTALS
LUM-BAR
INF. VE-NA CAVA

ANTERIOR FACIAL
INNOMINATE
INTERNAL MAMMARY
AXILLARY
ACCES. HEMIAZYGOS
AZYGOS
HEMIAZYGOS
CORONARY
SPLENIC
SUPERIOR MESENTERIC
INFERIOR MESENTERIC
ASCENDING LUMBAR
SPERMATIC OR OVARIAN
COMMON ILIAC
INTERIOR
EXTERIOR } → ILIAC
GREAT SAPHENOUS
FEMORAL
POPLITEAL
SMALL SAPHENOUS
DORSAL
VENOUS ARCH

———— SUPERFICIAL VEINS
·········· DEEP VEINS
═══════ PORTAL SYSTEM *

Figure 2–21. Venous system (diagrammatic).

vein in the body, extending from the foot to the groin. The saphenous vein has a long distance to lift blood against the force of gravity when an individual is in standing position. It is therefore susceptible to becoming dilated and stretched and the valves no longer function properly. When this occurs the vein is said to be varicosed.

37. Pulse and Blood Pressure

a. *Pulse.* This is a characteristic associated with the heartbeat and the subsequent wave of expansion and recoil set up in the wall of an artery. Pulse is defined as the alternate expansion and recoil of an artery. With each heartbeat, blood is forced into the arteries causing them to dilate (expand). Then the arteries contract (recoil) as the blood moves further along in the circulatory system. The pulse can be felt at certain points in the body where an artery lies close to the surface. The most common location for feeling the pulse is at the wrist, proximal to the thumb (radial artery) on the palm side of the hand. Alternate locations are in front of the ear (temporal artery), at the side of the neck (carotid artery), and on the top (dorsum) of the foot (dorsalis pedis).

b. *Blood Pressure.* The force that blood exerts on the walls of vessels through which it flows is called blood pressure. All parts of the blood vascular system are under pressure, but the term blood pressure usually refers to arterial pressure. Pressure in the arteries is highest when the ventricles contract during systole. Pressure is lowest when the ventricles relax during diastole. The brachial artery, in the upper arm, is the artery usually used for blood pressure measurement.

38. Lymphatic System

The lymphatic system consists of lymph, lymph vessels, and lymph nodes. The spleen belongs, in part, to the lymphatic system. Unlike the cardiovascular system, the lymphatic system has no pump to move the fluid which it collects, but muscle contractions and breathing movements aid in the movement of lymph through its channels and its return to the blood stream.

a. *Lymph and Tissue Fluid.* Lymph, fluid found in the lymph vessels, is clear and watery and is similar to tissue fluid, which is the colorless fluid that fills the spaces between tissues, between the cells of organs, and between cells and connective tissues. Tissue fluid serves as the "middleman" for the exchange between blood and body cells.

Formed from plasma, it seeps out of capillary walls. The lymphatic system collects tissue fluid, and as lymph, the collected fluid is started on its way for return to the circulating blood.

b. *Lymph Vessels.* Starting as small blind ducts within the tissues, the lymphatic vessels enlarge to form lymphatic capillaries. These capillaries unite to form larger lymphatic vessels, which resemble veins in structure and arrangement. Valves in lymph vessels prevent backflow. Superficial lymph vessels collect lymph from the skin and subcutaneous tissue; deep vessels collect lymph from all other parts of the body. The two largest collecting vessels are the thoracic duct and the right lymphatic duct. The thoracic duct (fig. 2–22) receives lymph from all parts of the body except the upper right side. The lymph from the thoracic duct drains into the left subclavian vein, at the root of the neck on the left side. The right lymphatic duct drains into a corresponding vein on the right side.

c. *Lymph Nodes.* Occurring in groups up to a dozen or more, lymph nodes lie along the course of lymph vessels. Although variable in size, they are usually small oval bodies which are composed of lymphoid tissue. Lymph nodes act as filters for removal of infective organisms from the lymph stream. Important groups of these nodes are located in the axilla, the cervical region, the submaxillary region, the inguinal (groin) region, and the mesentric (abdominal) region.

d. *Infection and the Lymphatic System.* Lymph vessels and lymph nodes often become inflamed as the result of infection. An infection in the hand may cause inflammation of the lymph vessels as high as the axilla (armpit). Sore throat may cause inflammation and swelling of lymph nodes in the neck (submandibular nodes below the jaw and cervical nodes posteriorly).

e. *Spleen.* The largest collection of lymphoid tissue in the body, the spleen is located high in the abdominal cavity on the left side (LUQ), below the diaphragm and behind the stomach. It is somewhat long and ovoid (egg-shaped). Although it can be removed (splenectomy) without noticeable harmful effects, the spleen has useful functions, such as serving as a reservoir for blood and red blood cells.

39. The Blood

Blood is the red body fluid flowing through the arteries, capillaries, and veins. It varies in color

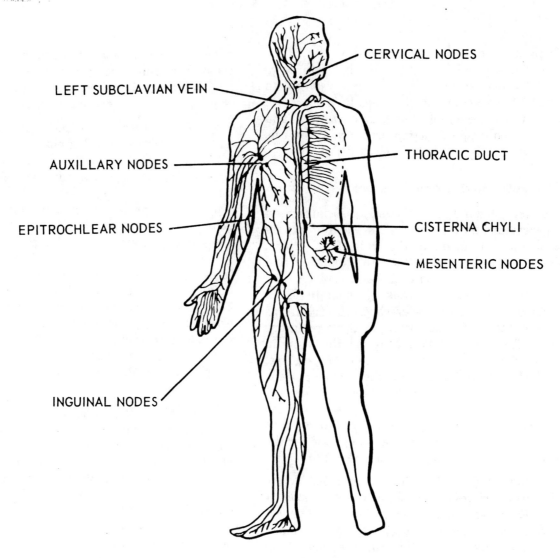

Figure 2–22. Lymphatic system.

CERVICAL NODES

LEFT SUBCLAVIAN VEIN

THORACIC DUCT

AUXILLARY NODES

EPITROCHLEAR NODES

CISTERNA CHYLI

MESENTERIC NODES

INGUINAL NODES

from bright red (oxygenated blood) when it flows from arteries, to dark red (deoxygenated blood) when it flows from veins. The average man has about 6000 ml. of blood.

a. Functions of Blood. The six major functions of blood are all carried out when blood circulates normally through the blood vessels. These functions are—

(1) To carry oxygen from the lungs to tissue cells and carbon dioxide from the cells to the lungs.

(2) To carry food materials absorbed from the digestive tract to the tissue cells and to remove waste products for elimination by excretory organs—the kidneys, intestines, and skin.

(3) To carry hormones, which help regulate body functions, from ductless (endocrine) glands to the tissues of the body.

(4) To help regulate and equalize body temperature. Body cells generate large amounts of heat, and the circulating blood absorbs this heat.

(5) To protect the body against infection.

(6) To maintain the fluid balance in the body.

b. Composition of Blood. Blood is made up of a liquid portion, plasma, and formed elements, blood cells, suspended in the plasma.

(1) *Plasma.* Making up more than one-half of the total volume of blood, plasma is the carrier for blood cells and carbon dioxide and other dissolved wastes. It brings hormones and antibodies (protective substances) to the tissues. Other components of plasma are water, oxygen, nitrogen, fat, carbohydrates, and proteins. Fibrinogen, one of the plasma proteins, helps blood clotting. When blood clots, the liquid portion that remains is serum. Blood serum contains no blood cells.

(2) *Blood cells.* The cellular elements in the blood are red cells (erythrocytes, or rbc), white cells (leucocytes, or wbc) and blood platelets (thrombocytes).

40. Red Blood Cells (Erythrocytes)

There are about 5,000,000 red blood cells in 1 cubic millimeter (cmm.) of blood. (One cmm. is a very small amount, about 1/25 of a drop). When viewed under a microscope, an individual red blood cell is disc-shaped. An rbc is the only mature body cell that has no nucleus; this fact is important in the diagnosis of some blood disease, because immature red blood cells which do have a nucleus under normal circumstances do not appear in the blood. When nucleated rbc are found, there is a special significance since this may indicate a type of anemia. Red cells are formed in the adult by the red bone marrow in special protected bone areas. Millions of red cells are thought to be destroyed daily, either in the liver, the spleen, the lymph nodes, or in the vascular system itself. In a healthy person, the rate of destruction is equaled by the rate of production, so that a red count of about 5,000,000 per cubic millimeter remains constant. Red blood cells have an average life span of about 90 to 120 days before becoming worn out in service.

a. Hemoglobin. A pigment, hemoglobin, gives red cells their color. Hemoglobin (Hgb) has the power to combine with oxygen, carrying it from the lungs to the tissue cells. Hgb assists in transporting carbon dioxide from the cells to the lungs. This transportation of gases (oxygen and carbon dioxide) is the principal function of red cells. The oxygen content gives arterial blood its bright red color. In order to carry oxygen, hemoglobin needs the mineral, iron, which is ordinarily available in a nutritionally adequate diet.

b. Anemia. The condition known as anemia is due to a reduction in number of red cells or a reduction in the hemoglobin content of red cells.

41. White Cells (Leucocytes)

White cells vary in size and shape, and are larger and much fewer in number than red cells. The average number in an adult is 5,000 to 10,000 in 1 cmm. of blood. Their function is primarily one of protection. They can ingest and destroy foreign particles, such as bacteria, in the blood and tissues. This function is called phagocytosis, and the white cells performing it are phagocytes. White cells are capable of ameboid movement and thus can pass through the walls of capillaries into surrounding tissues. This ability to enter tissue makes them very useful in fighting infection—an area of infection is characterized by a great increase of white cells which gather about the site to destroy bacteria. An example of this is seen in an ordinary boil (furuncle). The pus contained in the boil is made up largely of white cells, plus bacteria and dissolved tissue. Many of the white cells are killed in their struggle with invading bacteria.

a. Kinds of White Cells. There are several kinds of white cells. The most numerous, neutrophils, make up about 65 percent of all white cells and are called polymorphonuclear granulocytes. Certain very potent drugs interfere with the formation of these valuable cells, and the condition agranulocytosis (absence of granulocytes) develops. When drugs with this known toxic effect must be used in treatment of a disease, the doctor orders frequent white cell blood counts as an important part of the treatment. Neutrophils are produced by the red bone marrow.

b. Leucocytosis. In various diseases, the number of white cells in the blood stream may increase considerably, especially in acute infections. This increase is leucocytosis, and it is an important body defense response. A common condition where there is a leucocytosis is acute appendicitis. (A subnormal white count is known as leucopenia.)

c. Lymphocytes. Lymphocytes are white cells produced in lymphoid tissue. One type of lymphocyte is a monocyte, the largest white cells.

42. Blood Platelets (Thrombocytes)

Blood platelets, which are smaller than red blood cells, are thought to be fragments of cells formed in the bone marrow. Platelets number about 300,000 per cmm. of blood. Their main function is to aid in the coagulation of blood at the site of a wound. Platelets when injured release a substance to hasten formation of a blood clot.

43. Coagulation of Blood

a. Blood coagulation, or clotting, is the body's major method of preventing excessive loss of blood when the walls of a blood vessel are broken or cut open. When undisturbed, blood circulates in its vascular system without showing a tendency to clot. However, when blood leaves its natural environment, certain physical and chemical factors are changed and it begins to clot almost at once. At first the clot is soft and jellylike, but it soon becomes firm and acts as a plug, preventing the further escape of blood.

b. It takes 3 to 5 minutes for blood to clot, but sometimes it is necessary to hold back the clotting process. This is done with drugs called anticoagulants.

44. Hemorrhage

Hemorrhage is bleeding, particularly excessive bleeding, from blood vessels due to a break in their walls. It may be caused by a wound or by disease. Whatever its cause, it can be a serious threat to life and calls for prompt control. Hemorrhage can occur either externally or internally. External hemorrhage is bleeding that can be seen, such as bleeding from a wound. In external hemorrhage, blood escapes to the outside and spills onto the surface of some part of the body. Internal hemorrhage happens inside the body, spilling blood into tissues, a body cavity, or an organ. It can occur without any blood being seen outside the body. Bleeding in some internal areas is evident, however, when blood accumulates in tissues (forming a hematoma), or is vomited, coughed up, or excreted in urine or feces.

a. Effects of Hemorrhage. The effects of hemorrhage depend on the amount of blood lost, the rate of loss, and the area into which internal bleeding occurs. Generally, blood pressure drops and breathing and pulse rates become rapid. When blood is lost rapidly, as in bleeding from an artery, blood pressure may drop suddenly. If only small vessels are injured and bleeding is slow, a large amount of blood may be lost without an immediate drop in blood pressure.

b. Natural Measures to Control Hemorrhage. When a blood vessel is opened, the body reacts with measures to check bleeding. Two natural body responses to bleeding are clotting of blood and retraction and constriction of blood vessels. The muscle in an injured artery contracts, and if the artery is severed, the contraction pulls the damaged vessel back into the tissues, thus tending to close the leak. As a rule, these natural responses must be helped by artificial means for controlling hemorrhage and for restoring the blood. Artificial means for controlling external hemorrhage include two important first aid measures—elevation of bleeding extremities and applying pressure dressings.

45. Blood Types

All human blood may be divided into four main types or groups—O, A, B, AB. This system of typing is used to prevent incompatible blood transfusion, which causes serious reactions and sometimes death. Certain types of blood are incompatible or not suited to each other if combined. Two bloods are said to be incompatible when the plasma or serum of one blood causes clumping of the cells of the other. Two bloods are said to be compatible and safe for transfusion if the cells of each can be suspended in the plasma or serum of the other without clumping. Blood typing and cross-matching are done by highly trained laboratory technicians. Table 2–2 shows blood compatibilities and incompatibilities.

a. Importance of Blood Types. From table 2–2, it is evident that if the donor's blood is type "O" it is compatible with all types of recipient blood; or, in other words, type "O" is the universal donor. If the recipient's blood is type "AB", it is compatible with all types of donor blood, or, in other words, type "AB" is the universal recipient. When a blood transfusion is given, the blood type of both donor and recipient should be identical, and their compatibility must be proved by a cross-matching test. However, when blood of the same type is not available and death may result if transfusion is delayed, a type "O" donor (universal donor) may be used if the cross-matching is satisfactory.

Table 2-2. Blood Types

Donor	Recipient			
	O	A	B	AB
O	Compatible	Compatible	Compatible	Compatible
A	Incompatible	Compatible	Incompatible	Compatible
B	Incompatible	Incompatible	Compatible	Compatible
AB	Incompatible	Incompatible	Incompatible	Compatible

b. Rh Factor. In addition to blood grouping and cross-matching for compatibility, the Rh factor must be considered. The Rh factor is carried in red cells, and about 85 percent of all individuals have this factor and are, therefore, Rh positive. Individuals who do not have the Rh factor are Rh negative. As a general rule, Rh negative blood can be given to anyone, provided it is compatible in the ABO typing system, but Rh positive blood should not be given to an Rh negative individual.

Section VII. THE RESPIRATORY SYSTEM

46. Introduction

a. The cells of the body require a constant supply of oxygen to carry on the chemical processes necessary to life. As a result of these processes, a waste product, carbon dioxide, is formed that must be removed from the body. Oxygen and carbon dioxide are continually being exchanged, both between the body and the atmosphere and within the body, by the process known as respiration. The system which performs this exchange of gases is the respiratory system.

b. The respiratory system consists of the lungs and a series of air passages that connect the lungs to the outside atmosphere. The organs serving as air passages are the nose, the pharynx, the larynx, the trachea, and the bronchi. They carry air into the depths of the lungs and end there in thin-walled sacs, the alveoli, where carbon dioxide is exchanged for oxygen.

47. Structure and Function of the Respiratory System

a. Nose. The nose consists of two portions, one external and the other internal (nasal cavity). The external nose is a triangular framework of bone and cartilage covered by skin. On its under surface are the nostrils, the two external openings of the nasal cavity. The nasal cavity is divided in two by the nasal septum, and is separated from the mouth by the palate. Inhaled air is warmed, moistened, and filtered by the nasal cavity. The filtering is done by cilia of the mucous membrane lining the nasal passages. Cilia are numerous, long, microscopic processes which beat or wave together and cause movement of materials across the surface and out of the body. Ciliary movement is important in draining the sinuses.

b. Air Sinuses. Air spaces in several bones of the face and head open into the nasal cavity. They serve as resonance chambers in the production of voice and decrease the weight of the skull. These air sinuses (fig. 2–23) take the name of the bone in which they are found. They are lined with mucous membrane continuous with that lining the nasal cavity.

c. Pharynx. The pharynx, or throat, connects the nose and mouth with the lower air passages and esophagus. It is divided into three parts: the nasopharynx, the oropharynx, and the laryngopharynx. It is continued as the esophagus. Both air and food pass through the pharynx. It carries air from the nose to the larynx, food from the mouth to the esophagus. The walls of the pharynx contain masses of lymphoid tissues called the adenoids and tonsils.

d. Larynx. The larynx, or voice box, connects the pharynx with the trachea (fig. 2–23). It is located in the upper and anterior part of the neck. The larynx is shaped like a triangular box. It is made of 9 cartilages joined by ligaments and controlled by skeletal muscles. The thyroid cartilage is the largest. It forms the landmark in the neck called the "Adam's apple." Another of the cartilages is the epiglottis. During swallowing, the epiglottis closes the larynx, the soft palate closes the nasal cavity, and the lips close the mouth. Thus food is forced into the only remaining opening, the esophagus. Except during swallowing or when the throat is voluntarily closed, the air passages are wide open and air is free to pass from the mouth and nose into the lungs. Two membranous bands in the wall of the larynx are called vocal cords. Vibration of the vocal cords produce sounds. The cricoid cartilage, located just below the prominent thyroid cartilage, is joined to the thyroid cartilage by a membrane. The emergency procedure of cricothyroidotomy to produce an airway is performed by puncturing this connecting membrane.

e. Trachea. The trachea, or windpipe, is a tube held open by cartilaginous rings. It carries air from the larynx to the bronchi (fig. 2–24). The trachea is lined with cilia and mucous glands whose secretions provide a sticky film to keep dust and dirt out of the lungs.

f. Bronchi. The trachea divides to form the two bronchi. One bronchus enters each lung and there divides into many small air passages, called bronchioles or bronchial tubes which lead air into the final air spaces within the lungs.

g. The Lungs.

(1) The lungs (fig. 2–24) are the soft, air-filled, essential organs of respiration. They are elastic structures, almost filling the left and right

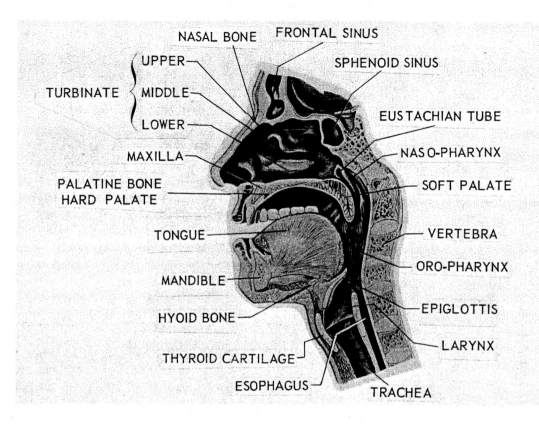

Figure 2-23. Upper respiratory tract.

sections of the thoracic cavity. The upper, pointed margin of each lung, the apex, extends above the clavicle. The lower border, the base, fits upon the dome-shaped surface of the diaphragm. Between the two lungs is the mediastinum (fig. 2–25), the central thoracic cavity containing the heart, great blood vessels, esophagus, and lower trachea. The right lung has three lobes; the left lung has two. Within each lobe are separate branches of the main bronchus, and the lobes themselves are divided into segments. The last subdivisions of the air passages to the lungs are alveoli, which are surrounded by networks of capillaries. The alveoli are air chambers.

(2) Each lung is inclosed by a membranous sac formed of two layers of serous membranes called the pleurae (or singly, pleura). One layer covers the lungs (visceral pleura); the other lines the chest cavity (parietal pleura). If air enters the pleural sac, it expands to form a large cavity and the lung collapses (fig. 2–25). This condition of air in the chest outside the lungs is called pneumothorax. If air can move through a hole into the chest, it is called open pneumothorax, a life-endangering condition. An open pneumothorax can result from a bullet wound, stab wound, or other injury that makes a hole in the chest.

48. Physiological Process of Respiration

The walls of the alveoli are very thin and it is here that oxygen passes into the bloodstream and carbon dioxide is taken from it. This exchange of oxygen and carbon dioxide in the lungs is called external respiration. The oxygen which enters the blood is carried by the red blood cells in chemical combination with hemoglobin. The blood, oxygenated in the lungs, returns to the heart, then is pumped through the arteries to the capillaries. Here oxygen from the blood passes to the tissue cells and carbon dioxide from the cells passes into the blood to be carried back by the veins to the heart. The exchange of gases between the capillary blood and the tissue cells is called internal respiration.

49. Mechanical Process of Respiration

The act of breathing, the cycle of inspiration and expiration, is repeated about 16 to 20 times per minute in an adult at rest. Breathing is regulated primarily by a respiratory center in the brain. The respiratory center is sensitive to changes in blood composition, temperature, and pressure, and adjusts breathing according to the body's needs.

a. Inspiration. This is an active movement. The diaphragm, the large, dome-shaped muscle form-

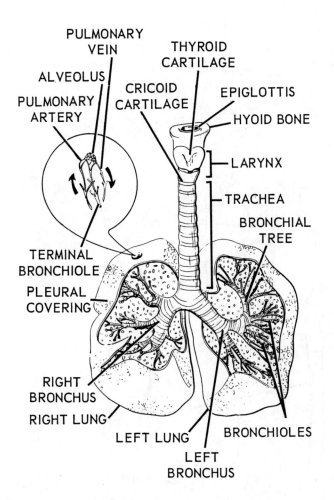

PULMONARY VEIN
ALVEOLUS
PULMONARY ARTERY
CRICOID CARTILAGE
THYROID CARTILAGE
EPIGLOTTIS
HYOID BONE
LARYNX
TRACHEA
BRONCHIAL TREE
TERMINAL BRONCHIOLE
PLEURAL COVERING
RIGHT BRONCHUS
RIGHT LUNG
LEFT LUNG
LEFT BRONCHUS
BRONCHIOLES

Figure 2–24. Lungs and air passages.

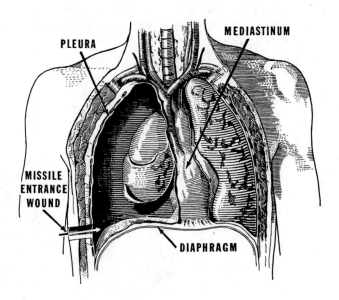

PLEURA
MEDIASTINUM
MISSILE ENTRANCE WOUND
DIAPHRAGM

Figure 2–25. Collapse of lungs by a sucking chest wound.

ing the floor of the thoracic cavity, contracts, flattening its domed upper surface and increasing the size of the cavity. At about the same time, muscles attached to the ribs (intercostals) contract to elevate and spread the ribs. This further increases the size of the cavity. Air rushes into the lungs and they expand, filling the enlarged cavity.

b. Expiration. At rest, during quiet breathing, expiration is a passive movement. The diaphragm, as it relaxes, is forced upward by intra-abdominal pressure. Muscles attached to the ribs relax, permitting the chest to flatten. These actions reduce the size of the thoracic cavity, allowing the elastic recoil of the stretched lungs to drive out the air. More air can be expelled from the lungs by forced expiration. This is done by contraction of the abdominal muscles, forcing the diaphragm upward, and of the muscles attached to the ribs, flattening the chest to compress the lungs and drive out the air. When breathing becomes forced, as with exercise, expiration also becomes active.

c. Volume. About 500 milliliters (1 pint) of air are inhaled during normal respiration. By deep inspiration it is possible to inhale an additional 1,500 milliliters.

d. Sounds. Sounds caused by air moving in the lungs change with some diseases. These changes, heard with a stethoscope, assist in diagnosis of diseases of the lungs such as pneumonia or tuberculosis.

Section VIII.   THE DIGESTIVE SYSTEM

50. Description

a. The digestive system is made up of the alimentary tract (food passage) and the accessory organs of digestion. Its main functions are to ingest and carry food so that digestion and absorption can occur, and to eliminate unused waste material. The products of the accessory organs help to prepare food for its absorption and use (metabolism) by the tissues of the body.

b. Digestion consists of two processes, one mechanical and the other chemical. The mechanical part of digestion includes chewing, swallowing, peristalsis, and defecation. The chemical part of digestion consists of breaking foodstuffs into simple components which can be absorbed and used by the body. In this process, foodstuffs are broken down by enzymes, or digestive juices, formed by digestive glands. Carbohydrates are broken into simple sugar (glucose). Fats are changed into fatty acids. Proteins are converted to amino acids.

51. Structure of Digestive System
   (fig. 2-26)

a. The alimentary canal is about 28 feet long, extending from the lips to the anus, and is divided as follows:

Mouth cavity:
   Teeth
   Tongue

Pharynx
Esophagus
Stomach
Small intestine
Large intestine (colon)
Rectum
Anus

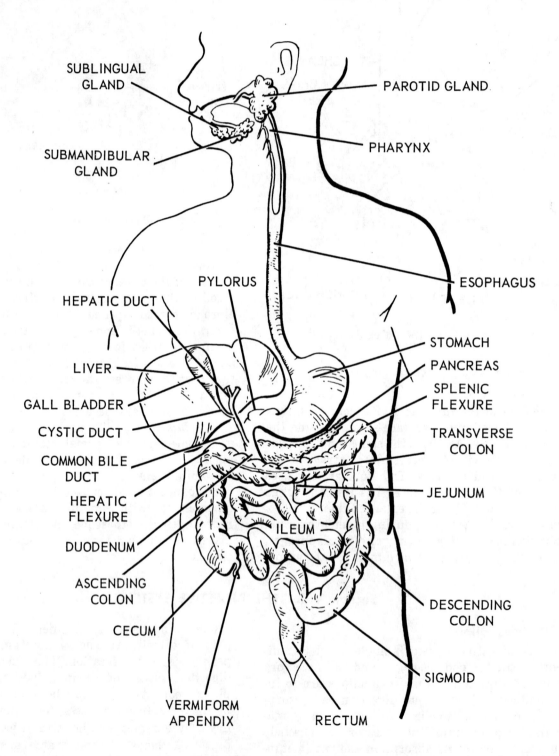

Figure 2-26. Digestive system.

b. The accessory organs that aid the process of digestion are: the salivary glands, pancreas, liver, gall bladder, and intestinal glands.

52. The Mouth

The mouth, or oral cavity, is the beginning of the digestive tract. Here food taken into the body is broken into small particles and mixed with saliva so that it can be swallowed.

a. Teeth.

(1) A person develops two sets of teeth during his life, a deciduous (or temporary) set and a permanent set. There are 20 deciduous teeth and these erupt during the first 3 years of life. They are replaced during the period between the 6th and 14th years by permanent teeth. There are 32 permanent teeth in the normal mouth; 4 incisors, 2 cuspids, 4 bicuspids, and 6 molars in each jaw. Each tooth is divided into two main parts: the crown, that part which is visible above the gums; and the root, that part which is not visible and which is embedded in the bony structure of the jaw. The crown of the tooth is protected by enamel. Tooth decay is from the outside in; once the protective enamel is broken, microorganisms attack the less resistant parts of the tooth.

(2) The primary function of the teeth is to chew or masticate food. Secondarily, the teeth help to modify sound as produced by the larynx and as used in forming words.

b. Salivary Glands. These glands are the first accessory organs of digestion. There are three pairs of salivary glands. They secrete saliva into the mouth through small ducts. One pair, the parotid glands, is located at the side of the face below and in front of the ears. The second pair, the submandibular glands, lies on either side of the mandible. The third pair, the sublingual glands, lies just below the mucous membrane in the floor of the mouth. The flow of saliva is begun in several ways. Placing food in the mouth affects the nerve endings there. These nerve endings stimulate cells of the glands to excrete a small amount of thick fluid. The sight, thought, or smell of food also activates the brain and induces a large flow of saliva. About 1,500 ml. of saliva are secreted daily. The saliva moistens the food, which makes chewing easier. It lubricates the food mass to aid in the act of swallowing. Saliva contains two enzymes, chemical ferments which change foods into simpler elements. The enzymes act upon starches and break them down into sugars.

c. Tongue. The tongue is a muscular organ attached at the back of the mouth and projecting upward into the oral cavity. It is concerned in taste, speech, mastication, salivation, and swallowing. After food has been masticated, the tongue propels it from the mouth into the pharynx. This is the first stage of swallowing. Mucus secreted by glands in the tongue lubricates the food and makes swallowing easier. Taste buds situated in the tongue make it the principal organ of the sense of taste. Stimulation of the taste buds causes secretion of gastric juices needed for the breaking down of food in the stomach.

53. Pharynx

The pharynx is a muscular canal which leads from the nose and mouth to the esophagus. The passage of food from the pharynx into the esophagus is the second stage of swallowing. When food is being swallowed, the larynx is closed off from the pharynx to keep food from getting into the respiratory tract.

54. The Esophagus

The esophagus is a muscular tube about 10 inches long, lined with a mucous membrane. It leads from the pharynx through the chest to the upper end of the stomach (fig. 2–26). Its function is to complete the act of swallowing. The involuntary movement of material down the esophagus is carried out by the process known as peristalsis, which is the wavelike action produced by contraction of the muscular wall. This is the method by which food is moved throughout the alimentary canal.

55. The Stomach

The stomach is an elongated pouchlike structure (fig. 2–26) lying just below the diaphragm, with most of it to the left of the midline. It has three divisions: the fundus, the enlarged portion to the left and above the entrance of the esophagus; the body, the central portion; and the pylorus, the lower portion. Circular sphincter muscles which act as valves guard the opening of the stomach. (The cardiac sphincter is at the esophageal opening, and the pyloric sphincter is at the junction of the stomach and the duodenum, the first portion of the small intestine.) The cardiac sphincter prevents stomach contents from re-entering the esophagus except when vomiting occurs. In the digestive process (fig. 2–27), two of the important functions of the stomach are—

a. It acts as a storehouse for food, receiving fairly large amounts, churning it, and breaking it down further for mixing with digestive juices. Semiliquid food is released in small amounts by the pyloric valve into the duodenum, the first part of the small intestine.

b. The glands in the stomach lining produce gastric juices (which contain enzymes) and hydrochloric acid. The enzymes in the gastric juice start the digestion of protein foods, milk, and fats. Hydrochloric acid aids enzyme action. The mucous membrane lining the stomach protects the stomach itself from being digested by the strong acid and powerful enzymes.

56. Small Intestine

The small intestine is a tube about 22 feet long. The intestine is attached to the margin of a thin band of tissue called the mesentery, which is a portion of the peritoneum, the serous membrane lining the abdominal cavity. The mesentery supports the intestine, and the vessels which carry blood to and from the intestine lie within this membrane. The other edge of the mesentery is drawn together like a fan; the gathered margin is attached to the posterior wall of the abdomen. This arrangement permits folding and coiling of the intestine so that this long organ can be packed into a small space. The intestine is divided into three continuous parts: duodenum, jejunum, and ileum. It receives digestive juices from three accessory organs of digestion: the pancreas, liver, and gall bladder (fig. 2–26).

a. Pancreas. The pancreas is a long, tapering organ lying behind the stomach. The head of the gland lies in the curve of the small intestine near the pyloric valve. The body of the pancreas extends to the left toward the spleen. The pancreas secretes a juice which acts on all types of food. Two enzymes in pancreatic juice act on proteins. Other enzymes change starches into sugars. Another enzyme changes fats into their simplest forms. The pancreas has another important function, the production of insulin (para 2–83).

b. Liver. The liver is the largest organ in the body. It is located in the upper part of the abdomen with its larger (right) lobe to the right of the midline. It is just under the diaphragm and above the lower end of the stomach. The liver has several important functions. One is the secretion of bile, which is stored in the gall bladder and discharged into the small intestine when digestion is

in process. The bile contains no enzymes but it breaks up the fat particles so that enzymes can act faster. The liver performs other important functions. It is a storehouse for the sugar of the body (glycogen) and for iron and vitamin B. It plays a part in the destruction of bacteria and wornout red blood cells. Many chemicals such as poisons or medicines are detoxified by the liver; others are excreted by the liver through bile ducts. The liver manufactures part of the proteins of blood plasma. The blood flow in the liver is of special importance. All the blood returning from the spleen, stomach, intestines, and pancreas is detoured through the liver by the portal vein in the portal circulation (fig. 2–17). Blood drains from the liver by hepatic veins which join the inferior vena cava.

c. Gall Bladder. The gall bladder is a dark green sac, shaped like a blackjack and lodged in a hollow on the underside of the liver. Its ducts join with the duct of the liver to conduct bile to the upper end of the small intestine. The main function of the gall bladder is the storage and concentration of the bile when it is not needed for digestion.

d. Ileum. Most of the absorption of food takes place in the ileum. The walls of the ileum are covered with extremely small, finger-like structures called villi which provide a large surface for absorption. After food has been digested, it is absorbed into the capillaries of the villi. Then it is carried to all parts of the body by the blood and lymph.

57. Large Intestine (Colon)

a. The large intestine is about 5 feet long. The cecum (fig. 2–26), located on the lower right side of the abdomen, is the first portion of the large intestine into which food is emptied from the small intestine. The appendix extends from the lower portion of the cecum and is a blind sac. Although the appendix usually is found lying just below the cecum, by virtue of its free end it can extend in several different directions, depending upon its mobility.

b. The colon extends along the right side of the abdomen from the cecum up to the region of the liver (ascending colon). There the colon bends (hepatic flexure) and is continued across the upper portion of the abdomen (transverse colon) to the spleen. The colon bends again (splenic flexure) and goes down the left side of the abdomen

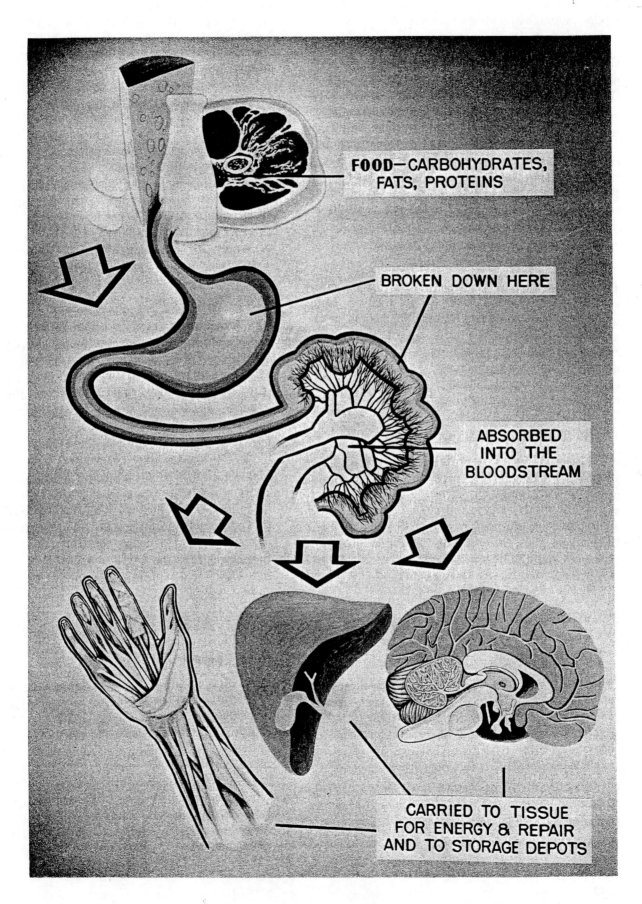

Figure 2-27. Assimilation of food.

(descending colon). The last portion makes an S curve (sigmoid) toward the center and posterior of the abdomen and ends in the rectum.

c. The main function of the large intestine is the recovery of water from the mass of undigested food it receives from the small intestine. As this mass passes through the colon, water is absorbed and returned to the tissues. Waste materials, or feces, become more solid as they are pushed along by peristaltic movements. Constipation is caused by delay in movement of intestinal contents and removal of too much water from them. Diarrhea results when movement of the intestinal contents is so rapid that not enough water is removed.

58. The Rectum and Anus

The rectum is about 5 inches long and follows the curve of the sacrum and coccyx until it bends back into the short anal canal. The anus is the external opening at the lower end of the digestive system. It is kept closed by a strong sphincter muscle. The rectum receives feces and periodically expels this material through the anus. This elimination of refuse is called defecation.

59. Time Required for Digestion

Within a few minutes after a meal reaches the stomach, it begins to pass through the lower valve of the stomach. After the first hour the stomach is half empty, and at the end of the sixth hour none of the meal is present in the stomach. The meal goes through the small intestine, and the first part of it reaches the cecum in 20 minutes to 2 hours. At the end of the sixth hour

most of it should have passed into the colon; in 12 hours all should be in the colon. Twenty-four hours from the time when food is eaten, the meal should reach the rectum. However, part of a meal may be defecated at one time and the rest at another.

60. Absorption of Digested Food
(fig. 2–27)

There is very little absorption in the stomach. Most absorption takes place in the small intestine. The final products of digestion pass through the mucous membrane lining of the gastrointestinal tract and are carried to the liver and from there to the rest of the body. There is marked absorption of water in the large intestine. The residue is concentrated and expelled as feces.

61. Defecation

The passage of feces is called defecation. It is begun voluntarily by contraction of the abdominal muscles. At the same time, the sphincter muscles of the anus relax and there is a peristaltic contraction wave of the colon and rectum. Feces are expelled as a result of all these actions. Feces consist of undigested food residue, secretions from the digestive glands, bile, mucus, and millions of bacteria. Mucus is derived from the many mucous glands which pour secretions into the intestine. Bacteria are especially numerous in the large intestine. They act upon food material, causing putrefaction of proteins and fermentation of carbohydrates. Although the bacteria normally in the large intestine serve a useful purpose internally, they are contaminants outside the intestine.

Section IX.   THE URINARY SYSTEM

62. Description

The urinary system (fig. 2–28), which filters and excretes waste materials from the blood, consists of two kidneys, two ureters, one urinary bladder, and one urethra. The urinary system helps the body maintain its delicate balance of water and various chemicals in the proportions needed for health and survival. During the process of urine formation, waste products are removed from circulating blood for elimination, and useful products are returned to the blood.

63. Kidney

a. The kidneys are bean-shaped organs (fig. 2–28), about 4½ inches long, 2 inches wide, and 1 inch thick. They lie on each side of the spinal column, against the posterior wall of the abdominal cavity, near the level of the last thoracic vertebra and the first lumbar vertebra. The right kidney is usually slightly lower than the left. Near the center of the medial side of each kidney is the central notch or hilum, where blood vessels and nerves enter and leave and from which the ureter leaves.

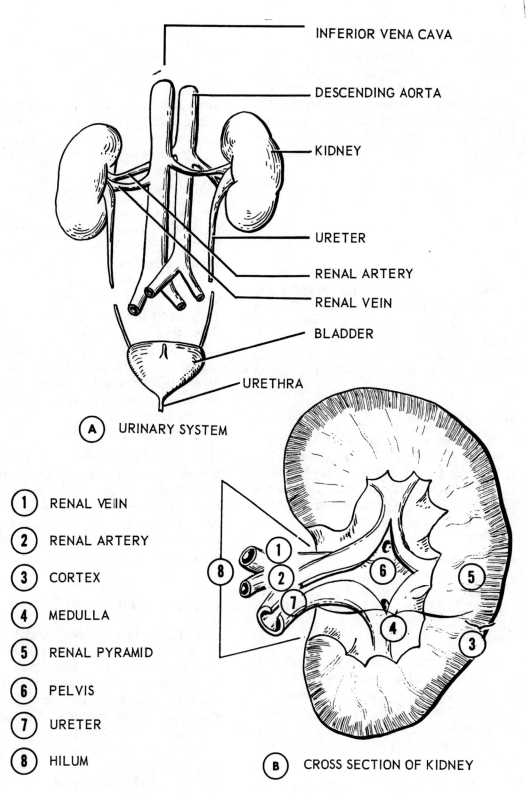

INFERIOR VENA CAVA

DESCENDING AORTA

KIDNEY

URETER

RENAL ARTERY

RENAL VEIN

BLADDER

URETHRA

(A) URINARY SYSTEM

① RENAL VEIN
② RENAL ARTERY
③ CORTEX
④ MEDULLA
⑤ RENAL PYRAMID
⑥ PELVIS
⑦ URETER
⑧ HILUM

(B) CROSS SECTION OF KIDNEY

Figure 2-28. Urinary system and cross section of kidney.

b. The kidney is composed of an outer shell or cortex, and an inner layer, the medulla. The cortex is made of firm, reddish-brown tissue containing millions of microscopic filtration plants, called nephrons. Each nephron is a urine-forming unit. The nephron units receive and filter all the body's blood about once every 12 minutes. During this period, they draw off and filter the liquid portion of blood, remove liquid wastes (urine), and return the usable portion to the circulation to maintain the body's fluid balance.

(1) Nephrons are very complicated struc-

tures. Each nephron has a capsule containing a cluster of capillaries called glomerulus. Leading from the capsule is a continuous looped tubule. The glomerulus filters the blood; the water, salts, waste products, and usable products pass from the capsule to the tubule; usable products and water are reabsorbed; and the final waste product, urine, drains from the last loop of the tubule. The glomerulus, the capsule, and the loops of tubule together form a nephron. Each part is essential for the coordinated filtration, reabsorption, and excretion process.

(2) Channels called collecting tubules form larger tubes and deliver the urine to the pelvis of the kidney.

64. Ureters

The pelvis of each kidney is drained by a ureter, a muscular tube extending from the hilus to the posterior portion of the urinary bladder. Ureters are smooth muscle structures, and urine is passed through each ureter by peristalsis. Drop by drop, urine passes into the bladder. Ureters are about 15 to 18 inches in length and about $1/5$ inch in diameter.

65. Urinary Bladder

The urinary bladder, a muscular sac located in the lowest part of the abdominal cavity, stores urine. Normally it holds 300 to 500 ml. The bladder is emptied by contraction of muscles in its walls which force urine out through the urethra.

66. Urethra

The urethra is the tube that carries urine from the urinary bladder to the external opening, the urinary meatus. In the male, the urethra will vary in length. Including the portion within the body, it is approximately 6 to $7\frac{1}{2}$ inches in length. It is divided into three areas: the prostatic which passes through the prostate gland; the membranous area, beneath the prostate; and the penile area (anterior), which passes through the penis (para 2–85). The female urethra, about $1\frac{1}{2}$ inch long, extends from the bladder to the meatus, which is located above the vaginal opening.

67. Urine

Normal urine is an aromatic, transparent (clear) fluid. The color of normal urine varies from amber or pale yellow to a brownish hue. Freshly voided urine has a characteristic aromatic odor, while stale urine has strong ammonia odor. The average quantity of urine excreted by a normal adult in 24 hours ranges from 1,500 to 2,000 ml., depending upon the fluid intake, amount of perspiration, and other factors. Urine contains protein wastes (urea), salts in solution, hormones, and pigments. (Normal urine should not contain blood, albumin, sugar, or pus cells.)

68. Urination

Urination is the discharge or voiding of urine. It is done by a contraction of the bladder and relaxation of the sphincters. In the adult, the act of voiding, although dependent on involuntary reflexes, is partly under voluntary control. Voluntary contraction of abdominal muscles usually accompanies and aids urination.

Section X. THE NERVOUS SYSTEM

69. General

a. The nervous system has two major functions, communication and control. It enables the individual to be aware of and to react to his environment. It coordinates the body's responses to stimuli and keeps body systems working together. (Stimuli are changes in environment that require adjustment of body activities.)

b. The nervous system consists of nerve centers and of nerves that branch off from them and lead to tissues and organs. Most nerve centers are in the brain and spinal cord. Nerves carry impulses from tissues and organs to nerve centers, and from these centers to tissues and organs. The neu-rons that carry impulses from the skin and other sense organs to the central nervous system are sensory neurons. They make the body aware of its environment. The neurons that carry impulses from the central nervous system to muscles and glands are motor neurons. They cause the body to react to its environment.

c. For study, parts of the nervous system may be considered separately as: the central nervous system, which consists of the brain and spinal cord; the peripheral nervous system, where the nerves are located outside the brain and spinal cord; and the autonomic nervous system, which influences the activities of involuntary muscle and gland tissue.

70. The Neuron and Nerves

a. The basic unit of the nervous system is the neuron, a cell specialized to respond to stimuli by transmitting impulses. Neurons differ in shape and function from all other body cells. Each neuron has three parts: a cell body and two kinds of processes extending from it (fig. 2–2 ⓓ). Many branched processes, the dendrites, conduct impulses toward the cell body. A single process, the axon, conducts impulses away from the cell body. Impulses are the messages carried by the processes. All communication between nerve cells is carried out through these dendrites and axons at the region of contact (synapse) between processes of 2 adjacent neurons.

b. The neuron processes, whether dendrite or axon, are called fibers. These nerve fibers are wrapped in an insulating material, the myelin sheath. In addition to the myelin sheath, nerve fibers that extend outside the brain and spinal cord (peripheral nerves) have an outside wrapping called neurilemma. The neurilemma and the nerve cell body are essential for nerve regeneration following injury. In time, if the nerve cell body has not been destroyed, a peripheral nerve fiber can regenerate.

c. Nerve cells and nerve processes are bound together and supported by special connective tissue cells called neuroglia. Neuroglia literally means nerve glue. Several different kinds of neuroglia cells help form nerve tissue.

d. Nerves, which appear as whitish cords, are bundles of nerve fibers bound together by a connective tissue sheath.

71. The Central Nervous System

The central nervous system (CNS) consists of the brain and spinal cord. These are delicate structures that are protected by two coverings, bones and special membranes. The brain is encased by the bones of the skull that form the cranium; the spinal cord by the vertebrae. The membranes enclosing both brain and spinal cord are the meninges.

a. The Meninges. Three layers of protective membranes, the meninges, surround the brain and spinal cord. The outer layer of strong fibrous tissue is called the dura mater. The middle layer of delicate cobwebby tissue is the arachnoid. The innermost layer, adherent to the outer surface of the brain and spinal cord, is the pia mater. Between the dura mater and arachnoid is the sub-dural space; between the arachnoid and pia mater is the subarachnoid space.

b. Cerebrospinal Fluid. In addition to protective bones and membranes, nature provides a cushion of fluid around and within the subarachnoid space, in the spaces within the brain called the ventricles, and in the central canal of the spinal cord. Cerebrospinal fluid, which is similar to lymph, filters out from networks of capillaries in the ventricles. It is formed constantly, circulated constantly, and part of it is reabsorbed constantly into the venous blood of the brain. At any one time, an adult has about 135 ml. of this fluid circulating, although over 500 ml. is produced daily. If anything interferes with its circulation or its reabsorption, the fluid accumulates. An abnormal accumulation of cerebrospinal fluid is hydrocephalus (water on the brain).

c. The Brain. The brain (fig. 2–29), a mass of nervous tissue, is the highest level of the nervous system. It coordinates activities of the entire body; carries on the learning, thinking, and reasoning processes; and directs voluntary movements of the body. The brain may be divided into three parts: the cerebrum, cerebellum, and the brain-stem, the last consisting of the forebrain, midbrain, pons, and medulla. The midbrain serves as a connecting pathway between the right and left halves of the cerebrum and also between the cerebellum and the rest of the brain.

(1) *Cerebrum.* The cerebrum is described as resembling many small sausages bound together. It is the largest part of the brain, divided, not quite completely, into two hemispheres. Each hemisphere has five lobes. The outer surface, or cortex, of the brain is made up of gray matter, which is composed of nerve cells. The white matter within the brain is made up of nerve fibers, which lead to and from the cell bodies in the gray matter. Certain areas of the cerebrum are localized for certain functions, but it is believed that no one area functions independently. In the frontal lobe is the motor area, which controls voluntary movements, the speech center, and the writing center. In the parietal lobe is the general sensory area which perceives sensations of heat, cold, touch, pressure, pain, and position. In the temporal lobe are the centers for hearing and smelling. In the occipital lobe is the visual center.

(2) *Cerebellum.* The cerebellum lies below the posterior part of the cerebrum. It coordinates muscular activity at an unconscious level. It also

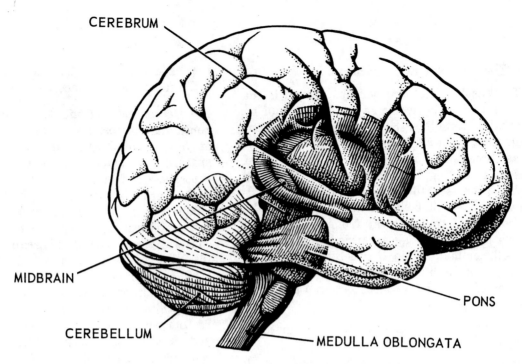

CEREBRUM

MIDBRAIN

CEREBELLUM

PONS

MEDULLA OBLONGATA

Figure 2-29. The brain, sagittal section.

coordinates with the cerebrum to produce skilled movements. The cerebellum helps control posture and controls skeletal muscles to maintain equilibrium. If the cerebellum is injured, movements will be jerky and trembly.

(3) *The pons.* The pons is a bridgelike structure, forming the part of the brain stem above the medulla. Nerve pathways between the spinal cord and other parts of the brain go through the pons.

(4) *The medulla.* The medulla oblongata, a bulblike structure attaching the brain to the spinal cord, is a part of the brain stem. It contains vital centers controlling heart action, blood vessel diameter, and respirations. Mechanisms controlling nonvital functions such as sneezing, hiccoughing, and vomiting are also functions of the medulla. Nerve fibers cross from one side to the other in the medulla, a fact that explains why one side of the brain is said to control the opposite side of the body.

d. The Spinal Cord. The spinal cord, protected by meninges and vertebrae, is about 18 inches in length. The cord is continuous with the medulla of the brain and terminates at a level between the first and second lumbar vertebrae (fig. 2-9).

(1) The meninges inclosing the cord continue down below the termination of the cord and are anchored at the sacrum and coccyx. This anatomical feature makes it possible for a physician to withdraw samples of cerebrospinal fluid without

danger of injuring the cord. When a patient is placed on his side and his back is arched by drawing his knees and chest together, the space between the fourth and fifth lumbar vertebrae is enlarged. A lumbar puncture needle can be inserted through the intervertebral space into the subarachnoid space to obtain spinal fluid for diagnostic tests. This feature also makes it possible to administer spinal anesthesia.

(2) The spinal cord has two major functions —conduction and connection. Many nerves enter and leave the spinal cord at different levels. These nerves all connect with nerve centers located within the spinal cord or with nerve centers in the brain. Nerve centers within the cord form the gray matter of the cord's inner core. Surrounding the gray matter are columns of nerve fibers, forming the white matter. The nerve fiber columns in the spinal cord are called tracts; these tracts connect the different levels of the nervous system. Tracts which transmit upward, the ascending tracts, are all sensory nerve fibers. Tracts which transmit impulses downward, the descending tracts, are all motor nerve fibers, controlling both voluntary and involuntary muscles. When the spinal cord is damaged, the extent of disability depends upon which nerve centers and which tracts are damaged.

(3) The soft spinal cord can be compressed by vertebrae fractures or by dislocation and displacement of vertebrae or vertebrae discs. If the

pressure can be relieved by surgical procedures or by traction, permanent damage may be avoided. Careful and knowledgeable moving and transporting of all patients suspected of having a spinal injury is essential to minimize injury to the spinal cord. If the cord is severed, or if all cord tracts have been damaged, patients lose feeling because sensory impulses cannot reach the brain; they are paralyzed, because motor impulses from the brain can no longer reach muscles located below the injury. Damage to the cord in the cervical area is particularly disabling because all of the cord tracts below the injury are involved. Disease, injury, or chemicals (drugs) can cause loss of function by interrupting the conduction and connection pathways.

(4) All sensory impulses coming into the cord do not have to travel all the way to the brain to get a motor impulse reaction. The gray matter in the spinal cord contains reflex centers, the places where incoming sensory impulses become outgoing motor impulses. There are reflex centers in both the brain and the spinal cord. The knee jerk is an example of a spinal cord reflex. When the doctor taps the patellar tendon, the sensation is transmitted to a segment of the spinal cord at the lumbar level, and a motor impulse causes extension of the lower leg. This kind of reflex is an involuntary response. If lumbar segments of the cord are damaged, the knee jerk is absent. The doctor tests for these different reflexes during a neurological examination because in certain diseases they deviate from normal.

72. The Peripheral Nervous System

The peripheral nervous system is composed of the nerves located outside the brain and spinal cord. Cranial nerves and their branches stem from the brain; spinal nerves and their branches stem from the spinal cord.

a. The Cranial Nerves. The 12 pairs of cranial nerves arise from the undersurface of the brain and pass through openings in the skull to their destinations (table 2–3). The nerves are numbered and have names that describe their distribution or their function; *for example,* the vagus nerve (fig. 2–30), the cranial nerve, is an important nerve in the autonomic nervous system, with both sensory and motor fibers distributed to organs in the thorax and abdomen. The cranial nerves supply organs of special sense, such as the eye, nose, ears, tongue, and their associated muscles, and also control muscles of the face, neck, thorax, and abdomen.

NOTE
Cranial nerves are usually indicated by Roman numerals.

b. The Spinal Nerves. The 31 pairs of spinal nerves arise from the spinal cord and pass through lateral openings between the vertebrae. Spinal nerves are numbered according to the level of the spinal column at which they emerge. The lumbar, sacral, and coccygeal nerves descend from the terminal end of the spinal cord and emerge in sequence from their respective vertebrae. These lower spinal nerves form the cauda equina (horse's tail) within the spinal cavity. Spinal nerves branch and subdivide into many lesser nerves after emerging from the spinal cavity.

(1) *Nerve plexuses.* A nerve plexus is a network of spinal nerve subdivisions that appear as tangled masses in areas outside the spinal cord. The brachial plexus (fig. 2–30) is in the shoulder region. Nerves emerging from this tangle go to the skin, the arm, and the hand. Pressure and/or

Table 2–3. The 12 Cranial Nerves

Number and name	Origin	Associated with—
I. Olfactory (sensory)	Nasal chamber	Sense of smell
II. Optic (sensory)	Retina	Sense of sight
III. Oculomotor (motor)	Midbrain	Eyeball muscles
IV. Trochlear (motor)	Midbrain	Eyeball muscles
V. Trigeminal (sensory and mixed).	Pons	(Three branches) eye, upper portion of face, ear, lower lip, teeth, gums.
VI. Abducens (motor)	Pons	Eyeball muscles
VII. Facial (mixed)	Pons	Facial muscles, middle ear, taste
VIII. Auditory (sensory)	Pons	Sense of hearing and balance
XI. Glossopharyngeal (mixed)	Medulla	Taste, swallowing
X. Vagus (mixed)	Medulla	Swallowing, hunger, speech muscles, breathing, heart rate, peristalsis, control of glands in stomach and pancreas.
XI. Spinal accessory (motor)	Medulla	Muscles of neck and upper back.
XII. Hypoglossal (motor)	Medulla	Muscles of tongue

stretching of the brachial plexus can cause paralysis of the arm and hand. If an unconscious patient's arm is allowed to dangle off a litter or bed, the plexus can be overstretched. Pressure from a plaster cast can also damage this area. The sacral plexus in the pelvic cavity supplies nerves to the lower extremity. The largest nerve in the body, the sciatic nerve, emerges from the sacral plexus. From the buttocks, the sciatic nerve runs down the back of the thigh; its branches supply posterior thigh muscles, leg, and foot. The sciatic nerve must be avoided when intramuscular injections are given into the buttocks.

(2) *Nerve fibers.* All spinal nerves carry both sensory and motor fibers. Some of the fibers supply skeletal muscle and others supply visceral (smooth) muscle. The spinal nerves are two-way conductors, and if anything happens to them, there can be both anesthesia, loss of sensation, and paralysis, loss of motion.

73. The Autonomic Nervous System

The autonomic nervous system is part of the nervous system that sends nerve fibers from nerve centers to smooth muscle, cardiac muscle, and gland tissue. Autonomic nerve fibers supply nerve impulses to body structures that are thought of as operating outside conscious control. Organs supplied are the heart, blood vessels, iris and ciliary muscles of the eye, bronchial tubes, parts of the esophagus, and abdominal organs. The autonomic nervous system is a part of the central and peripheral nervous system. It is not separate and independent. It has two divisions, sympathetic and parasympathetic. These divisions receive impulses from the CNS by way of the ganglia.

a. Ganglia are the relay stations of the autonomic nervous system. Neurons originating in the cord, or in the brain, conduct impulses to an autonomic ganglion. Other neurons conduct impulses from the ganglion to the tissue or organ. Ganglia of the sympathetic division are in a chain formation, like a string of beads, one on each side of the spinal column. Ganglia of the parasympathetic division are located in or near the organs to which they send impulses (table 2–4).

b. The sympathetic division regulates activities to prepare the body for maximum effort as a response to hazardous conditions. Sympathetic stimulation and response to stress go together.

c. The parasympathetic division regulates activities to conserve energy and to promote digestion and elimination.

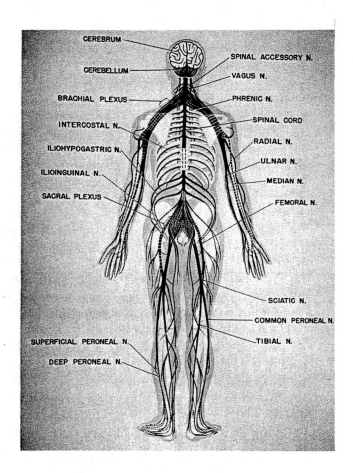

Figure 2–30. Principal nerve trunks.

74. Special Senses

Sensations of smell, taste, sight, hearing, and equilibrium are usually referred to as special senses because these sensations are received through specialized sense organs or receptors which are sensitive to specific types of stimuli. Other very important sensations such as touch, pressure, pain, heat, and cold are received through receptors widely distributed in the skin and underlying tissue and in viscera. Impulses from receptors for both special and other senses are carried by sensory nerve pathways to the cerebrum. There the impulses are converted into sensation and perception (awareness or consciousness of sensation). The parts of the sensory mechanism are (1) the sense organ or receptor, (2) the pathway by which the impulse is conducted into the central nervous system, and (3) the sensory center in the cerebrum. The sensory mechanisms of the special senses are summarized as follows:

a. Smell. Cells located in the olfactory membrane of the nose are stimulated by odors. The olfactory membrane is located in the uppermost part of the nose, in the area above the upper turbinates. Impulses from receptors for odors are

Table 2-4. *Functions of the Autonomic Nervous System*

Increased sympathetic tone results in—	Increased parasympathetic tone results in—
1. Dilation of pupils.	1. Contraction of pupils.
2. Decreased tones of ciliary muscles, so that the eyes are accommodated to see distant objects.	2. Contraction of ciliary muscles, so that the eyes are accommodated to see objects near at hand.
3. Dilation of bronchial tubes.	3. Contraction of bronchial tubes.
4. Quickened and strengthened heart action.	4. Slowed heart action.
5. Contraction of blood vessels of the skin and viscera so that more blood goes to the muscles where it is needed for "fight or flight."	5. Dilation of blood vessels.
6. Relaxation of gastrointestinal tract and bladder.	6. Increased contractions of gastrointestinal tract and muscle tone of bladder.
7. Decreased secretions of glands (except sweat glands which secrete more).	7. Increased secretions of glands (except sweat glands).
8. Contraction of sphincters which prevents emptying of bowels and bladder.	8. Relaxation of sphincters which allows emptying of bowels or bladder.

transmitted by the olfactory nerve to the temporal lobe of the brain. Although olfactory receptor cells are quite sensitive, they can also become fatigued, and odors that at first may be very noticeable may be less so upon continued exposure. Smell is considered a primitive sense and the detection of odors is more highly developed in animals than in man.

b. Taste. Sense organs for taste are taste buds located in the surface of the tongue. The primary taste sensations are sweet, sour, salty and bitter. The actual sensation of taste, particularly for distinctive flavors, is influenced by the sense of smell. Taste sensation is usually dulled when nasal membranes are congested or when the nostrils are pinched shut while eating foods. Impulses from taste receptors are transmitted by nerve fibers from two cranial nerves, facial and glossopharyngeal, to the temporal lobe.

c. Sight. Cells in the retina of the eye (fig. 2-3 Ⓐ) are stimulated by light rays entering the eye. These stimuli create impulses that are carried by the optic nerve to the visual center of the occipital lobe of the brain.

d. Hearing. Cells in the cochlea of the inner ear (fig. 2-32 Ⓑ) are stimulated by vibration of sound waves. These stimuli create impulses that are carried by the cochlear branch of the acoustic (auditory) nerve to the auditory center of the temporal lobe.

e. Equilibrium. In addition to receptors for hearing, the internal ear contains three semicircular canals which regulate the sense of equilibrium. Change in position of the head causes movement of fluid within the canals. The fluid movement stimulates nerve endings in the walls of the canals which send impulses to the brain by the vestibular branch of the auditory nerve.

75. The Eye

The eye is specialized for the reception of light. Each eye is located in a bony socket or cavity called the orbit, which is formed by several bones in the skull. The orbit provides protection, support, and attachment for the eye and its muscles, nerves, and blood vessels.

a. The Eyeball. The interior of the eye (fig. 2-31 Ⓐ) is divided into an anterior cavity (anterior to the lens) and a posterior cavity (posterior to the lens). A clear watery solution, the aqueous fluid, is formed and circulated in the anterior cavity. A transparent, semifluid material, the vitreous fluid, is contained in the posterior cavity. The globular form and firmness of the eyeball is maintained by its fluid contents, which also function in the transmission of light.

(1) *Eye tissue coats.* The eyeball has an outer coat, a middle coat, and an inner coat.

(a) *Outer coat.* The outer coat consists of a normally invisible, transparent anterior portion, the cornea, and a fibrous, white, nontransparent portion, the sclera, which is directly continuous with the cornea. The transparent cornea focuses and transmits light to the interior of the eye. The surface of the cornea must be moist at all times to maintain its transparency. The sclera helps to maintain the shape of the eyeball and protects the delicate structures within.

(b) *Middle coat.* The middle coat consists of the choroid, the iris, and the ciliary body. These three structures are referred to as the uveal tract. The choroid, the vascular middle layer of the eyeball, lies beneath the sclera and lines the posterior portion of the eye from the ciliary body to the optic nerve. The iris is a circular, colored, muscular membrane which is suspended between

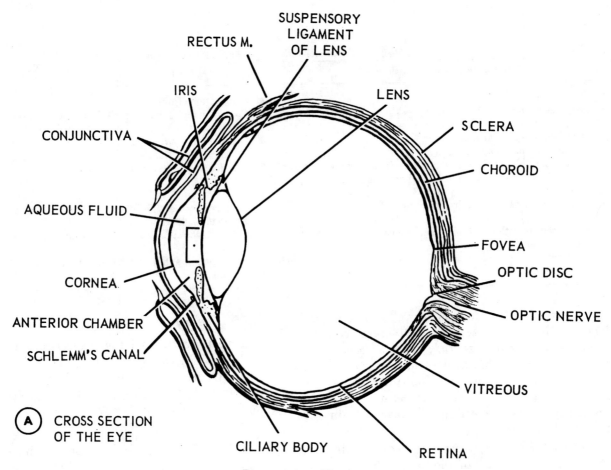

RECTUS M.

SUSPENSORY
LIGAMENT
OF LENS

IRIS

CONJUNCTIVA

LENS

SCLERA

CHOROID

AQUEOUS FLUID

FOVEA

OPTIC DISC

CORNEA

OPTIC NERVE

ANTERIOR CHAMBER

SCHLEMM'S CANAL

VITREOUS

(A) CROSS SECTION
OF THE EYE

CILIARY BODY

RETINA

Figure 2–31. The eye.

the cornea and the lens. The pigment material in the iris gives the eye its characteristic color. The round opening in its center is the pupil. The muscle structure of the iris adjusts the size of the pupil to adapt the eye to existing brightness of light. The ciliary body lies between the iris and choroid; it has a muscular function, changing the focus of the lens, and a secretory function, producing aqueous fluid.

(c) *Inner coat.* The inner coat is the retina, which lines the interior of the eye except toward its anterior inner surface. The visual nerve cells (rods and cones) are arranged closest together at the central portion of the retina, the macula lutea. A slight depression in the macula lutea, the fovea centralis, is in a direct line back from the center of the cornea and lens and is the area of the retina most sensitive to light. Medial to the fovea centralis is the area called the optic disc, the site of exit of the optic nerve and entry of the retinal artery. Here there is a natural defect in the retina; there are no visual cells at the exit of the optic nerve and in every eye there is, therefore, a physiological "blind spot." When the doctor examines

the interior of the eye with an ophthalmoscope, he can see the posterior surface of the retina and examine the appearance of the optic disc. The inner surface of the retina is in contact with the vitreous and the outer surface with the choroid. The condition known as "detached retina" means that some portion of the retina has become separated from the supporting choroid.

(2) *The lens.* The lens is a small, disc-shaped, transparent structure about 1/3 inch in diameter. It is situated immediately behind the iris and in front of the vitreous cavity. The lens is suspended in a capsule within the globe of the eye by a circular ligament, the suspensory ligament of the lens. This ligament is attached to the ciliary body. Muscular movements of the ciliary body affect the suspensory ligament and the consequent focus of the lens. The condition of "cataract" means that some portion of the lens has lost its transparency and has become cloudy or opaque.

(3) *Aqueous fluid.* The aqueous fluid is formed by a portion of the ciliary body and fills the two divisions of the anterior cavity of the eye, called the anterior and the posterior chamber.

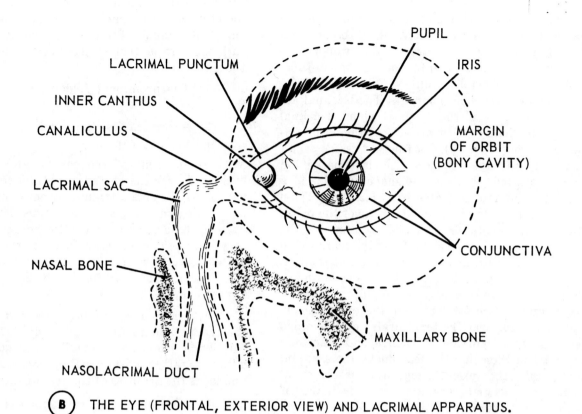

LACRIMAL PUNCTUM

INNER CANTHUS

CANALICULUS

LACRIMAL SAC

NASAL BONE

NASOLACRIMAL DUCT

PUPIL

IRIS

MARGIN
OF ORBIT
(BONY CAVITY)

CONJUNCTIVA

MAXILLARY BONE

Ⓑ   THE EYE (FRONTAL, EXTERIOR VIEW) AND LACRIMAL APPARATUS.

Figure 2–31—Continued.

Aqueous fluid is normally crystal clear for transmission of light rays and its formation and flow helps maintain the normal intraocular pressure. The aqueous fluid flows from the posterior chamber to the anterior chamber and drains by means of a series of channels into the venous blood. The largest of these drainage channels is the canal of Schlemm. Interference with the normal formation and flow of aqueous fluid can lead to development of excessively high intraocular pressure, a condition called glaucoma. Glaucoma will cause blindness. Fortunately, glaucoma can be detected by a tonometry examination, the measurement of internal eye pressure by means of a measuring instrument, a tonometer. With early detection, glaucoma can be treated successfully and blindness can be prevented.

b. *The External Eye and Accessory Structures.* Viewed from the surface of the body, the anterior surface of the eye and some of its accessory structures such as eyebrows, lids, lashes, and conjunctiva are readily visible. An additional essential accessory structure, the lacrimal (tear) apparatus, is indicated in figure 2–31 Ⓑ.

(1) *Eyebrows and eyelashes.* The eyebrow and lashes are usually considered to have a cosmetic (decorative) function, but the eyelashes also help protect against the entrance of foreign objects into the eyes. An eyelash becomes a foreign body itself if it becomes detached and falls on the eye surface. On the margin of the eyelids near the attachment of the eyelashes are the openings of a number of glands. Infection in these glands is commonly called a sty.

(2) *Eyelids.* The eyelids are thin, moveable, protective coverings for the eyes. The junctions of the upper and lower eyelids of each eye are canthi; the inner canthus (fig. 2–31 Ⓑ) is at the nasal junction and the outer canthus is at the temporal junction. A sheet of connective tissue called the tarsal plate maintains the shape of the eyelids. The tarsal plate and the orbicularis oculi muscle hold the eyelids in proper position against the eye; a levator (lifting) muscle opens the upper lid by pulling the lid upward into the orbit. The circular orbicularis oculi muscle closes the eyelids.

(3) *Conjunctiva.* The conjunctiva (fig. 2–31 Ⓑ) is a delicate mucous membrane which lines the inside of the eyelids and covers the front surface of the eyeball, continuing over the cornea as the corneal epithelium. The edge or margin where the conjunctiva overlaps the cornea is called the limbus; it is sometimes visible at the periphery of

the iris. The semitransparent conjunctiva appears while on the front surface of the eyeball where it covers the sclera and pink where it overlies lid tissue. Should the conjunctiva itself become inflamed or infected it appears red and swollen; one type of acute bacterial infection of the conjunctiva is commonly called "pinkeye."

(4) *The lacrimal apparatus.* The lacrimal apparatus consists of the lacrimal gland, lacrimal ducts (canaliculi), lacrimal sac, and the nasolacrimal duct (fig. 2–31 Ⓑ). Its function is the secretion and drainage of tears. The lacrimal gland (not illustrated) is about the shape and size of a small almond and is located in a small depression on the lateral side of the frontal bone of the orbit. Many small ducts drain tears secreted by the gland to the conjunctival surface; the tears drain downward and toward the inner angle of the eye. The normal regular blinking of the eyelids helps to spread the tears evenly to provide a lubricating, protective, moist film over the exposed surface of the cornea. The tears drain into openings near the nasal portion of each eyelid (lacrimal puncti) and then into the tear ducts, the sac, and finally into the nose through the nasolacrimal duct. This normal formation and drainage of tears is the natural way in which the eye surface is kept clean and moist.

(5) *Extraocular muscles.* In addition to the levator muscles of the eyelids and the orbicularis oculi, there are six sets of muscles located outside the eyeball. These muscles raise, lower, or rotate the eyeball within its socket. The muscles of the two eyes normally function in a coordinated manner so that both eyes move simultaneously and are aimed in the same direction. Divergence or crossing of the eyes is called strabismus.

76. The Ear

The ear, the organ of hearing, consists of three parts; the external ear, the middle ear (tympanic cavity), and the internal ear (the labyrinth). These divisions are commonly referred to as the outer ear, the middle ear, and the inner ear. They provide the reception and conduction of sound and contain one of the principal mechanisms for the maintenance of equilibrium. The structures of the ear, except the part protruding from the head, are situated within portions of the temporal bone of the skull.

a. The external ear (fig. 2–32 Ⓐ) consists of the shell-shaped portion of the ear, called the auricle or pinna, which projects from the side of the head and of the external acoustic meatus, which is the external auditory canal leading inward to-

ward the middle ear. The principal function of the external ear is the collection and conduction of sound waves to the middle and the inner ear. The auricle or pinna is composed of cartilage covered with membrane (called the perichondrium) and the skin.

(1) The prominent folded rim of the ear is the helix.

(2) A deep cavity, the concha, leads into the external auditory canal.

(3) In front of the concha and projecting backward over the entrance to the external auditory canal is a small, triangular eminence of cartilage called the tragus. The tragus protects, but does not touch, the entrance to the external auditory canal. The undersurface of the tragus is usually covered with soft hairs which help to prevent insects and other foreign bodies from entering the ear.

(4) The lobule, or lobe, is located inferior to the tragus and to the lowest point of the helix. The lobule contains no cartilage, is composed of adipose (fatty) tissue and of connective tissue, and lacks the firmness of the rest of the auricle.

b. The external auditory canal extends about 1¼ inches from its entrance at the bottom of the concha to the tympanic membrane, or eardrum, which closes its inner end. The canal is formed of two parts, its outer, or cartilaginous, part which is formed of cartilage and membrane; and its inner, or bony portion, formed by a passage in the temporal bone. The cartilage of the auricle is continuous with that forming the outer portion of the canal.

(1) Two or more deep fissures are present in

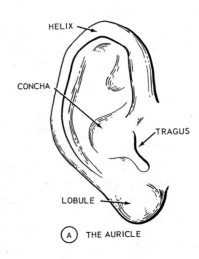

Figure 2–32. The ear.

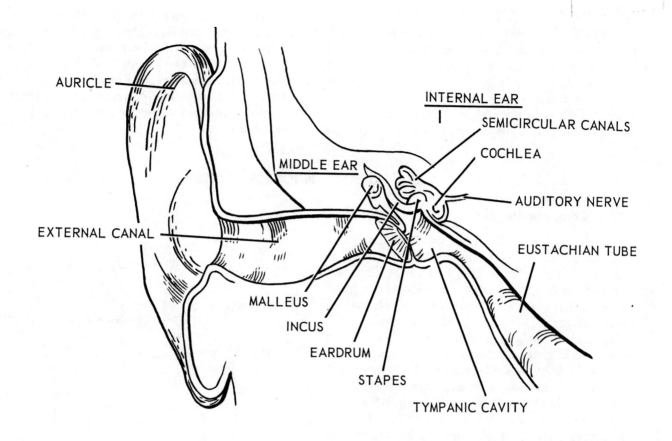

AURICLE

INTERNAL EAR

SEMICIRCULAR CANALS

COCHLEA

MIDDLE EAR

AUDITORY NERVE

EXTERNAL CANAL

EUSTACHIAN TUBE

MALLEUS

INCUS

EARDRUM

STAPES

TYMPANIC CAVITY

B   THE EXTERNAL, MIDDLE, AND INTERNAL EAR, FRONTAL VIEW

Figure 2-32—Continued

the anterior wall of the cartilaginous portion of the canal and are filled with fibrous membrane which allows for the flexibility of the canal. If the auricle (helix area) is pulled up and back, this portion of the canal straightens and may be examined or treated more easily. The entire passage is lined with skin. Near the entrance of the canal, the skin contains wax-producing glands and hair follicles. This wax, called cerumen, also helps to prevent the entry of foreign objects into the ear.

(2) The tympanic membrane, or eardrum, separates the inner end of the canal from the middle ear. The medical officer examines the external canal and the eardrum by means of a lighted instrument, an otoscope. The normal eardrum is translucent (partly transparent) and shiny gray (pearl-like). When inflamed, it appears pink or dull red.

c. The middle ear (tympanic cavity) is an irregular space in the temporal bone filled with air and containing the three ossicles of the ear: malleus (hammer), incus (anvil), and stapes (stirrup).

These bones conduct vibrations from the eardrum to the internal ear.

(1) The eustachian tube which connects the middle ear with the nasopharynx is about 1½ inches long. The trumpet-shaped opening of the eustachian tube into the pharynx remains closed except during the act of yawning or of swallowing, when it opens to admit air into the middle ear, thus performing its principal function of keeping the air pressure equal on either side of the eardrum. This is also an avenue of infection by which disease spreads from the throat to the middle ear.

(2) The roof or superior wall of the middle ear is composed of a very thin plate of bone which separates it from the dura. This bony plate is quite susceptible to fracture in head trauma and to spread of infection from the middle ear (otitis media), either of which can result in intracranial disease.

d. Internal ear (labyrinth). The internal ear contains receptors for hearing and equilibrium.

The receptor for hearing, the organ of Corti, lies within a structure called the cochlea which is coiled and resembles the shell of a snail.

(1) Sound waves, which pass through the external auditory canal, vibrate the eardrum and ossicles and are finally transmitted through the fluid of the inner ear. Nerve impulses travel through the acoustic (auditory) nerve from the organ of Corti to the auditory center of the cerebral cortex. The acoustic nerve is the final link in the chain of mechanisms which convey the sensation of sound to the brain for perception.

(2) The internal ear also contains three semicircular canals which control equilibrium. Change in the position of the head causes movement of the fluid within the canals and this fluid movement stimulates nerve endings in the wall of the canal. These nerve endings serve as receptors and transmit impulses along the acoustic nerve to the cerebellum.

Section XI. THE ENDOCRINE SYSTEM

77. Components

The endocrine system is made up of glands classified as glands of internal secretion (ductless glands). These glands are located in different parts of the body (fig. 2–33). Secretions produced by endocrine glands are hormones, which are secreted directly into the circulating blood, reach every part of the body, and influence the activities of specific organs and tissues, as well as the activities of the body as a whole. Small in quantity but powerful in action, hormones are part of the body's chemical coordinating and regulating system. There are six recognized endocrine glands—the thyroid, parathyroid, adrenals, pituitary (hypophysis), the testes or ovaries (male or female gonads, the glands of sex), and the pancreas.

78. The Thyroid

The thyroid gland, located in front of the neck, has two lobes, one on either side of the larynx. The hormone produced by the thyroid is thyroxin. This hormone is associated with metabolism, regulating heat and energy production in body cells. Thyroid gland cells need a mineral, iodine, to manufacture thyroxin. Iodine is ordinarily obtained from foods included in normal diet; however, certain geographical areas have an iodine deficiency. In these areas, iodized table salt can be used to insure an adequate amount of iodine for normal thyroid function. (This use of iodized salt is an example of a preventive health measure.) Disorders of thyroid function include hyperthyroidism, which, when severe, causes a dangerous increase in the metabolic rate; and hypothyroidism, an opposite condition, which causes physical and mental sluggishness. An enlargement of the thyroid gland is called a goiter. When the enlargement is a nodular tumor, it is called an adenoma. During a physical examination, the doctor may

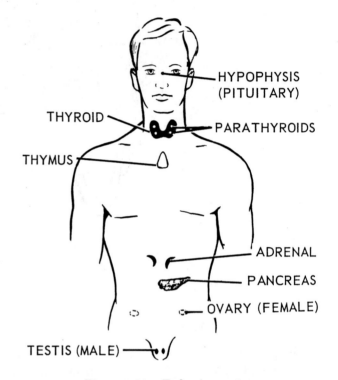

Figure 2-33. Endocrine system.

palpate the neck tissues to determine the size and consistency of thyroid tissue.

79. The Parathyroids

The parathyroid glands, usually four in number, are located on the posterior surfaces of the lobes of the thyroid gland. These glands produce the hormone, parathormone, which helps to regulate the amount of calcium in the blood. Calcium, normally stored in the bones, is released into the blood as required for normal nerve and muscle tissue function. When there is too little calcium in the blood, a type of muscle twitching called tetany develops. Because of the location of the parathyroid glands in relation to the thyroid, special observation for tetany may be required in the immediate postoperative period following thyroid surgery. Calcium is given by intravenous infusion to relieve the symptoms of tetany.

80. The Adrenal Glands

The two adrenal glands are located one above each kidney (suprarenal glands). Each adrenal gland actually functions as two separate glands, producing different hormones from its two parts, the medulla and the cortex. The medulla is the inner part of the adrenal gland. It produces epinephrine, the "fight or flight" hormone. The medulla is stimulated to produce epinephrine by the sympathetic branch of the autonomic nervous system in order to give the body the extra push it needs in responding to emergencies. The cortex, the outer part of the adrenal glands, produces a series of adrenocortical hormones, which include hydrocortisone. The adrenocortical hormones influence the salt and water balance of the body, the metabolism of foods, and the ability of the body to handle stress. The cortex of the adrenal glands requires stimulation by a hormone produced by the pituitary gland.

81. The Pituitary Gland

The pituitary gland, located deep within the skull, is also called the hypophysis. This small gland has two lobes, each producing distinctive hormones. The anterior lobe hormones stimulate other endocrine glands to produce their distinctive secretions; for this reason, the pituitary gland is called the master gland of the endocrine system. The four hormones produced by the anterior lobe of the pituitary have names with the suffix "trophic," meaning nourishing. Somatotrophic hormone (STH) means body nourishing. This hormone influences skeletal and soft tissue growth. Adrenocorticotrophic hormone (ACTH) stimulates the cortex of the adrenal gland to produce its cortisone-type hormones. Gonadotrophic hormone stimulates the normal development of the gonads, the testes or ovaries, and controls the development of the male and female reproductive systems. Thyrotrophic hormone stimulates the thyroid gland to produce its hormone. The posterior lobe of the pituitary gland produces a hormone that stimulates the contraction of the smooth muscle of the uterus, so it is important in childbirth. Another posterior lobe hormone which helps prevent excessive water excretion from the kidneys is called the antidiuretic hormone.

82. The Testes and Ovaries (the Gonads)

The male testes are located in the scrotum; the female ovaries, in the lower abdominal cavity. Hormones produced by these glands stimulate the development of sexual characteristics that normally appear at the development period called puberty (sexual maturity). They are responsible for the appearance of the secondary sexual characteristics: the pubic and axillary hair, the beard and the changing of the voice, and mammary (breast) development in the female. These hormones also help maintain the reproductive system organs in their adult state.

83. The Pancreas

Part of the pancreas functions as an accessory organ of the digestive system and part functions as an endocrine gland. Its endocrine gland function is carried out by groups of pancreas cells called the islands of Langerhans, which produce the hormone insulin. This hormone is necessary for the normal use of sugar by body cells. If insulin is not produced in sufficient amounts, the sugar normally present in the blood cannot be properly used by body cells, and the disease, diabetes mellitus, develops. A patient with diabetes mellitus requires continuous medical treatment—a combination of diet modification, education in modified living habits, and special medication as needed. As a medication, insulin must be given by hypodermic injection, because it is destroyed by digestive juices when taken by mouth. However, some patients requiring medication for diabetes mellitus can be treated with oral medications which are NOT insulin but which apparently stimulate underfunctioning pancreatic cells to produce insulin. An example of such a medication is tolbutamide (orinase). Other types of oral medication (such as phenformin) for diabetes promote the utilization of glucose by muscle tissue instead of stimulating underfunctioning pancreatic cells.

84. General

The male and female reproductive systems have their own specialized internal and external organs, passageways, and supportive structures. The parts and functions of these systems are designed to make the process of fertilization possible. The female cell, the ovum, must be fertilized by the male cell, the spermatozoa. The normal result of fertilization is reproduction. (Pregnancy and childbirth will be discussed in chapter 7.)

85. The Male Reproductive System

The major parts of the male reproductive system (fig. 2–34) are the scrotum, testis, epididymis, ductus deferens (also referred to as vas defere. or seminal duct), seminal vesicles, ejaculatory ducts, prostate gland, urethra, and penis. The penis, testes, and scrotum are referred to as external genitalia.

a. The Scrotum, the Testes, and the Epididymis. There are two testes, one on each side of the septum of the scrotum. A testis is an oval-shaped gland, about 1½ to 2 inches in length, which produces the male germ cells, spermatozoa (or sperm), and the male hormone, testosterone. Sperm are produced in great numbers, starting at the age of puberty. Although microscopic in size, each sperm has a head, which contains the cell nucleus, and an elongated tail for movement.

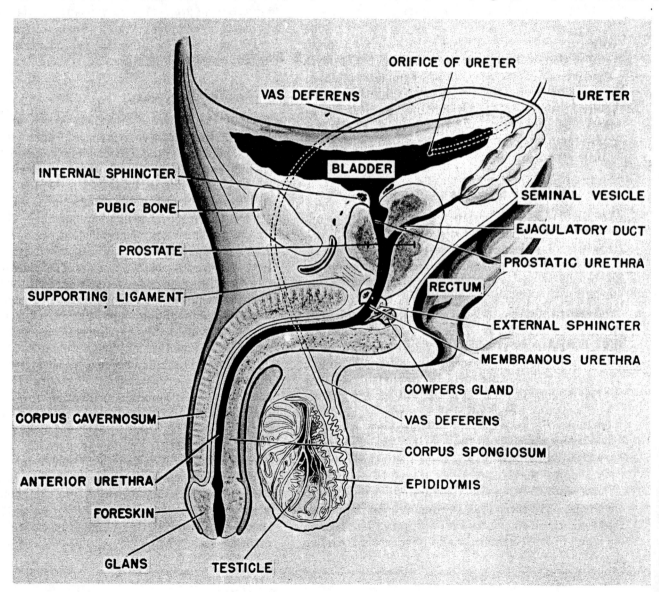

Figure 2–34. Male urogenital system.

Sperm travels from the testis to the tightly coiled tube, the epididymis. A continuation of the epidilymis is the ductus deferens (or vas deferens) (fig. 2–35).

b. *The Ductus Deferens.* This duct carries sperm from the scrotum to the pelvic cavity. As the duct leaves the scrotum, it passes through the inguinal canal into the pelvic cavity as part of the spermatic cord. Spermatic cords, one in each groin, are supporting structures. Each ductus deferens curves around the bladder and delivers the sperm to one of two storage pouches, called the seminal vesicles.

c. *The Seminal Vesicles and Ejaculatory Ducts.* The seminal vesicles are located behind the bladder. During the storage of sperm in these vesicles, secretions are added to them to keep them alive and motile. The secretions and the sperm form the seminal fluid, or semen. Ejaculatory ducts carry the seminal fluid from the seminal vesicles, through the prostate gland, to the urethra.

d. *The Prostate Gland.* This gland is located around the urethra at the neck of the bladder (fig. 2–35). Prostatic secretions are added to the seminal fluid to protect it from urethral secretions and female vaginal secretions. When the prostate gland becomes enlarged (hypertrophied), it can seriously constrict the urethra. The size and consistency of the prostate gland is determined by the doctor by means of a rectal examination.

e. *The Urethra and the Penis.* The urethra, a passageway for seminal fluid and for urine, has its longest segment in the penis. Several glands add secretions to the urethra, the largest being two bulbo-urethral (or Cowper's) glands (fig. 2–35). The terminal opening of the urethra is in the glans penis, which is surrounded by a retractable fold of skin called the foreskin, or prepuce. Surgical removal of the foreskin is circumcision, which is performed to reduce the possibility of an abnormal constriction of the glans, called phimosis, or to reduce the possibility of irritation from secretions that accumulate under the foreskin. The penis has spongy tissues which become distended from a greatly increased blood supply during penile erection.

86. The Female Reproductive System

The major parts of the female reproductive system (fig. 2–36) are the ovaries; fallopian tubes; uterus; vagina; and the external genitalia, the vulva. The supportive structures for the internal reproductive organs are a complicated arrangement of pelvic ligaments, which are formed in part, from folds of peritoneum that line the abdomino-pelvic cavity.

a. *The Ovaries.* These are described as two almond-shaped glands (fig. 2–37), one on either side of the abdomino-pelvic cavity. They produce female germ cells, ova, and female hormones, estrogen and progesterone. These hormones maintain

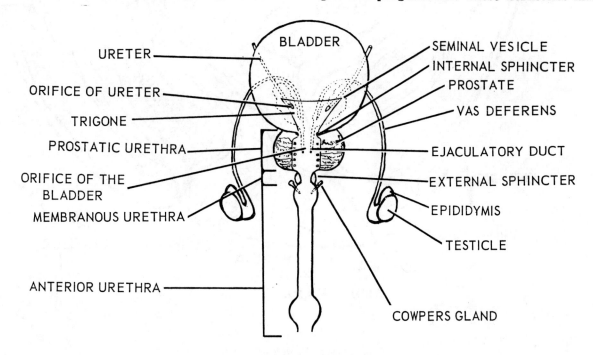

Figure 2–35. Diagram of male reproductive system.

the normal menstrual cycle An ovum is expelled from the surface of an ovary in a process called ovulation, which occurs about halfway between each menstrual period. An expelled ovum is picked up by the free end of a fallopian tube for transportation to the uterus.

b. *Fallopian Tubes.* There are two fallopian tubes (oviducts) each curving outward from the upper part of the uterus. About four inches in length, each tube has a free end which curves around, but is not attached to, an ovary. The fringed surface of the free end of the fallopian tube carries an expelled ovum into the tube, and the ovum moves slowly on its way to the uterus. If fertilization takes place, it normally occurs as the ovum moves through a tube. The male germ cell, the sperm, must therefore travel up the female reproductive tract in order to unite with the female germ cell, the ovum. Of the millions of sperm produced, only one must unite with one ovum for fertilization to occur.

c. *The Uterus.* The uterus, shaped somewhat like a pear, is suspended in the pelvic cavity, supported between the bladder and the rectum by its system of eight ligaments. The normal position of the body of the uterus is anteflexion (bent for-

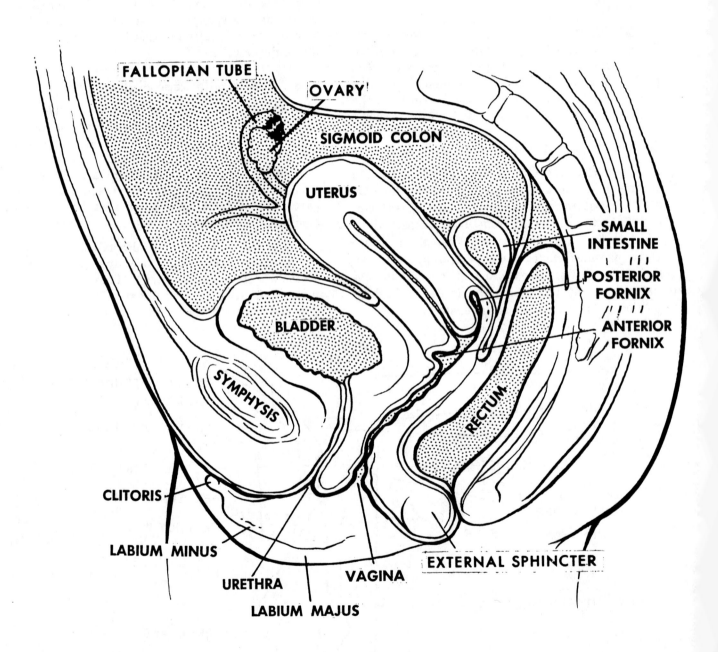

Figure 2–36. Female urogenital system.

ward over the bladder) (fig. 2–36). The uterus is about three inches long and three inches thick at its widest part. It has a thick wall of smooth muscle and a relatively small inner cavity. During pregnancy, it can increase about 20 times in size. The upper dome-shaped portion of the uterus is the fundus, the main part is the body, and the lower neck portion is the cervix (fig. 2–37). The cervix is a canal opening into the vagina. The inner lining of the uterus, the endometrium, undergoes periodic changes during the regular menstrual cycle, to make the uterus ready to receive a fertilized ovum. If the ovum is not fertilized, the endometrium gets a message from hormone influences and sheds its surface cells and built-up secretions. Some of the extra blood supply, the surface cells, and uterine secretions are eliminated as menstrual flow.

d. *The Vagina.* This muscular canal extends from the cervix of the uterus to the vaginal opening in the vestibule of the vulva. The vaginal canal is capable of stretching widely and serves as the birth canal. Part of the cervix protrudes into the uppermost portion of the vagina. An important part of a female pelvic examination is the physical examination of the visible surface of the cervix and vagina, plus a laboratory examination of cervical and vaginal secretions. A Pap (Papanicolaou) smear is made by obtaining these secretions for laboratory examination.

e. *The Vulva.* The several structures that make up the female external genitalia form the vulva. These are the mons pubis, the labia, the clitoris, and the vestibule. The labia, two parallel sets of liplike tissues, are the labia majora, the larger outer folds of tissue, and the labia minora, the smaller inner folds. The clitoris is located at the

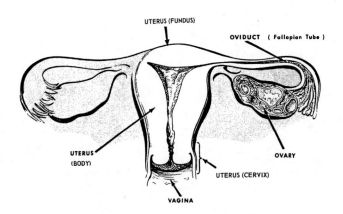

Internal Organs - Female Reproductive System

Figure 2–37. Female reproductive organs (frontal section).

upper meeting point of the labia majora and the labia minora. Between the labia minora is the vestibule, a shallow depression into which the urethra and the vagina open. The urethral opening is above the vaginal opening. A series of glands, which can become infected, open into the vestibule, the largest being the Bartholin glands at the vaginal opening.

87. Menstruation

In preparing to receive the ovum, the mucous lining (mucosa) of the uterus becomes soft and swollen and uterine blood vessels are dilated. If the ovum is not fertilized, the unneeded blood and mucosa are expelled from the uterus through the vagina. This process, called menstruation, begins at puberty and is repeated, except when interrupted by disease or pregnancy, about every 28 days until the age of 40 to 50 years.

GLOSSARY OF ANATOMIC SCIENCES

CONTENTS

	Page
Achilles Tendon ...... Concha	1
Costal ...... Iliacus	2
Iliocostal ...... Palmaris	3
Parietal ...... Ulna	4
Vastus ...... Zygoma	5

———

GLOSSARY OF ANATOMIC SCIENCES

ACHILLES TENDON

The tendon which attaches to the heel and originates from the muscles in the calf (gastrocnemius and soleus muscles).

ANCONEUS

This muscle extends from humerus in upper forearm to ulna in forearm. Its function is to straighten the elbow joint.

ARYEPIGLOTTIC

From the arytenoid cartilage to the epiglottis (the structure which closes the windpipe when swallowing). Its function is to close entrance to larynx.

ARYTENOID

From one arytenoid cartilage to other, its function is to close the larynx.

ASTRAGALUS

Located just below tibia and fibula (leg bones) in ankle. It connects with the heel bone.

ATLAS

First vertebra lying just beneath the skull.

AXIS

Second vertebra in neck, just below Atlas.

BRACHIALIS

Extends from upper and lower jaw bones to muscles about the mouth. Its function is to pull back angles of the mouth and tighten the cheeks.

BULBO-CAVERNOSUS

Extends from perineum (a point below the genitals) to penis. Its function is to compress urethra.

CALCANEUS

Heel bone.

CALVARIUM

Bones which form top of skull.

CAPITATE

Largest bone in wrist, located toward center of wrist joint.

CARPAL

Eight small bones of wrist greater multangular, lesser multangular, lunate, capitate, hamate, navicular, triquetrum, and pisiform bones.

CILIARY

Extends from membrane around iris to ciliary process of iris in the eye. Its function is to open and close the pupil of the eye.

CLAVICLE

Collarbone extending from sternum (breastbone) to shoulder tip.

COCCYX

Tailbone, the last vertebrae at base of spine.

CONCHA

Shell-shaped small bone located along the outer side of the nasal cavity.

COSTAL
   Ribs; 12 bones on each side, arising from the spinal column.
COXAE
   Hipbone; joins with sacrum and other hipbone to form the bony
pelvis. The Coxae is composed of 3 fused bones: ilium, ischium, and
pubis.
CRICOARYTENOID
   From cricoid cartilages to arytenoid cartilages in the neck. Its
function is to open and close the vocal chords.
CUROID
   Cube-shaped small bone of foot.

                              D

DELTOID
   Extends from the collarbone and the scapula, over the shoulder,
to the humerus in the upper arm. Its function is to lift the upper
arm away from the body.

                              E

ETHMOID
   Small bone located in front of base of skull, forming part of
orbit and nose. Within it are spaces, making up the ethmoid
sinuses.
EXTENSOR CARPI RADIALIS
   From humerus to bones of wrist. Its function is to straighten
the wrist.

                              F

FEMUR
   The thighbone, extending from hip to knee.
FIBULA
   Outer bone of leg, extending from knee to ankle
FLEXOR CARPI RADIALIS
   Extends from humerus to bones in front of the wrist. Its function
is to bend the wrist.
FRONTAL
   Bones of forehead, parts of orbit and nose.

                              G

GASTROCNEMIUS
   Extends down leg from femur to heel bone. Its function is to
bend ankle in downward direction and to help flex knee.

                              H

HAMSTRING
   Three large muscles extending down back of the thigh from ischium
to tibia below the knee. Its function is to flex the knee joint.
HUMERUS
   Arm bone, extending from shoulder to elbow.
HYOID
   Thin U-shaped bone beneath the chin and above the larynx.

                              I

ILIACUS
   Extends from pelvis bones to femur in the thigh. Its function is
to flex hip joint.

                               2

ILIOCOSTAL
From ribs to vertebral column. Its function is to straighten spinal column and bend trunk sideways.
ILLIUM
Part of hipbone, into which the femur fits.
INCUS
The anvil. One of 3 small bones of middle ear, adjacent to ear-drum.
ISCHIUM
Part of hipbone

L

LONGISSIMUS
Extends up back near spine. Its function is to straighten spine.
LONGUS CAPITIS
Extends from vertebrae in neck to base of the skull. Its function is to flex the head.

M

MALAR
Cheekbone; the zygoma.
MALLEUS
The hammer. One of 3 small bones of middle ear; adjacent to ear-drum.
MANDIBLE
Jawbone. Attached to the skull at the temperomandibular joint in front of the ear.
MASSETER
Extends from cheekbone to the lower jawbone. Its function is to close the mouth.
MAXILLA
Upper jawbone. Makes up part of the face, orbit, nose, etc.
METACARPAL
The 5 bones of the hand to which the finger bones are attached.
METATARSAL
The 5 bones of the foot to which the toe bones are attached.

N

NASALIS
Maxillary bone of face to bridge. Alters expression of face.
NAVICULAR
Small bones of the hands and feet; shaped like a boat.

O

OBTURATOR
Extends from bones of pubis to femur (thighbone). Rotates thigh outward.
OCCIPITAL
The back and part of base of the skull.

P

PALMARIS
Extends down front of forearm to palm of the hand. Helps to flex the wrist and make "hollow of the hand."

PARIETAL
    This bone makes up part of the side and top of the skull.
PATELLA
    The kneecap.
PELVIS
    The bony pelvis is made up of the hipbones, sacrum, and coccyx.
PHALANGES
    The bones of the fingers and toes.
PUBIS
    The bone in front of the pelvis.

R

RADIUS
    Long bone on outer side of the forearm, extending from elbow to
wrist.

S

SACRUM
    Five fused vertebrae in lower back which make up the back part
of the bony pelvis.
SCALENE
    Extends from vertebra in the neck to the first and second ribs.
Bends the head and neck sideways.
SCAPULA
    The shoulder blade (wingbone).
SPHENOID
    Irregularly shaped bone making up front portion of the base of
the skull and parts of the orbit and nose.
SPLENIUS
    Extends from the vertebrae in the chest and the neck to back of
the head. Straightens the head and spine.
STAPES
    The stirrup. One of 3 small bones of middle ear adjacent to
the eardrum.
STERNUM
    The breastbone.

T

TALUS
    The same as the astragalus.
TARSAL
    The same as the foot bones.
TEMPORAL
    The bone forming front portion of the side of the skull and part
of the base.
    Extends from temple to lower jaw. Closes the mouth.
TIBIA
    The large inner bone of the leg, extending from knee to the ankle.
(It is responsible for weight bearing.)
TURBINATE
    Three bones located on the outer side of the nasal cavity.

U

ULNA
    The long bone on the inner side of the forearm, extending from
the elbow to the wrist.

4

VASTUS

It extends down the entire front of the thigh to the kneecap and tibia in the leg. Its function is to straighten the knee.

VOMER

This bone forms the back segment of the nasal septum which separates the two sides of the nose.

ZYGOMA

The cheekbone; the malar bone.

———

GLOSSARY OF MICROBIOLOGY

Contents

Page

ACID-FAST BACTERIA .... ANAPHYLACTIC SHOCK   1

ANAPHYLAXIS ...... BACTERIOPHAGE   2

BALLISTOSPORES ...... COCCI   3

COLIFORM GROUP ...... DIPLOID NUCLEUS   4

DISINFECTANTS ...... FERMENTATION   5

FISSION .... IMHOFF TANK   6

IMMUNITY .... LYSIN   7

MANTOUX TEST ...... MYCELIUM   8

NATURAL IMMUNITY ......PATHOLOGY   9

PERITRICHIC ...... PROTOZOA   10

PSYCHROPHILES ...... SEPTIC TANK   11

SEPTICEMIA ...... SUPPURATION   12

SYMBIOSIS....... ...... UREASE   13

VACCINE .... ZYGOTE   14

GLOSSARY OF MICROBIOLOGY

A

ACID-FAST BACTERIA - Bacteria that strongly resist decoloration with acid-alcohol after being stained with a hot dye such as carbol fuchsin. Mycobacterium tuberculosis is a typical example.

ACQUIRED IMMUNITY - Immunity that an individual obtains after a period of natural susceptibility.

ACTIVATED SLUDGE PROCESS - A method of sewage purification in which a little "ripe" sewage is added to the fresh sewage to be treated, which is then submitted to extensive aeration.

ACTIVE IMMUNITY - Immunity in which the immunizing agent is produced by the metabolism of the immunized individual.

AEROBES - Organisms that can grow in the presence of air.

AGAR - (1) A polysaccharide material extracted from sea weeds.
(2) A common term applied to a culture medium solidified with this material, such as nutrient agar.

AGGLUTINATION - The clumping together of bacteria through the action of agglutinins homologous with them.

AGGLUTININS - A kind of antibody that causes the clumping together of the corresponding antigen particles, such as bacterial bodies.

ALGAE - Thallophytic plants that carry on photosynthesis with the aid of chlorophyll or other pigment.

ALLERGY - A state of hypersensitivity to a foreign substance such as protein.

AMMONIFICATION - The formation of ammonia from organic compounds.

AMPHITRICHIC - With a tuft of flagella at each end of the cell. Resulting from cell division but not not separation of two sister cells each carrying flagella at one end. Terminal flagellation.

AMYLASE - The enzyme that hydrolyzes starch to maltose. Diastase. Ptyalin.

ANAEROBES - Organisms that cannot grow in the presence of air. ANAEROBIOSIS - Life in the absence of free oxygen.

ANAPHYLACTIC SHOCK - The response of the body to the injection of a substance to which the body is abnormally sensitive.

ANAPHYLAXIS - A state of hypersensitiveness to a foreign protein or other substance, brought about by an initial injection of the substance.

ANOREXIA - Loss of appetite.

ANTAGONISM - A relationship between species of microorganisms in which one kills or injures the other. Antibiosis.

ANTIBIOTIC - A substance produced by a living organism which will inhibit or destroy other forms of life, expecially pathogenic micro-organisms. Examples are penicillin, streptomycin, bacitracin, etc.

ANTIBODY - A substance produced by the body under the stimulus of an antigen and capable of reacting with it *in vitro*.

ANTIGEN - A substance, usually a foreign protein, that, if injected into the body, stimulates the production of an antibody such as antitoxin.

ANTISEPTIC - A chemical substance that, in the strength used, will inhibit the activities of microorganisms without killing them.

ANTITOXIN - An antibody that has the power of neutralizing the effects of the homologous toxin that served as an antigen for its production.

ASCOSPORES - Spores produced in definite numbers, usually eight, by free cell formation within a sac or ascus.

ASCUS - The spore-bearing sac of the *Ascomyeetest* ATTENUATED - Made weaker than normal, or less pathogenic.

AUTOCLAVE - An apparatus used for heating materials under steam pressure. Similar in principle to a pressure cooker.

AUTOLYSIS - Self-digestion due to the action of enzymes upon the tissues that produced them, as the over-ripening of bananas and other kinds of fruit, or the breakdown of dead bacterial cells.

AUTOTROPHIC BACTERIA - Bacterial that can live without a supply of organic matter, and can obtain energy from inorganic materials, or in some instances from sunlight.

B

BACTEREMIA - The presence of bacteria in the blood stream. Septicemia.

BACTERIOLYSIS - The disintegration of bacterial cells.

BACTERIOPHAGE - A specific virus capable of destroying living bacteria.

BALLISTOSPORES - Asexual spores formed by yeasts of the family *sporobolo-myceta-ceae.* They arise on sterigmata and are shot off by a drop excretion mechanism.

BARRIERS OF INFECTION - Mechanical obstructions, such as skin and mucous membranes, that prevent pathogenic organisms from reaching a vulnerable region.

BROWNIAN MOVEMENT - The movement of visible particles by the bombardment of molecules of the suspending fluid.

BUDDING - A method of cell division in which a small area of the cell wall softens and protoplasm including a nucleus is forced out and is later cut off by constriction, thus forming a new cell.

BUTTER CULTURE - A pure culture or a definite mixture of bacterial species added to cream after pasteurization to give desire flavor and consistency to the butter made from it.

BY-PRODUCTS - Substances that remain after certain elements have been removed for use by the organism, e.g., nitrites, after oxygen has been removed from nitrates.

C

CAPSULE - A thickened slime of layer of carbohydrate material surrounding the cell wall of many species of bacteria.

CARBOHYDRASES - The group of enzymes that hydrolyze complex carbohydrates to simpler ones. The amylolytic group.

CARRIER OF DISEASE - A person or animal that harbors the orga-isms of disease without showing symptoms.

CATEGORIES - The several group names - orders, families, genera, etc. - used for classifying living things.

CELLULASE - The enzyme that hydrolyzes cellulose into cellobiose.

CHEMOSYNTHESIS - The obtaining of energy by the oxidation of inorganic substances, followed by its use for the building of organic compounds.

CHEMOTAXIS - The ability of organisms to respond to chemical stimuli by moving toward or away from the region of greatest concentration.

CHLAMYDOSPORES - Thick-walled spores formed by a rounding up of cells of a mycelium.

CHROMOGENESIS - The production of pigment.

COCCI - Bacteria that are spherical or nearly so.

COLIFORM GROUP - All aerobic and facultatively anaerobic gram negative non-spore-forming rods which ferment lactose with gas formation.

COLIPHAGE - A specific bacteriophage that is capable of destroying *Kechericha* coli.

COLONY - A visible collection of bacteria resulting from the multiplication and growth of a single individual.

COLUMELLA - A dome-shaped, non-sporeforming structure extending upward from the sporangiophore into the base of a sporangium, as in *Rhizopus*.

COMMENSALISM - A relationship between species of organisms in which one receives benefit and the other neither benefit nor harm. Metabiosis.

COMPLEMENT - A thermolabel, non-specific constituent of the normal blood of man aiding in the destruction of all kinds of bacteria.

CONDENSER - A large lens beneath the stage of a microscope, for concentrating light on the object from below.

CONIDIA - Fungus spores cut off from the tips of hyphae by constriction.

CONIDTOPHORE - A stalk arising from the vegetative mycelium and supporting sterigmata that produce one or more conidia.

CONJURATION - The union of two gamete cells in sexual reproduction.

CONSTRICTION - A method of cell division in which the cell is cut in two by a circular furrow surrounding it.

D

DARK-FIELD ILLUMINATION - A method of illuminating objects for microscopic examination whereby the object is made to appear luminous against a dark background.

DECAY - The destruction of organic materials through the action of enzymes produced by microorganisms.

DEHYDROGENASES - A group of enzymes that remove hydrogen from compounds and thus -produce the effect of oxidation.

DENITRIFICATION - The formation of free nitrogen or nitrous oxide from nitrates.

DICK TEST - A skin test to determine, whether a person is susceptible to scarlet fever.

DIFFUSE NUCLEI - Nuclei composed of chromatin material scattered throughout the cytoplasm rather than enclosed within a nuclear membrane.

DIPLOID NUCLEUS - A nucleus having a complete number of paired chromosomes for the species. See *Haploid*.

DISINFECTANTS - Chemical substances capable of killing pathogenic microorganisms.

E

EFFLUENT - Partially or completely treated sewage flowing out of any sewage treatment device.

ELECTRON MICROSCOPE - A microscope similar in principle to the compound light microscope but which uses electrons instead of light as a source of radiation.

ENDOENZYMES - Same as intracellular enzymes.

ENDOTOXINS - Toxins that remain within the cells that produce them and do not stimulate the production of corresponding antitoxins.

ENVIRONMENT - The composite of all conditions surrounding an organism.

ENZYME - A biological catalyst.

EPIDEMIOLOGY - The science of tracing the sources from which diseases spread.

ETIOLOGY - The science of causes, e.g., causes of disease.

EXCRETIONS - Substances that have become so changed in composition through metabolism that they are no longer useful to the organism that produced them and are cast off, e.g., carbon dioxide.

EXOENZYMES - Same as extracellular enzymes.

EXOTOXINS - Toxins that diffuse from the cells that produce them into the surrounding medium. They are antigenic and stimulate the formation of antitoxins.

EXTRACELLULAR ENZYMES - Enzymes that diffuse out of the cells that formed them. Exoenzymes.

F

FACULTATIVELY ANAEROBIC - Organisms that can grow in either the presence or absence of air.

FACULTATIVELY PARASITIC - Organisms that can live either as parasites or as saprophytes.

FALSE BRANCHING - A kind of branching of filaments in which the cells do not branch, but the branch of the filament is held to the main filament by a common sheath surrounding both.

FERMENTATION - A process carried on by microorganisms whereby organic materials, usually carbohydrates, are decomposed with the formation of acids and sometimes carbon dioxide and alcohol.

FISSION - A method of cell division by constriction in which two daughter cells of equal size are formed.

FLAGELLA - Slender protoplasmic strands that extend from the cell and serve as organs of locomotion.

FUNGI IMPERFECTI - A heterogeneous group of fungi that have no sexual stage. Apparently most of them are degenerate. *Ascomycetes.*

FUNGUS - A thallophytic plant that lacks chlorophyll and is of filamentous structure.

G

GAMETES - Two haploid cells that unite in sexual reproduction.

GENOTYPE - The sum total of the determinants controlling the reaction range of an individual or a cell.

GROWTH -   (1) Increase in size of an individual.
             (2) Increase in numbers of microorganisms.
             (3) A visible mass of microorganisms formed by reproduction and enlargement.

H

HANGING DROP - A drop of liquid suspended for study from the under side of a cover glass mounted on a slide with a depression in the surface.

HAPLOID NUCLEUS - A nucleus having a complete number of single chromosomes for the species. See *Diploid.*

HUMUS - Organic matter decomposed to such an extent that its original structure is no longer recognizable.

HYDROLASES - Enzymes that bring about chemical change by the addition of water that goes into chemical union with the substance acted upon.

HYPERSENSITIVITY - An abnormally high degree of sensitiveness to foreign substances such as proteins.

HYPERTROPHY - The abnormal multiplication of cells resulting in the formation of nodules, tumors, etc.

HYPHAE - Branches of a fungus mycelium.

I

IMHOFF TANK - A specially constructed septic tank having a flow chamber above and a sludge chamber below.

IMMUNITY - The ability of an animal or plant to resist disease even when the pathogenic organisms or their products reach a vulnerable region.

IMPRESSED VARIATION - A kind of variation brought about by some recognizably unfavorable condition.

INFLAMMATION - A morbid condition characterized by swelling, redness, and pain, usually in a localized region.

INFLUENT - Sewage, treated or partially treated, flowing into any sewage treatment device.

INOCULUM - Material containing microorganisms and used for the inoculation of media or hosts.

INTERMITTENT STERILIZATION - A sterilization process involving the heating of the material to a temperature of 80-100 C for a time up to an hour on each of three successive days. Fractional sterilization. Tyndallization.

INTERMOLECULAR RESPIRATION - A form of respiration in which oxygen is taken from one kind of molecule and used to oxidize another.

INTRACELLULAR ENZYMES - Enzymes that remain within the cells that produced them. Endoenzymes.

INTRAMOLECULAR RESPIRATION - A form of respiration in which there is a rearrangement of atoms within the molecule resulting in a release of energy.

INVOLUTION FORMS - Cells of microorganisms large in size and of unusual form. Generally considered abnormal.

IRON BACTERIA - Bacteria that contain ferric hydroxide in the stalk or the sheath.

IRRITABILITY - The capacity of an organism for response to change in the environment.

L

LENS - A piece of glass or other transparent substance used for magnifying or reducing the apparent size of objects.

LIPOLYTIC ENZYMES - Enzymes that hydrolyze fats into fatty acids and glycerol.

LOPHOTRICHIC - With flagella in a tuft at one end of the cell. Terminal flagellation.

LYOPHILIZE - To dry a protein, usually from the frozen state, in such a way so it is still soluble. As applied to microorganisms it involves the freezing and drying of the organisms so that many of the cells will remain viable for long periods of time.

LYSIN - An enzyme or other substance that breaks down or dissolves organic substances.

M

MANTOUX TEST - A tuberculin test in which the tuberculin is injected intradermally.

MASS MORPHOLOGY - The morphology of bacterial groups, colonies, etc., as contrasted with individual cells.

MECHANISM OF INFECTION - The means by which microorganisms produce disease.

MESOPHILES - Bacteria that grow best at moderate temperatures, having an optimum of 25°C to 45°C.

METABIOSIS - Same as commensalism.

METABOLISM - Any chemical change brought about by a living thing in its use of food.

MICROAEROPHILIC - Organisms that require free oxygen of less concentration than that found in the atmosphere.

MICROMANIPULATOR - A complicated piece of apparatus used for fine dissection under the microscope, or for single cell isolation.

MICRON - A unit of measurement having a value of 0.001 of a millimeter.

MICROORGANISMS - Forms of life that are microscopic in size, or nearly so.

MICROPHILES - Bacteria having a narrow temperature range for growth.

MILLIMICRON - 0.001 micron or 0.000001 mm. A unit of measurement often used in designating the size of virus particles.

MITOSIS - Division of a cell with a diploid nucleus in which all of the chromosomes divide, resulting in two diploid daughter cells.

MOLD - A saprophytic fungus that is of simple filamentous structure.

MONOTRICHIC - With a flagellum occurring at one end of the cell. Terminal flagellation.

MORBIDITY - The frequency of occurrence of cases of a disease.

MORPHOLOGY - That branch of biological science that deals with qualities that appear to the eye - size, form, color, etc.

MORTALITY - The percentage of deaths among those afflicted with a disease.

MUTATION - A change from some parental character occurring in the offspring. More permanent than variation.

MYCELIUM - The branching, thread-like structure that makes up the vegetative body of a fungus.

N

NATURAL IMMUNITY - Immunity that an individual possesses by virtue of its race or species. Immunity present from the beginning of life of the individual.

NECROSIS - The death of tissues.

NITRATE REDUCTION - The formation of nitrites or ammonia from nitrates.

NITRIFICATION - The formation of nitric acid or nitrates from ammonia.

NITROGEN FIXATION - The formation of nitrogen compounds from free nitrogen.

NON-SYMBIOTIC NITROGEN FIXATION - Fixation of nitrogen by organisms living independently, as *Azotobacter* and *Clostridium*.

NOSEPIECE - The portion of a microscope into which the objectives are screwed.

O

OBJECTIVE - The system of lenses in a compound microscope that is used next to the object to be studied.

OCULAR - The combination of lenses at the top of a compound microscope. Also called an eyepiece.

OIDIA - Thin walled spores formed by the separation of undifferentiated cells of a mycelium.

OPSONINS - Antibodies which make bacteria more readily ingested by phagocytes.

OSMOSIS - The tendency of fluids to pass through a membrane that separates two portions of different concentration.

P

PARASITES - Organisms that obtain their food from the living substance of other organisms.

PASSIVE IMMUNITY - Immunity in which the immunized individual does not produce its own immunizing agent but receives it from one with active immunity.

PASTEURIZATION - Heating at a temperature that will kill most objectionable microorganisms, excepting sporeforming bacteria and thermophiles.

PATHOGENICITY - The ability to produce disease.

PATHOGENS - Organisms that cause disease in other forms of life.

PATHOLOGY - A study of the abnormal conditions that occur in the tissues as a result of disease.

PERITRICHIC - With flagella distributed all over the cell body. Lateral flagellation.

PHAGOCYTES - Leucocytes or other living cells that have the power of ingesting bacteria.

PHENOL COEFFICIENT - The killing strength of a disinfectant, relative to that of phenol.

PHOTOGENESIS - The production of light. Phosphorescence.

PHOTOSYNTHESIS - The formation of carbohydrates from simpler food materials, using light as a source of energy.

PHYSIOLOGY - That branch of biological science which deals with the functions and activities of living things - nutrition, growth, reproduction, irritability, etc.

PLAQUES - Clear zones in streaks of bacterial growth resulting from the lysis of bacteria by bacteriophage.

PLANE OF DIVISION - The direction in which a cleavage furrow divides a cell.

PLASMODESMID - A protoplasmic strand extending from one bacterial cell to another.

PLASMOLYSIS - The shrinkage of cell contents through the withdrawal of water by osmotic action.

PLEOMORPHISM - Exhibiting several forms or shapes. Polymorphism.

PLEUROPNEUMONIA GROUP - Microorganisms that grow in cell-free culture media with the development of polymorphic structures as rings, globules, filaments, and minute reproductive bodies.

POLYMORPHISM - Exhibiting several forms or shapes. Pleomorphism.

PORTALS OF INFECTION - Openings through which pathogenic organisms pass into the body of the host.

POST-FISSION MOVEMENTS - Movements of cells following fission, whereby the two adjacent cells are finally separated.

PRECIPITINS - A kind of antibody that forms a precipitate with an antigen that was previously in solution.

PROCESSING - Preliminary treatment, canning, and sterilization of foods. The term is often used for a single one of these operations such as sterilization.

PROTEOLYSIS - The destruction of proteins by enzymes.

PROTEOLYTIC ENZYMES - Enzymes that hydrolyze proteins and related compounds.

PROTOZOA - Unicellular members of the animal kingdom.

PSYCHROPHILES - Bacteria that grow best at relatively low temperatures, having an optimum of 15°C to 20°C.

PUTREFACTION - The chemical decomposition of proteins and related compounds, usually with the production of disagreeable odors.

R

R-COLONIES - Colonies that have a rough surface, although belonging to a species that usually produces smooth colonies.

REFLECTED LIGHT - Light that strikes the surface of an object being studied with a microscope and is reflected back into the lens.

RENNIN - The enzyme that changes the soluble casein of milk into the solid paracasein in the presence of calcium.

RESOLVING POWER - The ability of a lens to reveal fine detail. It is measured in terms of the least distance between two points at which they can be identified as two rather than as a single blurred object.

RESPIRATION - Any chemical reaction whereby energy is released for life processes.

RICKETTSIAE - Microorganisms that are obligate intracellular parasites or that are dependent directly on living cells. They are not ultramicroscopic but are adapted to intra-cellular life in arthropod tissue.

ROPY MILK - Milk that is viscid because of the presence of capsule forming bacteria such as *Alcaligenee visconsus*.

S

SAPROPHYTES - Organisms that use non-living organic matter for food.

SCHICK TEST - A skin test to determine whether a person is susceptible to diphtheria. Similar to the Dick test for scarlet fever.

S-COLONIES - Colonies that have a smooth surface, although belonging to a species that may produce rough-surfaced colonies.

SECONDARY INVADERS - Saprophytic organisms that invade the body of a host in the wake of a pathogenic species.

SECRETIONS - Substances that serve a useful purpose to the organisms that produce them, e.g., enzymes.

SEPTATE MYCELIUM - A mycelium subdivided into cells by cross-walls or septa.

SEPTIC TANK - A deep vat or chamber used for the anaerobic treatment of sewage.

SEPTICEMIA - The presence of bacteria in the blood stream. Bacteremia.

SEWERAGE - The system employed for the handling of sewage.

SLIME LAYER - A carbohydrate layer surrounding all bacterial cells which, if it becomes extensive, is called a capsule.

SLUDGE - The mass of solids remaining after a sewage treating process is completed or wet sewage solids which have been deposited by sedimentation.

SOURCES OF INFECTION - Places from which disease-producing organisms were acquired by the host.

SPECIFICITY - The limitation of a species of microorganism to one species of host, or to at least a small number.

SPONTANEOUS COMBUSTION - Ignition of material by heat generated through its oxidation.

SPONTANEOUS GENERATION - The origin of living things from nonliving materials.

SPORANGIA - Sacs in which fungus spores are formed. SPORANGIOPHORE - A stalk that produces a sporangium.

SPORANGIUM - A sac that contains spores, usually numerous and indefinite in number.

SPORE -   (1) A simple reproductive body of a lower plant, capable of growing directly into a new plant.
            (2) Among bacteria, a thick-walled resistant cell.

STERIGMATA - Tiny stalks that produce spores at their tips, as in *Aspergillus, Penicillium,* and mushrooms.

STERILIZATION - Killing microorganisms, usually by means of heat.

STOCK CULTURE - Cultures of microorganisms kept as a reserve for future use.

STREAK CULTURES - Cultures made by applying the organisms with a loop or other instrument to the surface of a medium, usually agar slanted in a test tube.

STRICT PARASITES - Organisms that require a living host.

STRINGY MILK - Milk that contains tough stringy clots as it is drawn from an inflamed udder.

SULFUR BACTERIA - Bacteria that use sulfur or hydrogen sulfide for food and oxidize it. Some forms store granules of sulfur in their cells.

SUPPURATION - The formation of pus.

SYMBIOSIS - A relationship between species of organisms whereby each receives some form of benefit.

SYMBIOTIC NITROGEN FIXATION - Nitrogen fixation by bacteria living symbiotically with higher plants.

SYMPTOMS - Functional disturbances brought about by diseased conditions.

SYNERGISM - The ability of two or more species of organisms to bring about chemical changes that neither can bring about alone.

T

THERMODURIC BACTERIA - Organisms capable of withstanding high temperatures.

THERMOGENESIS - Heat production by microorganisms.

THERMOLABILE - Destroyed by a temperature below the boiling point of water.

THERMOPHILES - Bacteria that grow best at relative high temperatures, having an optimum of 55C or higher.

THERMOSTABLE - Resistant to heat at the boiling point of water or thereabout.

TOXEMIA - A condition characterized by toxins in the blood.

TOXINS - Poisonous substances of complex nitrogenous composition produced by bacteria and some higher organisms.

TOXOID - A detoxified toxin that remains antigenic and can be used to confer active immunity.

TRANSMITTED LIGHT - Light that passes through the object that is being studied with a microscope.

TRICKLING FILTER - A sewage purification plant in which the sewage is sprayed onto a layer of crushed rock or similar material to provide an extensive surface or aeration.

TUBERCULIN TEST - A test to determine whether a person or animal has been infected with *Mycobacterium tuberculosis*.

U

ULTRAMICROSCOPE - A microscope that reveals very minute objects by the use of light that strikes them obliquely and is reflected into the objective.

UREASE - The enzyme that hydrolyzes urea into ammonium carbonate.

V

VACCINE - Anything which, if injected into the body, causes it to develop active immunity.

VARIATION - The departure of the offspring from the parent with respect to some character. Usually more temporary than mutation.

VECTORS OF DISEASE - Insects or other forms of animal life that transfer pathogenic organisms from host to host.

VEHICLE OF INFECTION - Food or water containing pathogenic microorganisms.

VIRULENCE - In bacteriology, the ability to produce disease.

VIRUSES - Etiological agents of disease, typically of small size, most being capable of passing filters that retain bacteria, increasing only in the presence of living cells, and giving rise to new strains by mutation, not arising spontaneously.

W

WIDAL TEST - The agglutination test for typhoid fever.

WINOGRADSKY TEST - A soil test for fertility by determining its suitability for growing *Azotobacter.*

Y

YEAST - A kind of fungus which has been reduced to a more or less unicellular state by loss of mycelium.

Z

ZYGOSPORE - The zygote of certain kinds of fungi and algae, e.g. *Rhizopus, Mucur* and *Spirogyra.*

ZYGOTE - A diploid cell formed by the union of two haploid gamete cells in sexual reproduction.

———

ANSWER SHEET

TEST NO. ______________ PART ______ TITLE OF POSITION ______________________________
(AS GIVEN IN EXAMINATION ANNOUNCEMENT - INCLUDE OPTION, IF ANY)

PLACE OF EXAMINATION ______________________________ DATE ______
(CITY OR TOWN) (STATE)

RATING

USE THE SPECIAL PENCIL. MAKE GLOSSY BLACK MARKS.

1 A B C D E	26 A B C D E	51 A B C D E	76 A B C D E	101 A B C D E
2 A B C D E	27 A B C D E	52 A B C D E	77 A B C D E	102 A B C D E
3 A B C D E	28 A B C D E	53 A B C D E	78 A B C D E	103 A B C D E
4 A B C D E	29 A B C D E	54 A B C D E	79 A B C D E	104 A B C D E
5 A B C D E	30 A B C D E	55 A B C D E	80 A B C D E	105 A B C D E
6 A B C D E	31 A B C D E	56 A B C D E	81 A B C D E	106 A B C D E
7 A B C D E	32 A B C D E	57 A B C D E	82 A B C D E	107 A B C D E
8 A B C D E	33 A B C D E	58 A B C D E	83 A B C D E	108 A B C D E
9 A B C D E	34 A B C D E	59 A B C D E	84 A B C D E	109 A B C D E
10 A B C D E	35 A B C D E	60 A B C D E	85 A B C D E	110 A B C D E

Make only ONE mark for each answer. Additional and stray marks may be counted as mistakes. In making corrections, erase errors COMPLETELY.

11 A B C D E	36 A B C D E	61 A B C D E	86 A B C D E	111 A B C D E
12 A B C D E	37 A B C D E	62 A B C D E	87 A B C D E	112 A B C D E
13 A B C D E	38 A B C D E	63 A B C D E	88 A B C D E	113 A B C D E
14 A B C D E	39 A B C D E	64 A B C D E	89 A B C D E	114 A B C D E
15 A B C D E	40 A B C D E	65 A B C D E	90 A B C D E	115 A B C D E
16 A B C D E	41 A B C D E	66 A B C D E	91 A B C D E	116 A B C D E
17 A B C D E	42 A B C D E	67 A B C D E	92 A B C D E	117 A B C D E
18 A B C D E	43 A B C D E	68 A B C D E	93 A B C D E	118 A B C D E
19 A B C D E	44 A B C D E	69 A B C D E	94 A B C D E	119 A B C D E
20 A B C D E	45 A B C D E	70 A B C D E	95 A B C D E	120 A B C D E
21 A B C D E	46 A B C D E	71 A B C D E	96 A B C D E	121 A B C D E
22 A B C D E	47 A B C D E	72 A B C D E	97 A B C D E	122 A B C D E
23 A B C D E	48 A B C D E	73 A B C D E	98 A B C D E	123 A B C D E
24 A B C D E	49 A B C D E	74 A B C D E	99 A B C D E	124 A B C D E
25 A B C D E	50 A B C D E	75 A B C D E	100 A B C D E	125 A B C D E

ANSWER SHEET

TEST NO. _____ PART _____ TITLE OF POSITION _____

(AS GIVEN IN EXAMINATION ANNOUNCEMENT - INCLUDE OPTION, IF ANY)

PLACE OF EXAMINATION _____ DATE _____

(CITY OR TOWN)   (STATE)

RATING

USE THE SPECIAL PENCIL.   MAKE GLOSSY BLACK MARKS.

Make only ONE mark for each answer.   Additional and stray marks may be counted as mistakes.   In making corrections, erase errors COMPLETELY.